Citizens in Conflict

The sociology of town planning

Books from Hutchinson in the Built Environment Series include:

An Introduction to Transportation Studies: M. J. Bruton
An Introduction to Town and Country Planning: John Ratcliffe
An Introduction to Regional Planning: John Glasson
An Introduction to Town Planning Techniques: Margaret A. Roberts
The Dynamics of Urbanism: P. F. Smith
The Spirit and Purpose of Planning: Edited by M. J. Bruton

Jointly with the Open University:

Future of Cities: Edited by Andrew Blowers, Chris Hammett and Phillip Sarre

Citizens in Conflict

The sociology of town planning

J. M. Simmie

Hutchinson of London

For N.B. – California

Hutchinson and Co (Publishers) Ltd
3 Fitzroy Square, London W1

London Melbourne Sydney Auckland
Wellington Johannesburg and agencies
throughout the world

First published June 1974
Reprinted 1976
Reprinted 1978

Printed in Great Britain by litho at The Anchor Press Ltd
and bound by Wm Brendon & Son Ltd
both of Tiptree, Essex

ISBN 0 09 119650 7 (cased)
0 09 119651 5 (paper)

Contents

List of figures and tables viii
Acknowledgements ix
Preface xi

1. **Concepts and definitions** 1

Town planning 2
The origins of sociology 7
The nature of sociology 9
Forms of social interaction 10
The application of sociology to town planning 12
An outline of sociology in town planning 14
References 16

2. **Co-operative society** 17

Understanding society 17
The application of structural-functionalism in town planning 20
Social ecology 23
The specification of sub-systems 27
Systems theory 33
Normal society 37
Conclusions 42
References 43

3. **A socio-political perspective on British town planning** 47

The need for perspective 47
A theoretical perspective 48
Contemporary formulations of conflict theory 55

Empirical evidence 63
Victorian Britain and the development of social and spatial conflict 64
Politics and change 73
The effects of the introduction of statutory town planning 74
Wartime change and the Welfare State 80
Conclusions 80
References 82

4. **Social conflict and spatial inequality** 85

Conflict and the structure of society 85
Social structure and social class 86
Economic resources and social class 88
Social class and spatial structure 99
Social and physical mobility 109
Conclusions 116
References 116

5. **Power, planning and distributional equity** 119

Professionals and the public interest 119
Different conceptions of the public interest 121
The politics of planning 127
Hidden mechanisms of redistribution 131
Politics and redistribution 134
Participation and the acquisition of scarce resources 136
Redistribution in the market place 141
The effects of town planning on distribution 145
Town planning and the legitimate use of power 149
Conclusions 154
References 156

6. **Social action and ideological conflict** 160

Rationality versus ideology 160
Rational action 161
Functional rationality 165
Town planning in practice 167
Substantial rationality 169
Social action and ideology 171

Socialist ideology 175
The ideologies of town planning 180
Town planning as co-ordination 184
Alternative planning 193
Conclusions 198
References 199

7. The planning of change 203

The price of criticism 203
Conflict and planning 207
Planning the distribution of resources 209
Planning the power structure 219
Politics and the power structure 220
Bureaucracy and the power structure 223
Planning ideological change 226
References 228

Subject index 231
Author index 237

Figures and Tables

Figure 1. Forms of social interaction 11
Figure 2. Effect of town planning on the price of land 77
Table 1. Great Britain 1966, social class structure 87
Table 2. United Kingdom 1961 and 1969, distribution of wealth by groups of owners 89
Table 3. United Kingdom 1961 and 1969, changes in categories of wealth 90
Table 4. Great Britain 1961 and 1970, persons receiving national insurance benefits 92
Table 5. Percentages of national insurance beneficiaries also receiving national assistance/supplementary benefit 93
Figure 3. The poverty cycle 98
Table 6. England and Wales/Great Britain 1963–70, housebuilding costs and prices 101
Table 7. England and Wales 1966–70, dwellings completed 103
Table 8. Weekly costs of accommodation under different types of tenure 104
Table 9. Social class, tenure and conditions of housing 107
Table 10. Great Britain 1960 and 1970, stock of dwellings by tenure 115

Acknowledgements

Any book such as this owes a great debt not only to the friends and colleagues of the author but also to all those writers who have forced him to think and take notice of what they have said. As far as the latter are concerned, their contributions are gratefully acknowledged in the references in the text.

As far as the former are concerned, I should like to thank my students in Berkeley, California, where it all started, for stimulating me to translate our seminars into a book. I should also like to thank Professors David Donnison and Peter Willmott for their patient encouragement and criticism, both of which have had a great influence on the final form of the book. I also owe a great debt to Madge Bridge, Rosanne Kyriakides and Cathy Mills for all their splendidly stoical work in typing and retyping the various drafts, sometimes several times, before they reached their completed form. Trinet Scheltinga-Koopman also rendered great assistance by checking all the final drafts and searching for the material I have used in a number of the individual chapters.

Preface

Citizens in Conflict has sprung from two main sources of inspiration. The first is that after some ten years of involvement in town planning practice and education, and after an initial period where it seemed that town planning held out material prospects of contributing to desirable planned social change in cities, I have become increasingly disillusioned with its promise. This disillusionment has come about mainly through the analysis of the effects of town planning on different groups in the population. These seem to have been particularly severe on those least able to help themselves, either because they lack economic resources and political power or because they do not speak the same language or share the same values as town planners. The paradox has developed that, while the demonstrated effectiveness, from its clients' points of view, of the outputs from town planning is the only satisfactory criterion of success, all too often town planners measure their success in terms of plan inputs and the esteem they acquire among their professional colleagues. It is becoming decreasingly appropriate to describe them as public servants.

The second source of inspiration for this book came from a visit made in 1970 to the University of California at Berkeley. There the atmosphere and approach to town planning were completely different from what I had been used to in this country. Many of the controversies were stimulated by the so-called 'War on Poverty' initiated under the Kennedy Administration. The questions being asked seemed to be some years in advance of the issues holding the attention of town planners here. In the first place, the whole concept of a multi-fronted attack on poverty was not something that British town planners or even social administrators had formulated as a major objective in the 1960s. In the second place, the questions being asked about this programme seemed to be far in advance of 'permissible' criticism in Britain. For example, no plan could be produced without demands to know what it did for the blacks and the poor. Increasingly, voices were heard accusing the warriors of being the main beneficiaries of the programmes rather than those they were intended to help. On returning to this country it seemed appropriate to ask some of these questions here.

As the work progressed, the basic questions emerged as to who gains and who loses from the effects of town planning in particular, and social policy in general; and is the distribution of these gains and losses fair or just? Most of the book is addressed to these two fundamental questions.

Before answering them, however, it seemed necessary to ask why town planners do not habitually ask these questions anyway. The answer seemed to be that their implicit theoretical stance directly precluded consideration of such issues. Thus it has been necessary to make a critique of this stance and develop an alternative. The stance which is criticised is that which sees society as composed of primarily co-operative social interaction. The alternative that is advanced is based on conflict theory which sees society primarily as a constantly changing balance of opposed forces, particularly as represented in economics, politics and ideology. Such a framework points clearly to the questions of distribution and justice.

Some attempt is made to suggest answers to these questions in the last chapter. They are, of course, mostly outlines and ideas which would have to be researched, tried out and evaluated in much more detail before becoming general programmes. They do, however, point to the problem of achieving any general objectives by the use of single-interest professions and bureaucratic departments. Hence a prerequisite for adequate planning in our cities is a radical change in the institutions responsible for planning processes. Without this, I suspect that someone will be able to write the same kind of book after each new decade of planning.

James Simmie
London

1. Concepts and definitions

The study of theory in the social sciences is a peculiarly difficult enterprise. Unlike those in the natural sciences, the units whose behaviour one is trying to explain have the ability to conceal their real motives or actions and also to change them either according to circumstances or when paradoxes are brought to their attention, in some cases by social scientists. The latter are also constrained in their understanding by being inextricably part of what they are trying to explain. The position of the social theorist is a little like that of a player/coach in a football team who is trying to explain to his side, while in earshot of the opposition, the causes of their defeat during a match. Both teams can alter the pattern of their play as a result of his explanation; this alteration then renders his first explanation an incorrect approximation of the following state of play, and may or may not lead to his team's success in that particular match. Either way, his theories about the most effective action in future matches will also have to be altered according to the eventual outcome of today's game.

However much he may pretend to be otherwise, the social theorist is not an impartial observer on the terraces. His commitment to social science will always stem from some interest and he would not be able to explain phenomena without such an interest. A person who does not care about the outcome of a football game and is prepared to offer gratuitous advice to both sides cannot really understand what motivates the players to pursue a small round object with such dedication, emotion and seemingly irrational sacrifice. Thinking, and therefore theorising, require involvement and conceptual prejudice before objects and their actions can take on any real meaning.

Most important theories in the social sciences are therefore based on the prejudices or values of their proponents. They rest on intuitive intellectual leaps of startling perspicacity and relevance to their time which are subsequently developed and expounded on the basis of their originator's immersion in relevant knowledge. In contrast, much 'theorising' which claims to be value-free and often empirical can only achieve an approximation of both these states at once by being so trivial as to constitute little more than the mysterious or banal statement of the obvious.

In theorising about theory one is therefore treading a difficult path between sophisticated prejudice and mystified banality. In producing a sociological analysis of town planning, these difficulties are compounded by the fact that a strong line of thought in Britain believes that there is no such thing as town planning theory anyway. In order to progress with such an analysis, some clear definitions of the subjects of study are needed, together with an outline of what aspects of these subjects are to count as significant from the point of view of sociological explanation. Such study may start with conventional definitions of town planning and sociological explanation, but there is no reason why it should not stray into other preserves if these offer more relevant explanations of the phenomena under investigation. Traditional definitions of sociology and town planning will be used as a starting point for analysis but the ensuing arguments will also cross the traditional boundaries of public administration, political science and economics.

In seeking to explain the economic, political and social foundations of town planning, such transgressions are a necessary virtue rather than illegitimate incursions. While they will inevitably be seen as the latter by purists in the individual disciplines concerned, the reader must judge for himself whether a satisfactory explanation of the complex interactions between planners and their environment would be forthcoming on the basis of any purist's attack from the basis of a single subject of study.

Town planning

The activity which is to be analysed should be turned to first. When one considers that the activities of town planning are enshrined in legislation, one might think that there should be no difficulty in defining them. Thus, legally, the 1947 Town and Country Planning Act required county and county borough councils, to produce development plans showing, on broad lines only:

1. the allocation of land for different uses such as housing, industry and open space . . . and

2. the approximate future position of such things as schools and roads for which land needed to be reserved.[1]

Right from the start, however, there has been disagreement among planners themselves as to what these requirements implied in practice, how the law should be interpreted and where it should be altered. The legal definition of town planning is only an approximation of what town planners do and is even farther removed from what some of them think they ought to do.

The major division of opinion centres on what is required to actually produce a plan for location and land use. The 'official' view of the late 1940s as expressed then by the Town Planning Institute, 'was that to plan was to express in a drawing the form of existing or proposed land uses and buildings'.[2] Keeble also argued that town planning was 'concerned with the arrangement of land uses and communication routes in the most satisfactory practicable form'.[3] This view was restated by the Institute and enshrined in its 'education' policy in the 1960s, under the influence of Kantorowich, who said that town planning 'is dedicated to the promotion of an efficient and life-enhancing relationship between man and his physical environment'.[4] This was also the view expressed in the early 1970s by Kitchen and Perry who said that, 'We are talking about physical planning, which we regard as a discipline and a professional activity in its own right, primarily responsible for the physical aspects of the total development process.'[5]

By this time, however, such a view already required further definition in the light of the new statutory arrangements introduced in the 1968 Town and Country Planning Act as a result of the recommendations of the 1965 report of the Planning Advisory Group. The Act distinguished between local and structure plans. Local plans were concerned with the physical aspects of areas traditionally the preserve of architects, surveyors and engineers. Structure plans include, among other things:

1. The principal physical and economic characteristics of the area of the authority (including the principal purposes for which

land is used) and, so far as they may be expected to affect that area, of any neighbouring areas.

2. The size, composition and distribution of the population of that area (whether resident or otherwise).

3. . . . the communications, transport system and traffic of that area . . .[6]

Nevertheless, despite this apparent broadening of the 'total development process' the 1970 Development Plans Manual stressed, as McLoughlin points out, 'that the ultimate purpose of planning is to create an efficient physical structure and a good environment . . . This indicates that in the opinion of the Manual's authors the social and economic goals should be satisfied through physical solutions.'[7]

The physical planning definition of town planning, while it has been modified over the last few decades, still stresses the coordination of the visible, often man-made aspects of the environment as being the main concern of planners. For this reason their plans are still expressed as either detailed or generalised maps, diagrams and drawings concerned with the location and design of physical land uses. The relevance of such an approach to town planning has been challenged at least since the Second World War.

It has been challenged mainly by those who have started with the problems of society as they saw them and have then looked around for ways of diminishing or abolishing them. As early as 1947 Silkin called for 'a new approach to training to correspond to the vast changes taking place in our conception and our practice of planning'.[8] These changes were outlined in 1950 by the Schuster Report. There it was argued that 'planning is now primarily a social and economic activity limited but not determined by the technical possibilities of design'.[9] Fifteen years later this assertion had had little effect on town planning or the education of planners, so that Burns again argued that in contrast to physical definitions of planning, the activity was, in reality, 'a highly complex operation where such things as primary road networks, modal splits, social satisfactions, politics, employment difficulties, housing standards and leisure problems, are all interwoven and all require specialist analysis to formulate properly a comprehensive plan'.[10] A further contribution was made to this idea in 1969 when Hall argued that there was a view opposed to the idea that there is something called planning and this is town and country planning and that this is the province of the Town Planning Institute. Some of us feel that planning is a near universal condition of modern life and that town and country planning is only one particular aspect of it.[11]

Support for this view was forthcoming from the growing debate on the structure, organisation and purposes of local government in general. For example, Friend and Jessop indicated, on the basis of their work in Coventry, the interrelatedness of decisions made by the various committees of the City Council and the importance of general strategic planning above and beyond the work of the town planning department and committee.[12] As yet there is no statutory framework for such planning and indeed such a framework could well be more of a hindrance than a help, particularly to innovation.

Nevertheless, under stimulation from the Maud report on the Management of Local Government and the use of management consultants in authorities such as Liverpool, Hull and Greenwich, a new kind of structure planning has grown up over the last five years or so. Corporate planning, as it is called, 'developed out of a desire to improve management and decision-making in local government as a whole'.[13] Its 'interest is in all of the activities of an authority, and within this area of concern its interest in social, economic and physical systems is very broad with no particular emphasis of subject matter'.[14] Its central activity is concerned, however, mainly with the co-ordinated allocation of a local authority's budget in such a way that waste and duplication are minimised and the general purposes of the authority are achieved.

A situation has arisen where some local authorities are producing three separate but overlapping kinds of plan. Local, structure and corporate plans all have their effects on the nature of towns and cities although concentrating on design, location and management, respectively. This situation led Eddison and Stewart to argue in 1971 that,

An authority cannot pursue separate policies in structure planning from corporate planning without giving up the claim to be one organisation. An authority cannot pursue separate policies in structure planning from corporate planning if it is in any way concerned with the impact of its activities on the environment. An authority cannot afford to build up two separate planning systems. The real issue is how the relationship should be worked out.[15]

Their proposed resolution of this dilemma was the inappropriately titled community plan. 'It would secure, in so far as it was possible to secure, that the various organisations which affect the life of the community would plan their activities together. Perhaps the local authority should take the initiative in creating the framework within which this should happen.'[16] In 1972 McLoughlin and Thornley proposed a somewhat similar procedure with the more appropriate title of policy planning. They argued that, 'There should be a central planning procedure within the authority from which a variety of planning procedures within the authority would be derived and to which they would contribute.'[17]

Clearly the 1970s are a time of change in town planning. Old certainties about what constituted the activity are dissolving, and to call oneself a town planner no longer gives the same clues to one's occupation as it did even in the 1960s. A town planner employed by a local authority may now be working on exercises called local, structure, corporate or policy plans. The outputs from all four are different both in the form they take and in the ways in which they seek to influence the environment.

The current confusion does not end there, for not only can a town planner be working on different kinds of plan but he may also be working at quite different scales. Partly due to the strong vertical links between local authority planners and Whitehall, their activities may be set in the context of national, regional or even sub-regional plans. These latter types of plan, associated mainly with the Labour Administration of the 1960s, imposed even more serious strains on old conceptions of physical plans than did the debate taking place at local authority level. In the end it proved impossible to produce regional plans either within the context of local administration or the approach of the physical planner. Thus the regional and sub-regional plans of the 1960s gave further impetus to change and also highlighted the importance of economic and demographic factors beyond the traditional conceptions of town planning.

In trying to analyse the theories and effects of town planning from a sociological point of view, one is faced with a subject which currently has no clear and generally accepted definition. As this is not an empirical study of contemporary, up-to-the-minute planning practice, however, it is legitimate to confine the analysis to published information available in the early 1970s. This means that one is therefore discussing mainly physical or, as it has become known, structure planning and the areas where this central activity overlaps with local and corporate planning. For the purposes of this analysis, town planning is defined as structure planning and includes its immediate administrative context and local effects.

The origins of sociology

The problem of finding a generally accepted definition of sociology is not less than discovering one for town planning. Again this is largely because the central concerns of the discipline have changed over time. This may be illustrated by tracing its origins, which lie in political philosophy, the philosophy of history, biological theories of evolution and movements for social and political reform. These have all contributed to the development of sociology as a relatively distinct activity in its own right and at different periods in its development have predominated as the central themes of concern.

Sociology developed first as a new point of view within traditional philosophy. It sprang from the fusion of two previously opposed points of view in Western thought, namely, positivism and organicism. Organicism, as the name suggests, constructs its picture of society on the basis of an organic model. In metaphysics it refers to the attempt to explain the world, reality, or even the universe as a kind of organism. This line of thought has its roots in the idealistic Western philosophies propounded by men like Plato (427–347 B.C.), Aristotle (384–322 B.C.), Hegel (1770–1831), Schopenhauer (1788–1860) and Nietzsche (1844–1900). In contrast, positivism is associated with the rise of science. It is a term which refers to the line of thought which attempts to explain the world almost exclusively in terms of measurable experiences and the facts, forces and energies which underlie them.

These idealistic and scientific lines of thought came closer to sociology as it is known today in the work of Burke (1729–97) and Spencer (1820–1903), propounding a reactionary view of society, and in the 'scientific socialism' of Saint-Simon (1760–1825), Owen (1711–1858), J. S. Mill (1806–73), Proudhon (1809–65), Blanc (1811–82) and Marx (1818–83). All these writers either experienced or were influenced by either the French Revolution or the English Industrial Revolution. Nevertheless it was left to Comte (1798–1857) to synthesise organicism, positivism and idealism and to coin the word 'sociology' to represent this evolving area of study.

Yet another line of thought bearing on the development of sociology was the philosophy of history through the writings of Ferguson (1723–1816), Saint-Simon and Hegel. These writers strongly influenced Comte and Marx, and through them some of the important strands in modern sociology. Again, the French Revolution and the English Industrial Revolution were instrumental in sparking off this new line of enquiry which contributed the notions of development, progress, historical periods and social types. The philosophy of history was also responsible for contributing the idea that society is something different from the state or political society. In Ferguson's *Essay on the History of Civil Society* (1767) he talks of society as a system of related institutions and seeks to distinguish between different types of society and stages in their development.

An unintentionally more sinister influence on the study of society have been biological theories of evolution. These stem from the publication, in 1859, of Darwin's (1809–82) *Origin of Species* which emphasised the idea of change over time by means of natural selection. These ideas lead to some crude comparisons between social structure and living organisms. Thus Darwinists have argued that those people who survive and prosper are therefore the fittest to do so; racialists have applied the same contention to whole races; and eugenicists have argued that the character of society is due to the genetic makeup of its individuals. While there may be some truth in all these assertions, they should always be regarded with suspicion as they usually cloak *a priori* judgements on the part of their protagonists.

Another strand in the origins of sociology was movements for social and political reform. The main instrument of these movements was the social survey, which sought to extend the methods of the natural sciences into the study of human affairs and also to measure the effects of the industrial revolution on those who seemed to benefit least from it.

All these philosophical, intellectual and practical traditions were interwoven in different ways during the nineteenth century by

Comte, Marx and Spencer, whom many consider to be the founding fathers of modern sociology.

The nature of sociology

Despite the emergence of sociology as a field of study during the nineteenth century, it was not, and in some cases is still not, recognised as such by, for example, the universities. This is partly because the actual data which it uses, and seeks to explain, are human behaviour and its results. These data are the same as those used by psychologists, economists, political scientists and historians. The difference lies not in the raw material but in the theoretical terms and context within which the data are explained.

The main thrust of sociological theory is aimed at explaining the social relations which exist between human beings and also the nature of the societies in which they find themselves. This requires a clear definition of social as opposed to other kinds of relationships and also of the term society when used in this context. One of the early 'great' sociologists, Durkheim (1858–1917), was alert to these problems. He defined a social fact as 'every way of acting which is general throughout a given society, while at the same time existing in its own right independent of its individual manifestations'.[18] Examples of social facts are marriage, law, custom, religion, morality, etc. Sociology is therefore concerned with explanations of such facts as the social relationships occurring in the family, the reasons why men devise and maintain legal systems or obey the 'laws' of custom, religion, morality and so on. It is also concerned with explaining why these facts are different in different societies and what it is about the circumstances of a particular society which leads to the development of particular social relationships. This latter phrase, social relationships, has been defined by Weber (1864–1920). He said that in his work,

> The term social relationship will be used to denote the behaviour of a plurality of actors in so far as, in its meaningful context, the action of each takes account of that of others and is oriented in these terms. The relationship thus consists entirely and exclusively in the existence of a probability that there will be, in some meaningfully understandable sense, a course of social action.[19]

Weber is thus responsible for the classic definition of sociology as the science of social action. The description seeks to interpret and grasp the significance of the subjective meaning of social action. It tries to comprehend and organise the subjective meaning of human actions into concepts. Finally, it searches for causal explanations of these actions. Social action is defined as

a form of human conduct . . . consisting of an internal or external attitude which is expressed by acting or refraining from action. It is action when man assigns a certain meaning to his conduct, and the action is social when, by the meaning he gives it, it relates to the behaviour of other persons, and is oriented towards their behaviour.[20]

In practice social action takes the form of social interaction. This occurs when, given a number of individuals or groups, their actions are reciprocally oriented towards one another. Thus social action is seldom, if ever, one-way and directed at totally passive recipients. It is more likely to be a regular and reciprocal activity.

Sociology may therefore be defined as a search for the significance of social interaction, the organisation of the significance into concepts and the development of causal explanations of these organised forms of social interaction.

Forms of social interaction

There are four main parameters of the forms of social interaction. These are total co-operation, total anomie, total alienation and total conflict. In practice any actual social interaction will be something less than totally one or the other of these forms and to that extent will contain different degrees of all of them. Usually, however, one or two of them will predominate. These contentions may be illustrated diagrammatically as shown in Fig. 1.

Figure 1 illustrates in an extremely simplified way the main parameters of social interaction. Within those parameters the social interaction taking place between *A* and *B* is basically co-operative. They share roughly the same values and aspirations and find that these may be achieved by co-operation. The kind of society that they create by their reciprocal interaction may also be conceptualised as relatively co-operative and integrated. Their perceived individual interests are served by such an arrangement. They are not, however, totally co-operative, integrated and happy in their

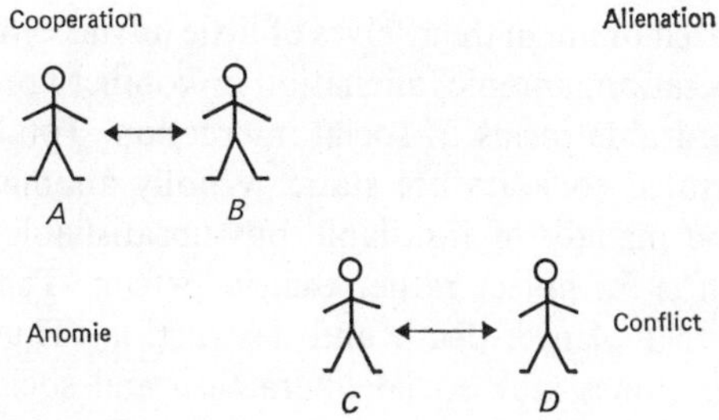

Figure 1 Forms of social interaction

interaction, and therefore have not created a completely static and unchanging society. Thus, from time to time small tensions and disputes arise which, when resolved, result in a slightly new form of social interaction and society. In the case of *A* and *B* these tensions are characterised as mainly anomic, that is, they arise either because their economy cannot be sufficiently regulated by them, and a poor crop, for instance, leads to some dispute as to how it is to be divided between them, or one of them is never satisfied with his share of the crop anyway. Their general co-operation is therefore marked from time to time by structural or mental changes which result in some discontent but not necessarily relevant remedial action.

In contrast, the social interaction between *C* and *D* is usually characterised by conflict. They do not share many values and aspirations and each seeks to organise their society in such a way that it serves mainly his interests. This continuing dynamic tension often leads to changes in the form of their social interaction and hence to changes in their society. The ability to initiate or resist such change depends to a large extent on the ownership or control of economic resources or political power. In order to prevent such a situation leading to continuous, violent and destructive interaction, *C* and *D* co-operate to some extent by establishing institutionalised conflict in forms which do not normally lead to the ultimate destruction of one or the other of them. Such a society may also be characterised by an element of alienation. To the extent that alienation exists, *C* or *D* or even both live and work in such a way that they do not fulfil their true potential as human beings. To this extent, in their social interaction they treat each other as things rather than people and spend much of their time engaged in sub-human action, like working on an assembly line, in order to create objects for which an artificial demand is created or are in themselves of little intrinsic value anyway.

Total co-operation, anomie, alienation or conflict are all therefore relatively undesirable forms of social interaction. Totally co-operative and integrated societies are static. Wholly anomic individuals suffer from the malady of insatiable but unsatisfiable aspirations. Alienated man is an object rather than a person. The ultimate in conflict leads to violence, death and destruction. Thus most individuals at most times seek social interaction and societal arrangements which are less than any of these extremes. The degree to which they are able to succeed in this search depends upon the complexity of society, the different positions that individuals and groups occupy, and their ability to comprehend and organise society according to their values and aspirations. To the extent that these factors are different either for different individuals and groups in a particular society or in different societies, so the characteristics of social interaction within a society or in different societies will themselves differ.

The application of sociology to town planning

Having outlined the definitions of town planning, the origins of sociology and the nature of sociological analysis, it is now necessary to argue what would constitute a sociological analysis of town planning. Basically, it would involve the analysis of the relationships between the purposes of planners and the purposes of individuals and groups in society, and the effects of these relationships.

To use the terminology outlined above, the sociological analysis of town planning is therefore concerned with seeking causal explanations of the meaningful social interactions which take place between physical or structure planners, their institutional environment, individuals and groups in society; and to seek the evidence of these meaningful social interactions in the social and physical effects they have on society as a whole, particular groups, individuals, or environments.

Thus, in their professional capacity, town planners form a relatively distinct group among all the groups which constitute a society. The social interaction which they initiate with or between these groups depends upon their knowledge and understanding of the nature and purposes of the groups; the ability of these other groups to get administrative agencies to satisfy their values and aspirations; the relationships between the planners' understanding of these circumstances and their own normative positions; and the interests of planners themselves.

Therefore, in order to produce a sociological analysis of town planning one needs to grasp the nature of the dynamic interactions between a number of continually changing complex variables. It is necessary to analyse the kind of social interaction taking place between the main groups in society and to identify the balance between co-operation, anomie, alienation and conflict. It is then important to specify the relationships which exist between this dynamic balance, government, and administration. These reference points may then be compared with the town planners' understanding of them to see whether their comprehension of the society in which they operate is 'relevant' and consequently whether their programmes of action are effective. Whether the latter is the case, however, will depend not just on accurate understanding but also on the planners' normative judgements based on this understanding. Finally, it will be instructive to assess whose interests are served by town planning. In all this analysis the main objective is to identify relevant groups and their purposes. The main evidence of their existence and aspirations will be differences in access to, and possession of, scarce and desirable resources, power and status. The main criteria for the selection of relevant data in these areas will be whether or not they fall within the influence of physical, structure planning.

As all these factors are subject to continued but varying rates of change, in part due to their own interaction with one another, their analysis poses two major problems. The first is that as there are no *a priori* reasons for supposing that clear cause-and-effect chains exist, there is no obvious merit in starting the analysis at any particular point. The choice of starting point depends primarily on what the analyst is trying to explain and what order will make this explanation most clear. The second problem is that as all the factors exist in a dynamic and changing relationship with one another it is not possible to specify exactly what those relationships are at this point in time. It is only possible to trace them historically up to the very recent past and to project this understanding into the present and the immediate future. Analysis which starts with the present and concerns itself with the future is likely to be pure fancy which may or may not materialise according to who believes it and what circumstances they find themselves in.

An outline of sociology in town planning

This analysis of town planning will consider the foregoing definitions, concepts and caveats and start with the town planners' understanding of society. For many physical, structure planners this incorporates a vague and often implicit belief that the interaction between different groups in British society is based on co-operation and generally shared values and aspirations. This is therefore assumed to be the 'normal' state of society, and as such it is also the kind of social interaction which it is a purpose of planning to seek. This means that there is a close relationship between 'facts' and 'values' as far as many planners are concerned. The 'fact' is that normally society is co-operative and the 'value' is therefore that it ought to be co-operative. The policies which often flow from this understanding and normative judgement are concerned with creating economically and socially 'balanced' and integrated communities. The main purposes of these communities are economic and administrative efficiency. These are thought to be generally acceptable goals as they bring equal benefits to all members of the community. Failure to accept this situation or the main problem to be overcome in mobile, new or changing communities is implicitly assumed to be anomie. The answers to anomie are often sought in increased opportunity, choice and regulation.

The evidence for these understandings and normative judgements is to be found in the acceptance of ecological theories of urbanisation and urbanism, the adoption of systems theory and attempts to create neighbourhoods and communities. The intimation of their inadequacy is to be found in the degree to which such policies stimulate alienation or conflict rather than co-operation. To the extent, for example, that society is not normally characterised by co-operation and therefore deviance is not anomie, so policies based on those implicit understandings will exacerbate rather than remove the kinds of social interaction of which planners do not approve. Increased regulation in these circumstances is more likely to lead to alienation or conflict than to co-operation.

If, in contrast to what many physical, structure planners believe, British society is normally characterised by conflict between different groups who do not share the same values and aspirations and who can be identified by their differential possession of resources, power and status, then a wholly different set of policy problems present themselves. In the first place, this explodes the consensus over the normative propositions which should guide policies. Instead of simply being a question of how generally agreed objectives are to be achieved, planning then becomes first a problem of why some objectives rather than others should be sought. If these conflicting objectives spring from the different interests of different groups then they are also not just philosophical differences of opinion but critical disputes about which groups get what and how much.

The second problem is that such disputes are not normally settled by the intervention of the kind of rational, apolitical, professional umpires that many planners claim to be but by the competitive success of different groups in the market place and in politics. In such circumstances the planner may find himself more determined than determining in the policies he may adopt vis-à-vis the physical environment.

The third problem which social conflict brings for the planner is that rationality, political neutrality and the public interest do not serve as adequate doctrines on which to base the practice of planning. They are superseded by ideology as the guiding and combined understanding, normative judgement and practice theory of different groups and professionals alike. To the extent that planners accept one ideology rather than another, so the planners represent some groups or social classes rather than other groups and social classes. That is, planners who have their own ideology are likely to serve their own interests rather than those of other bodies.

It is therefore critical for planners to have a clear, explicit and accurate understanding of the nature of social interaction in their particular society and also some equally clear and explicit normative evaluations of the conditions resulting from the nature of society. Without these, a great deal of planning will either be counter-productive in that it will create the very conditions it seeks to remove; it will not greatly alter what would have happened had it not existed as a government activity; it will serve the interests of those groups with most resources, power and status rather than those with least; and the main extra beneficiaries of such a system will be the planners themselves rather than any other groups in society.

These then are the issues with which sociology in town planning is concerned. They may be summarised as the goals of town planning, its socio-political context, the causes of spatial inequality, power and distributional equity, ideology, and the problems of planning change. These are the topics which will be explored in the following pages.

References

1 J. J. Clarke, *The Gist of Planning Law*, Macmillan (1964), p. 5
2 C. Cockburn, *Opinion and Planning Education*, Centre for Environmental Studies Information Paper No. 21 (London, 1970), p. 20
3 L. B. Keeble, 'Planning education', *Planning Outlook*, **V** (4), (1962)
4 R. H. Kantorowich, 'Education for planning', *Journal of the Royal Town Planning Institute*, May (1967), 175–81
5 T. Kitchen and J. Perry, 'Planning education and planning research', *Journal of the Royal Town Planning Institute*, December (1971), 455–7
6 Town and Country Planning Act 1968, Part I
7 J. B. McLoughlin and J. Thornley, *Some Problems in Structure Planning: a literature review*, Centre for Environmental Studies Information Paper No. 27 (London, 1972), p. 12
8 L. Silkin, Address as Minister of Town and Country Planning to the Town and Country Planning Summer School at Reading University, *Town Planning Institute* (1947)
9 Ministry of Town and Country Planning, *Report of the Committee on Qualifications of Planners*, Prepared by a committee under the chairmanship of Sir George Schuster, HMSO (1950), Cmnd. 8059
10 W. Burns, Contribution to a discussion following the Presidential Address, *Journal of the Royal Town Planning Institute*, November (1965)
11 Regional Studies Association. Report of a conference on the theme: the new planning courses. *Regional Studies Association*, July (1969)
12 J. K. Friend and W. N. Jessop, *Local Government and Strategic Choice*, Tavistock (1969)
13 J. B. McLoughlin and J. Thornley, *op. cit.* (1972), p. 16
14 *ibid.*, p. 17
15 J. D. Stewart and T. Eddison, 'Structure planning and corporate planning', *Journal of the Royal Town Planning Institute*, **57** (1971), 367–9
16 *ibid.*
17 J. B. McLoughlin and J. Thornley, *op. cit.* (1972), p. 19
18 E. Durkheim, *The Rules of Sociological Method*, Collier Macmillan (1966), p. 1
19 M. Weber, *The Theory of Social and Economic Organisation*, Free Press of Glencoe (1964)
20 *ibid.*

2. Co-operative society

Understanding society

A common strand in the way that a number of different disciplines seek to understand the nature of social interaction is based on the notion that society is a fundamentally co-operative collection of groups and individuals virtually all sharing roughly the same values and aspirations. This belief is to be found in sociology, political science, biology and physical or structure planning; the latter is hereafter referred to as town planning. Orlans argues, for example, that,

> most New Town planners regarded community centres and neighbourhood units as a means of integrating the diverse activities of individuals and families into an organic social whole of progressively larger dimensions – the community, town, region, and nation – and rationalised this goal in terms of a structural-functional or organic sociology . . . often that of Geddes and Mumford, in which individuals and groups in a society are likened to the parts of a mechanical system or the organs of an organism whose specialisation contributes to the harmonious functioning of the whole.[1]

Such a view of society draws on the nineteenth century tradition of organicism as exemplified by Spencer. It has been formalised as a school of thought in sociology by Radcliffe-Brown (1881–1955), Malinowski (1884–1942), Durkheim, Parsons and his disciples. The idea of society as an organism composed of functionally interrelated parts was first developed explicitly by anthropologists. It was a concept which was used to explain why particular societies survived relatively unchanged.

Radcliffe-Brown defined function as 'the contribution which a partial activity makes to the total activity of which it is a part. The function of a particular social usage is the contribution it makes to the total social life as the functioning of the social system.'[2] Malinowski argued that the 'functional theory' which was built on such propositions

aims at the explanation of anthropological facts at all levels of development by the part which they play within the integral system of culture, by the manner in which they are related to each other within the system, and by the manner in which this system is related to the physical surroundings.[3]

The classic example of such an analysis applied to society is contained in Durkheim's treatise, *The Division of Labour in Society*, first published in 1893. The language of the co-operative understanding of society contains many references to the words: function, integration, system, culture and lately structure.

The formulation of the grand theory based on the assumption that society is mainly characterised by co-operative social interaction is now mainly to be found in the works of Parsons and his disciples and is called structural-functionalism. Parsons, for example, argues that human actions may be analysed according to the part they play in four action systems. These are nature, personality, culture, and the social system.

The social system consists of a plurality of interacting persons motivated in terms of a tendency to the optimisation of gratification and whose relation to their situations, including each other, is defined and mediated in terms of a system of culturally structured and shared symbols.[4]

Each system has built-in restorative processes which tend to maintain a given 'normal' state of interaction. These consist of an adaptive, instrumental, object-manipulation sub-system; an expressive, consummatory, goal-gratification sub-system; a latent, pattern-maintenance, meaning-integration and energy regulation sub-system; and an integrative, expressive, sign-manipulation sub-system.

McLeish summarises the functions of these sub-systems. As he says,

Society must provide for the utilization of the resources available to it: this means,

1. That society must be adaptive. Individuals and groups in society must be able to recognise and be impelled towards certain ends perceived as possible gratifications of felt needs.

2. The group must be organised towards goal-attainment. The social unit must be preserved from disintegration by disruptive tendencies, i.e.

the specific patterns of activities, beliefs and values of society must be guarded from violent and destructive change.

3. A combination of processes must reinstate the latent patterns of order and work to maintain tension at a manageable level. The different social units must mutually adjust themselves to each other in a continuous way so that their contribution to the effective function of the system can be maximised.

4. An integrative sub-system is needed to facilitate internal adjustments and to adapt the system to the demands of the changing external situation.[5]

The social system is seen as being structured into four main sub-systems and as capable of explanation in terms of the interactions between the adaptive, integrative, goal-attainment and pattern maintenance sub-systems.

Inputs to the social system are said to come specifically from the cultural, personality and behavioural systems. There is said to be *no direct input from the physical environment to the social system.* Instead, interactions between the social system and the physical environment are mediated via the behavioural system. In other words, individuals may react to the physical environment but social systems do not. It is only in so far as the social system is composed of two or more individuals who may be reacting as individuals to the physical environment that the latter has any effect on the functioning of the social system as such.

Inputs to the social system are said to consist of:

1. Codes for the organisation of information.
2. Need dispositions in the form of adequacy, conformity and nurturance.
3. Plastic potentiality, i.e. physiological capabilities.
4. Values which are generated from within the social system itself.

They enter the social system from the cultural to the adaptive sub-system; from the personality to the goal-attainment sub-system; and from the behavioural organism to the integrative sub-system. Such an analysis of society has been worked out in its most sophisticated form in its application to social change in the *British Industrial Revolution* by Smelser. According to the theory, the end result of the utilisation of these inputs in a co-operative social system is the accomplishment of 'tasks'. In accomplishing these 'tasks' money, commitment, power and communication are also used.

The formalisation of the understanding of co-operative social interaction in the school of sociological thought known as structural-functionalism requires a number of elements as given. It requires a large measure of internal consistency in all of the sub-systems and inputs. It requires a large measure of agreement among individuals and groups as to their ends. It requires that social goals are not radically or violently disputed. It requires that different social groups adjust to each other so that the overall goals of society are achieved. It requires a mechanism for insuring that these consistencies are maintained. At the same time, there must be some general consistency in codes of behaviour, the needs of individuals and groups, roughly similar abilities, and internally consistent values and aspirations. It assumes therefore both that society is co-operative and that it needs co-operation. In other words, what is ought to be. It therefore has an in-built tendency to admire and sustain the status quo.

The application of structural-functionalism in town planning

The general school of thought exemplified by structural-functionalism is applied to town planning theory with increasing sophistication. Its chronological development parallels, at a later date, that found in sociology. It is to be found first in the use of an organic analogy, next in the specification of units via the use of ecological analogies, then in the delineation of sub-systems in terms of particular kinds of groupings and finally in systems theory which is the equivalent in town planning theory of structural-functionalism in sociology. Both manifestations of the same kind of understanding have implicit underlying assumptions about the normal or natural states of societies and towns.

The use of an organic analogy in town planning goes back to the origins of that idea in Western philosophy. As Herbert says,

> The Pythagorean search for an underlying universal order and harmony found expression in Hippodamian planning principles; and the neo-Platonic philosophy of the Renaissance led to the designing of ideal towns which reflected the harmonious structure of the universe and all creation.[6]

Utopian town plans in post-industrial Britain reflected both this same concern for order and the meaning attached to life. The concern for order may be seen both in their physical attributes of regular patterns and segregation of land uses. The meaning they attached to life is illustrated both by the permitted cultural pursuits concerned primarily with education and self-improvement, and by their relationship to the industrial social-class structure. In the latter they accommodated their planners' traditional, feudal and organic view of society in which each member had his allocated, understood and accepted place. The resulting physical plans reflected these beliefs in the kind of provision that was made for work and housing, leisure and education.

Such an understanding of society, while correctly reflecting the social relationships of the time, fails to recognise that these relationships change during the passage of time, and also tends to enshrine what exists with a metaphysical justification simply because it exists. The results are static town plans unable to cope with the processes of growth and change in society, and provision for the continuation of a set of social relationships which may or may not be desirable.

The use of the organic analogy in British town planning has also contributed materially to the flourishing of paternalism. Once, for example, the town planner has seized upon the metaphysical meaning of society and the kind of order which would contribute to its realisation, a whole collection of social objectives for town plans spring to his mind. British town plans are accordingly filled with highly debatable assertions of what contributes to human happiness and hence should form the objectives of the plans. As Herbert points out,

> It has motivated the garden city movement and inspired the concept of the greenbelt and the green wedge. City park systems, nature reserves, national parks, and recreation areas have, through this analogy, become an accepted part of the planners' responsibility. It has led to the desire to limit the size of the town, and indirectly to the satellite city idea, and it has promoted the concept of regionalism.[7]

It has furthermore lead to the spread of the garden suburb, low-density housing developments and urban sprawl. In short, the emphasis upon organicism in the planners' understanding of society is materially responsible for the anti-urban animus of British town planning.

Much of the responsibility for the prevalence of the nature analogy in British town planning lies with Howard, Geddes, the Garden City Movement and the Town and Country Planning Association. In many ways, however, they correctly reflect the commonly held nineteenth century view of the relative merits of rural as opposed to urban life. Thus, the English romantic poets eulogised nature as both the true and desirable in life; the reformers criticised urban living conditions; and the decision making élites in British society were exposed to these views during the course of their education. Consequently the town planning doctrines initiated by Howard struck receptive chords even if these were not immediately supported financially.

The fundamental weakness of the organic analogy, however, is that cities are not made by nature nor do they grow and change in the same way or time scale as do natural organisms. It is also probably misleading to assume that there is some ideal form of social and physical arrangement which is the natural form that cities do or should take. Certainly there is no reason to suppose, on the basis of the 'natural' behaviour of individuals and the choices they have made leading to the phenomenal growth of large urban settlements over the last century and a half, that the garden city or suburb is more 'natural' than large, high density and centralised forms of settlement. Indeed, it could be argued that the anti-urban aspects of British town planning arising from the nature analogy are, in fact, themselves 'un-natural'.

It could be posited, for example, that to arrest the growth of cities by the crude encircling device of the green belt is unnatural. Not only does this device promote artificial land scarcity, but also it entrains a whole range of subsequent policies such as the development of satellite towns and the limitation of their and other towns' size – a limitation which is based on implicit and untested assumptions about the 'natural' size and conditions of urban settlements. The results merely substitute some physical gains to set against the economic and social advantages of large urban concentrations.

The physical gains arising from the application of town planning policies based on the nature analogy are, however, mainly improvements by default. That is to say, they are seen as gains relative to the conditions prevailing particularly in the inner areas of cities because town planners have failed to achieve much in the way of the 'satisfactory' use of land in those areas. Instead, they have preferred to apply the more 'negative' aspects of their professional activities to existing development and their more 'positive' and tangible efforts to the utopian, irrational, but politically acceptable creation of pseudo-urban conditions either on the periphery of existing settlements or in the midst of green fields.

Social ecology

After the early adoption of a crude organic analogy by town planners during the early part of the twentieth century – in practical terms resulting in garden cities and suburbs – a more sophisticated interest in the interrelationships between the different parts of settlements grew up as a result of the work of the inter-war Chicago School of sociology.

The creation of a climate of opinion, among town planners, receptive to the work of the Chicago School owes much to Geddes. A professor of Botany at St Andrews University, Geddes 'was one of those pioneer thinkers who emphasised the relation between the physical and the biological on the one hand, and the social, on the other'.[8] His influence on British town planning has done much to foster the organic analogy in general and the acceptance of its ecological variation in particular.

During the nineteenth century, Vetch[9] and later Booth[10] noticed that the populations of English cities tended to be segregated by social class. The result was that the spatial arrangement of these populations reflected their position in the social class structure. During the inter-war period, Burgess studied the processes leading to the social segregation of different groups in Chicago.[11] Four such processes could be identified:

1. Concentration and deconcentration;
2. Centralisation and decentralisation;
3. Invasion and retreat;
4. Succession and withdrawal.

The first, concentration and deconcentration, reflected changes in the distribution of the population in space resulting either from unequal volumes of migration between one area and another or from differences in the rates of natural increase between different areas. Centralisation and decentralisation resulted from increasing or decreasing dominance by the city or its central area over the surrounding metropolitan region as the number and types of services performed within the region came to be more or less exclusively found at the centre. The third, invasion and retreat, resulted in the segregation of residential from commercial or industrial land, or of different types of residential areas. Invasion denoted the arrival in an area, for the first time, of new social groups and land users not previously found in the area. Finally, while invasion represented the movement of groups through space, Quinn[12] regarded succession as a movement through time within the same space and as the final stage of a sequence beginning with invasion. From the point of view of the ecological social structure of cities, invasion and retreat, succession and withdrawal are the most significant processes.

According to Burgess, the processes operated as follows:

> 1. invasion, beginning often as an unnoticed or gradual penetration, followed by
> 2. reaction, or the resistance mild or violent of the inhabitants of the community, ultimately resulting in
> 3. the influx of newcomers and the rapid abandonment of the area by its old-time residents, and
> 4. climax or the achievement of a new equilibrium of communal stability.[13]

Note the organic assumption that the ultimate and natural state of social interaction is not the possibly violent clashes between different groups during the process of change but the eventual stable equilibrium. This stable equilibrium is what Burgess saw reflected in his classic statement on the spatial structure of cities.

He argued, that

> as a result of industrial and commercial growth on the one hand, and of the corresponding residential motive of escape, on the other, the city tends to take form and to become organised on a pattern approximately that of concentric zones . . . These zones are:
>
> 1. The Central Business District Zone;
> 2. The Zone in Transition;
> 3. The Zone of Workingmen's Homes;
> 4. The Residential Zone;
> 5. The Commuters' Zone.[14]

In summary, he defined the characteristics of these zones as follows:

> The central business district tends in American cities to be at once the center of retail, financial, recreational, civic and political activities ... The zone in transition . . . [is] an interstitial area in the throes of change from residence to business and industry. This region is the port of first entry for incoming racial and incongruent groups . . . The zone of workingmen's homes finds its location at that distance beyond the factory belt surrounding the central business district, which is still accessible, often within walking distance, to the worker ... The better residential zone is inhabited by the families of persons engaged in professional and clerical pursuits . . . The commuters' zone comprises the suburban districts of the city which combine the atmosphere of village residence with access by rapid transit or by automobile to the downtown metropolitan center for work, shopping, and entertainment.[15]

Virtually all subsequent analyses of the socio-spatial characteristics of cities have been adaptations of these basic propositions.

The first major modification was proposed by Hoyt.[16] He studied the shifts, which took place between 1900 and 1936, in lccation of fashionable residential areas in six American cities. He concluded that cities developed in sectors rather than zones. This reflected the radial lines of communication centred on the industrial and commercial nucleus of a city. Later Harris and Ullman[17] pointed out that many large cities have more than one such nucleus so that zonal or sectoral growth might emanate from more than one such centre. Despite a great deal of subsequent investigation, ably documented by Johnston,[18] this remains the basic contemporary, conventional wisdom.

This concept was responsible for a number of studies conducted in the United Kingdom during the 1960s. Among these, it was shown by Collison[19] for Oxford, Robson[20] for Sunderland, Jones[21] for Belfast, Westergaard[22] for Greater London and Mann[23] for the North of England that the socio-spatial arrangement, at least in these areas, did indeed follow a zonal, sectoral or multiple nucleated form. From studies such as these, town planners in Britain have become concerned with social segregation, an emphasis on the spatial arrangement of cities as a determinant of this segregation, a belief that zonal and sectoral growth is the 'natural' form of city growth and that the different social and economic spatial attributes of cities are organically related to one another.

These assumptions may be challenged. The most important early critique of the ecological understanding of cities was produced by Firey.[24] He criticised this understanding as idealised description, empirical or methodological rationalism. He argued that,

> Though vague concentric and sector patterns are apparent in certain types of land use, the more important is the variation of land use within these zones . . . There are . . . some rough cartographic patterns to be found now and then in land uses, which are just tangible enough to make the concentric-sector theories plausible. Indeed, if there were not, it would be something of a mystery how such theories had come to be formulated.[25]

In general, however, it may be argued that to impose simplified patterns of regularity on the often random and chaotic socio-spatial patterns of cities does less than justice to an explanation of these complexities.

Indeed, the explanatory power of the ecology theories is, again, as Firey points out, very low indeed. 'Nowhere in the theory is there a definite statement of the *modus operandi* by which people and groups are propelled to their appointed niches in space.'[26] Consequently, it does not offer a satisfactory explanation of why specific socio-spatial patterns exist or how and why the residential choices made by individuals create and maintain or change them. In fact, according to Firey, ecological theories assume away the need to explain these problems by implicitly asserting that physical space possesses qualities which are wholly devoid of cultural values and that social systems passively comply with spatial distance.

Research conducted by the author into the motives for residential change in Southampton[27] shows that these assumptions are unwarranted. The investigation showed that any explanation of the socio-spatial structure of cities resulting from the residential choices made by their inhabitants would have to take into account differences in market situations, values and aspirations of individuals situated differently in the social structure. Thus, far from the resulting structure of cities being devoid of social and cultural significance, they will, in fact, reflect just these characteristics of society.

This being the case, a further implicit assumption of the ecological analogy as a basis for understanding the city must be questioned. In its classical formulation it assumes the existence of an unmitigated capitalist economy and that the zonal or sectoral patterning of cities is based on competition in the market place for the use of land. Even in a mixed economy like that found in Britain, once this condition no longer holds, any concentric or zonal growth may be so altered as to render theories reflecting these features irrelevant. The location of local authority housing in Sunderland, for example, was shown by Robson[28] to distort the concentric and zonal patterns of the city to such an extent that it had to be removed from maps attempting to demonstrate such patterns.

Finally, in the discussion of the social ecology of cities, it should be noted that such theories are essentially conservative in their organicism. Despite their discussion of the processes of growth and change they uniformly envisage a subsequent equilibrium in which a new, 'normal' balance is struck in the residential location of the populations of cities. The natural condition of cities is therefore assumed to be based on organic relationships in which each individual knows the plot to which he may aspire and moves there, accepting not only the justice of his allocation but also the 'eventually' peaceful reactions of his fellow citizens. Town planners accepting this understanding of cities plan accordingly.

The specification of sub-systems

Running almost concurrently with the developing interest in the inter-relationships between citizens, found in British town planning as a result of the influence of social ecologists, has been the attempt to specify and plan for the units and sub-systems which are interrelated. This interest developed chronologically immediately before and after the Second World War. In its simplest form it postulates that the basic unit is the family; groups of families form communities which may be happily accommodated in neighbourhoods, and cities are composed of numbers of neighbourhoods. The basic planning function is therefore to arrange and link these cells hierarchically in the most felicitous physical form. Accordingly, a great deal of British town planning theory and practice has been concerned with the family and neighbourhood.

According to Herbert, 'the neighbourhood unit concept constitutes a new orthodoxy'.[29] It also derives from the Chicago School.

Its progenitor, Perry, was influenced by the work of Cooley, Park, Burgess, Woods and Wood – all members of that School. They 'were concerned with the weakening of social bonds in the rapidly expanding cities, with the substitution of indirect for direct social relations, and the development of . . . anomic society'.[30] The town planning answer to these problems advanced by Perry in 1923 was the neighbourhood unit.

Perry's neighbourhood was:

1. to be of a size necessary for the maintenance of one primary school;
2. to have boundaries which clearly defined and articulated it within the town;
3. to have open spaces to provide for recreational needs;
4. to provide for educational and social needs having service areas which were coincident;
5. to have local shops, preferably on the perimeter of the unit;
6. to have an internal street system, related to traffic load and segregated from the external, peripheral through traffic routes.

It bore a marked resemblance to the ward organisation suggested by Howard in his 'ideal formulation of the garden city plan'.[31] It is not surprising, therefore, that the idea was taken up by the Community Centres and Associations Survey Group of the National Council of Social Service in 1943, who recommended that,

> All development of housing policy should be based on the neighbourhood unit, regarded as a community with a maximum of about 2000 dwellings, and thus comprising between 7000 and 10 000 persons, and furnished with the communal facilities required for the full development of the life of the neighbourhood.'[32]

This view was enshrined in the official Dudley Report of 1944.[33]

In the light of the social characteristics of pre-war housing and war-time experiences, British town planners added the notion of social balance or mix to the original neighbourhood concept. Again this recommendation may be found in the 1943 report from the National Council of Social Service. They say,

> In the interest of social variety, and in order to enable families of different backgrounds and experiences to continue to mix in peace-time as they are now mixing during war, each neighbourhood unit should be socially

balanced, containing houses of different types and sizes inhabited by families belonging to different income groups.[34]

In other instances the concept of balance is used to refer to the proportions of families in different stages of their life-cycles as in the recent experiment reported by Barlow and Ramsdale. According to their diagnosis, 'Many of the physical and social problems that face existing new towns and large estates stem directly from the unbalanced age and household structure of their population.'[35] They go on to argue that these undefined physical and social problems can be alleviated. They assert that,

The theoretical ideal would give a stationary population, i.e. the population total would not change over the years, births would equate with deaths, and there would be a constant number of school children, of persons of working age and of retired persons.[36]

They recognise that, short of euthanasia, this 'ideal' is impractical and go on to recommend and execute a 'second best' alternative in which 'the population of the new development would be balanced according to age and size of family, in relation to Sunderland as a whole'.[37] Again, for unspecified reasons, the contemporary demographic structure of Sunderland is taken as the 'norm' for which the planner is to strive irrespective of the characteristics of those most in need of public authority housing.

It is impossible to escape the impression that far from being the answer to the anomie (itself open to serious question as an adequate analysis) of urban society, the neighbourhood unit and social balance are primarily devices of administrative convenience. They benefit the planner rather than the planned. Thus, as Barlow and Ramsdale assert, their main justification is that they 'allow accurate planning for, and optimum use of, social investment in the form of housing, roads, schools, cultural and entertainment provision'.[38] But, more accurately, they provide a simplification of the complexities of social interaction in settlements which makes it easier for the town planner to attempt to forecast the demands for the future use of land and the other resources he is responsible for allocating.

Not only is the socially balanced neighbourhood unit more of an administrative convenience than a relevant response to the social interactions of cities, but also it is based on false assumptions. As

Rex argues, 'The metasocial assumptions on which . . . planners . . . seem to draw are so trivial that they appear to be nothing more than the rationalizations of what they are forced to do by their masters or what they do simply for reasons of expediency.'[39]

In the first place, the assumption derived via Perry and the Chicago School that urban life is characterised by anomie and that what people therefore want and need is assistance in organic and functional integration, is inaccurate in two ways. It is not confirmed by empirical evidence nor is it demonstrated that anomie offers a more relevant conceptualisation of urban pathology than does alienation.

In Britain, during the late 1950s, a series of community studies showed that some areas of cities were not characterised by anomie while many of the products of town planners based on this false assumption were. Many of these studies have been admirably analysed by Klein in her book *Samples from English Cultures*. In it she argues that, in many of the working-class areas studied,

> The networks of component families are often so close-knit, and the relationships within the local population group so clearly distinguished from external relationships that the local population can almost be called an organised group. The members' activities are known to all. None can escape the sanctions of gossip and public opinion. In these conditions, people tend to reach consensus on norms and exert a consistent informal pressure on each other to conform. This is the way a tradition is perpetuated relatively immune from change as long as the network remains intact.[40]

This may be a description of an alienated group as attested to by the kind of industrial conflict experienced by dockers and mineworkers, but it is certainly not anomie. This kind of description, often generalised from communities containing many such workers, is not, however, characteristic, particularly during the early years, of new neighbourhoods created by town planners. As Klein says,

> On the estates there is often nowhere to go out to . . . the other men on the estates are not lifelong friends and the home is more attractive. The home and the family become more important emotionally and in some ways cost less money for their maintenance than the traditional male group does.[41] Most deeply felt of all is the reduction of interaction with other members of the extended family.[42]

To be fair, not all new residents of the creations of town planners regard their old communities as ideal. Norris, for example, found that 'a large minority thought back with disapproval and remembered quarrels, too much mixing, too much popping in and out'.[43]

Either way, however, the evidence is not consistent with the assumption that urban life is necessarily anomic for, whether they approve of it or not, residents in traditional working-class communities are shown to be subject to processes of social control. In the creations of town planners, especially during the first few years, these processes are absent or changed. Consequently, as Rex argues, in these circumstances town planning creates 'a sense of purposelessness and normlessness and anomie far worse than anything which existed in industrial cities which had reached maturity'.[44] Thus, 'Instead of planning becoming the means of overcoming anomie, it has become its instrument.'[45] While this may be an accurate description of many of the results of town planning, it is still based on the fundamental misconception that the communities which form the planners' clients are anomic. The evidence cited does not support this assumption. They may be alienated from other groups in society but they are clearly not anomic. In so far as anomie is to be found in urban society it is more often a feature of residentially mobile populations, whether enforced or voluntary, rather than of non-mobile groups with traditional social and residential associations. In so far as the town planner is an agent of residential mobility, he may also be the agent of anomie.

It is often the case, therefore, that in new towns and suburbs, as Orlans remarks, 'Planners often try to repair with one hand what they have damaged with the other – that is, they try to remedy conditions which are themselves (in part) a consequence of previous remedies.'[46] The neighbourhood unit is an attempt to do just this and the socially balanced neighbourhood is an attempt to create something which is not and never has been a characteristic of cities nor satisfies its inhabitants. Hutchinson, for example, examining the balanced community features of Willesden, found that almost two-thirds of his informants would have preferred single-class streets to streets of mixed social classes.[47]

Even if these criticisms of the application of the organic analogy in the form of the neighbourhood community unit are rejected, its implementation requires the surmounting of further difficulties.

Foremost among these is what kind of community town-planners are trying to create. In this connection, Kuper poses some critical questions. Speaking of the 'sense of neighbourhood' he asks,

Is it expressed when residents in an area join together to resist the appropriation of land for the building of a hostel by the local authority? And what is the ideal relationship between sentiment for the town as a whole and sentiment for the neighbourhood? Or again, is the ideal neighbourhood-feeling an awareness and knowledge by the residents of the intimate behaviour of neighbours and a social control exercised by gossip and extending to the items displayed on the wash-line? Or are there degrees of neighbourhood sentiment, and if so, what degree of intimacy and affective ties is desired?[48]

Dennis also points to the confusion that exists about what actually constitutes a neighbourhood community. He says,

The community may denote merely the houses and people located in a given area, even when there are few relationships of any kind, whether institutionalised or informal, manifest or latent . . . In text books the term often means an area which contains all or most of the elements of a complete social system . . . Others reserve the term for situations in which there is present a common opinion on topics of common interest . . . There is finally the idea of community as involving interaction of a certain degree and quality.[49]

Even if it is thought desirable to create neighbourhood communities, without a clearer definition than the conflicting views portrayed by Kuper and Dennis, it will not be possible to devise the means to achieve the end. Thus a fundamental criticism of the organic analogy, as applied to the neighbourhood community by British town planners, is that they cannot be created without the arbitrary adoption of some partial, inadequate or tendentious definition of what constitutes a satisfactory final state of the community.

In view of the paradoxes surrounding the creation of neighbourhood communities, it is instructive to examine some of their consequences which are not usually mentioned by their advocates. Glass argues that,

the idea of social balance may be used to introduce wise middle-class councillors into predominantly working-class areas which, together with the dispersal to the periphery of urban areas of large portions of the working class reduces the possibilities for the development of class consciousness and conflict.[50]

Orlans also concludes

> that many garden city and new town planners merely translated into sociological terms and architectural forms middle and upper-class ideologies of a conservative or liberal-reformist nature, and that the balanced community concept thus served the forces of law and order, middle-class morality, and the social and political status quo.[51]

Systems theory

The latest version of the planning equivalent of structural-functionalism is systems theory. It comes nearest to the identification of sub-systems and their functional interrelationships and often seeks to express these relationships in quasi-mathematical form. Like structural-functionalism, systems theory also inherits the positivist tradition in the social sciences. An analogy is drawn between the normal, systematic functions of animal life and plant life and those of the city. It is therefore assumed that the process of city life are systematically related; that given sufficient information, these relationships can be identified; and that town planning is concerned with the rational manipulation of these identified processes with a view to achieving more desirable ends than those which arise without the interference of town planners.

Prominent among the pioneers of the systematic analogy in British town planning are McLoughlin[52] and Chadwick.[53] The former, in a paper delivered to the Town and Country Planning Summer School held in Belfast in 1967 explicitly draws attention to the analogy between animal and plant systems and the application of this view to planning.

> Consider [he writes] a herd of buffalo roaming the plains. We can regard the herd as a system and each animal as a component – they interact with one another as individuals and they have a corporate identity. But each buffalo is a system too – comprised of heart, lungs, liver, brain, muscles and nerves. If we were studying the species we might wish to look upon each of the thousands of herds as a component in the system of buffalo ecology – itself only a sub-system of the total ecology of the plains . . .[54]

This view – via the application of general systems theory, operations research, systems analysis, cybernetics and traffic engineering – he seeks to develop in town planning. To do this planners are advised to foresee how the system might evolve – how it would develop if left severely alone, and also what the outcomes of many different kinds of stimuli and intervention might be. McLoughlin quotes Mitchell as illustrating what town plans developed on the basis of the systematic view would be like. They would 'be plans for the nature, rate, quantity and quality of urban change – for a process of development. They will be expressed in dynamic rather than in static terms. They will start with present conditions and point the direction of change.'[55]

Chadwick develops the same analogy. He correctly argues that a prerequisite of town planning is 'that it provides a better performance than laissez-faire, or the free play of the market'.[56] He then claims that operations research provides the technology for 'optimising the performance'[57] of the systems with which planning deals, and that town planners should concern themselves with 'the optimisation of the real world system by seeking optimisation of the conceptual system'.[58] Systems analysis has now become so widespread among British town planners that it may be seen as the conventional wisdom of contemporary planning. This position is unmerited.

In the first place there is no evidence that the systematic analogy is appropriate when applied to the city. It would be necessary to know much more about how and why cities, or more properly their inhabitants, behave in the way that they do before it could be argued that this behaviour may either be adequately studied or explained by systems theory. What the systems theorists have done is to take a method for examining, by simplifying, complex interrelationships found in clearly defined institutions and organisational arrangements, and applied this method to the study of urban settlements. It is pure assertion that methods for studying herds of buffalo or the maximisation of the output of industrial and commercial organisations bears any relationship to the interaction between inhabitants of cities. Having made this assertion, however, it is quite likely that the systems theorists will be able to demonstrate some relevance in the application of their theories to the city, simply because that is what they are looking for. This, however, would be the case with almost any *a priori* application of theory to the city.

A second criticism of the systematic analogy in British town planning is that it reflects the belief that any subject only awaits the diligent application of sufficient time and resources to become susceptible to numerate explanation. Again this is a belief which, given the present state of knowledge about cities, may or may not be true in their case. However, this belief is not something that can be assumed without argument or evidence. On the contrary, the impression of irrationality, chaos and anarchy found in cities leads the introspective analyst to doubt the suitability of systematic and numerate analysis of the interactions between their inhabitants. The bewildering variety of their personal interrelationships and decisions seem quite unsusceptible to causal explanation by a theory which both simplifies and concentrates on the analysis of processes and virtually ignores the importance of motivation.

Even if one accepts the systematic analogy in planning, its efficacy as an explanatory tool is limited by its own logical requirements. Thus, to study systems requires their definition. This can only be done with relatively closed systems such as a particular commercial concern or government agency. In a situation of complexity such as that found in cities it is just not possible to define the boundaries of relevant systems. It is not possible, for example, to enumerate all the social ramifications of moving large numbers of people from one part of a city to another in a redevelopment scheme. This being the case, systems theorists are forced to abandon the attempt to define significant closed systems and to talk instead of open systems. By this device they are really arguing that it is possible to look at a part of the system that is the city without having to define its boundaries or enumerate precisely its inputs and outputs. This argument has much the same force that a biological thesis, which said that it was relevant to study the heart without defining its external structure or its related cardio-vascular system, would have. Furthermore, it may be doubtful whether the concept of an open system constitutes a rigorous use of the systematic analogy. Indeed, one is entitled to ask whether the open system is, correctly speaking, a system at all.

Both structural-functionalism and systems theory are inherently conservative, require a high degree of unanimity on values and aspirations, break down as explanatory theories when social interaction is characterised by conflict rather than co-operation, provide obscure definitions of social reality and therefore weak explanations of it anyway, cannot account for the all important phenomenon of social change and generate no exogenous principles for the normative evaluation of existing or proposed states of society. These factors help to explain why the theories are favoured even in countries where, for example, sociology is a proscribed discipline. The fact is that they can be used to support the status quo regardless of what that situation is.

Thus, if one studies the processes of organisation and change in the city by using an analogy which axiomatically assumes a moving equilibrium situation (changing gradually over time on account of feedback from its various sub-systems, all embraced by a given set of values) then radical, large scale, violent or unusual change must be seen as alien to the existing system. This applies as much in communist as in capitalist systems. Consequently, the 'correct' response to any of these problems will be to react against them in favour of the status quo ante.

Similarly, systems theory or structural-functionalism can only describe situations where there is a degree of unanimity on values, codes, needs and similarities in individual abilities. These conditions are generally only fulfilled either in static and primitive societies or where most people prefer the status quo.

This is not the case in advanced, industrial and capitalist societies: As any casual observer may see in such societies, there is conflict between groups over their values and aspirations, and their ability to satisfy these in terms of the acquisition of scarce and desirable resources and power. While a crude total dichotomy between capital and labour is not found in capitalist society, nevertheless, elements of both these groups are always to be found in conflict and always in dispute over the allocation of resources and power. In such circumstances assumptions about internally generated values and unanimity are not satisfactory *a priori* foundations upon which to construct any theory about the way in which different groups interact.

Not only do systems theory and structural-functionalism provide inherent support for the status quo and fail to explain conflict, but also, in order to avoid some of these problems, they produce obscure definitions of social sub-systems. In their attempts to demarcate social as opposed to individual behaviour or in their exclusion of the discussion of different purposes among different groups, they tend to gloss-over or ignore important avenues of explanation. At the same time, what is left constitutes a very vague approximation of the way in which individuals know that they lead their lives. Not many people would intuitively agree, for example, that the nature of the society in which they found themselves was the result of the collective interaction of their and other people's attempts at goal-attainment, latent pattern maintenance, adaptation and integration.

Such theories also fail to come to grips with the crucial question of social change. This is because they rest on the assumption that people co-operate with each other mainly in order to ensure the survival of the group. In fact, in competitive societies a tendency to do quite the reverse may be observed. The motivation of individual self-interest looms large in such circumstances and only regulations and prudence prevent the development of greater rather than less conflict.

Finally, the most important reason why structural-functionalism and systems theory must be regarded as inadequate ways of understanding and making decisions about social interaction is that they lack any explicit and exogenous normative reference points. Their implicit normative stance is, however, that whatever is ought to be. Consequently, whatever diverges from what is, ought to be brought back to something like the status quo ante. This therefore excluded all the most important debates about the nature of society. Liberty, equality, fraternity and justice are all precluded from serious disputation. For example, the authorities in South Africa and Czechoslovakia are equally happy to allow the study of Parsons and equally unhappy to permit public and dissident debate.

Normal society

For policy makers the main problem which arises if their understanding of society and cities is based on structural-functionalism and systems theories is that this understanding carries with it implications of what is 'normal', and therefore impels a particular way of recognising what is thought to be abnormal and also how such abnormalities should be treated. This means that if the understanding of what is normal is inadequate, then what is abnormal will be relatively incorrectly diagnosed and consequently the policies followed to restore the status quo will not be particularly effective. In the case of town planning this usually means that abnormal social interaction, or lack of it, is often described as anomie rather than alienation and the consequent policies sometimes create greater alienation than co-operation. In this, town planners have been influenced in their understanding of urban society by the studies of urbanism issuing from the Chicago School. As Morris points out, this 'approach to urban sociology . . . begins with patterns of social behaviour rather than with the size of the population units . . . The key objective . . . is to study the processes through which a particular society encourages or discourages the development of cities . . .'[59] Foremost in the initiation of such studies is Wirth, whose article 'Urbanism as a way of life'[60] represents one of the founding seminal works along with those of Simmel[61] and Weber.[62]

One of the main themes in the article by Wirth is the lack of close personal relationships between the inhabitants of cities. He records the following: the likelihood that there will be weak bonds among co-residents; little chance of knowing many citizens personally; a highly developed division of labour associated with the treatment of relationships as means-to-ends; the impossibility of assembling all the residents in one place and the consequent reliance placed on indirect mass communication; close but socially superficial physical contacts, and a general absence of close sentimental and emotional ties between co-workers and co-residents. In short, Wirth says,

> The distinctive features of the urban mode of life have often been described sociologically as consisting of the substitution of secondary for primary contacts, the weakening of bonds of kinship, and the declining social significance of the family, the disappearance of the neighbourhood, and the undermining of the traditional basis of social solidarity. All these phenomenon can be substantially verified through objective indices.[63]

Accordingly,

> Personal disorganisation, mental breakdown, suicide, delinquency, crime, corruption, and disorder might be expected under these circumstances to be more prevalent in the urban than in the rural community.[64]

This view precisely echoes and reinforces those held by utopians and garden city advocates in British town planning. Wirth thus provided them with a coherent exposition of the nature of urban society which not only confirmed their definition of the problem but also lent the weight of a member of a prestigious school of sociology to their diagnosis.

Sociology provides two alternative explanations of the possible causes of such characteristics where they exist. On the one hand there is the concept of anomie originated by Durkheim and on the other the notion of alienation associated with Marx. Both imply a strong sense of the natural as opposed to anomic or alienated society, so that to adopt one or the other is either to accept a particular state of society towards which individuals should be directed or to indicate the implicit values of the analyst.

In general, British town planners have accepted variations of Durkheim's anomic analysis of the 'pathological' characteristics of cities said to exist by Wirth. As Lukes points out, anomie 'refers first to the relationship of the individual to elements of his social environment and second to his state of mind'.[65] In his book *The Division of Labour*, Durkheim uses anomie

> to characterise the pathological state of the economy, this sphere of collective life which is, in large part, freed from the moderating action of regulations, whether latent or active, the state of war is necessarily chronic and each individual finds himself in a state of war with every other. In *Suicide* it is used to characterise the pathological mental state of the individual who is insufficiently regulated by society and suffers from the malady of infinite aspiration.[66]

In defining the remedy for such a situation, Durkheim joins the doctrine also espoused by Hobbes and Freud by asserting, as Lukes points out, that 'man is a bundle of desires, which need to be regulated, tamed, repressed, manipulated and given direction for the sake of social order'.[67]

For Durkheim, the division of labour is not antithetical to the development of social order and in fact, when properly regulated by relevant rules and institutions, is the major source of solidarity in modern industrial society. Consequently, increases in the division of labour and the size of the market result in the growth of cities and the decline of intimate personal relationships as diagnosed by Wirth, but require town planners, among others, to increase the amount of regulations and moral institutions for the return to 'normality'. What is important to note here is that this diagnosis of the social malaise of city life implies a set of relationships which are 'normal' and therefore the kind of social relationships that policy makers should seek to achieve. In this instance 'normal' city life would be based on a highly developed division of labour regulated by institutions and generally accepted codes of behaviour. In other words, the goals of town planners accepting an anomic analysis of urbanism are predetermined by this analysis, and consist of promoting a systematically related society based on common values and generally accepted regulations which Durkheim would call mechanical solidarity. In practice such a conception of the 'natural' or 'normal' city life might more accurately be described as yet another example of the use of sophisticated organicism by town planners in their diagnosis and treatment of the problems of urban settlements.

In contrast, Marx's analysis of the same problems using the concept of alienation leads to a different set of propositions about the 'natural', 'normal' and therefore desirable conditions of society. Lukes notes that Marx distinguishes four aspects of alienated labour:

1. The relationship of the worker to the product of labour as an alien object which dominates him. Thus, the more the worker expends himself in work the more powerful becomes the world of objects which he creates in face of himself, the poorer he becomes in his inner life, and the less he belongs to himself.

2. The relationship of labour to the act of production, with the result that the work is external to the worker, that it is not part of his nature, and that, consequently, he does not fulfil himself in his work but denies himself, has a feeling of misery rather than well-being, does not develop freely his mental and physical energies but is physically exhausted and mentally debased. The worker, therefore, feels himself at home only during his leisure time, whereas at work he feels homeless. His work is not voluntary but imposed, forced labour. It is not the satisfaction of a need, but only a means for satisfying other needs.

3. The alienation of man from himself as a species-being, from his own active function, his life-activity, which is a free, conscious activity. Man is thus alienated from his own body, external nature, his mental life and his human life.

4. The alienation of man from other men. When man confronts himself he also confronts other men . . . in the relationship of alienated labour every man regards other men according to the standards and relationships in which he finds himself placed as a worker. Social relations are not relations between individual and individual, but between worker and capitalist, between farmer and landlord, etc. Further, men's lives are divided up into different spheres of activity . . .[68]

These characteristics of alienated labour are strikingly like those portrayed as the nature of urban social relationships by Wirth above. But, while Durkheim regards the regulated division of labour in society as the norm towards which anomic man should be directed, Marx regards it, partly, as the cause of alienation. Thus, as Lukes says,

Durkheim sees the division of labour as being (when properly regulated) the source of solidarity in modern industrial society: the prevalence of anomie is due to a lag in the growth of the relevant rules and institutions . . (while) in Marx's thinking (alienation is) what characterizes precisely those states of the individual and conditions of society which Durkheim sees as the solution to anomie: namely, where men are socially determined and constrained, when they must conform to social rules which are independent of their wills and are conditioned to think and act within the confines of specialized roles.[69]

The paradox facing town planners in this situation is that if they accept Durkheim's analysis of the causes of anomie in urban life and attempt to reintegrate individuals into the 'natural', 'normal' and organic society postulated by their structural-functionalist systems theory on the one hand; and if Marx's analysis of alienated man is more valid than Durkheim's on the other; then town planners will be helping to create precisely those social interrelationships they consider undesirable. Thus, if Marx is correct, the attempt to meet the undesirable attributes of urban life, portrayed by Wirth, by increased regulation and imposed social values will probably lead to greater rather than less alienation in the urban settlements of modern industrial society. Examples of the effects of planning blight, the movement of populations and town planners' attitudes to 'problem' areas show that this is often the case. In each of these instances the actions of British town planners have a tendency to increase alienation rather than reduce anomie. This alone should cause town planners to speculate on the validity of structural-functionalism and systems theories as adequate conceptions of 'normal' social interaction and also on anomie as an explanation of what is 'abnormal'. At any rate, there is clearly enough doubt about these theories to warrant the exploration of what it would mean in terms of understanding social interaction and producing normative plans for its alteration if society was in reality based on conflict rather than co-operation.

Conclusions

It has been argued that the main planks of the home-spun sociology of town planners are insecure. They are selectively culled from a general strand in sociological theory known as structural-functionalism. This asserts that society is basically a co-operative and integrated collection of groups, most of whom subscribe to the same kinds of values.

On the basis of this assumption town planners have developed incorrect versions of what constitutes normal and abnormal social interaction. On the basis of these assumptions, programmes and remedies have been constructed.

The answer to 'anomie' is seen as the reintegration of individuals into society via such mechanisms as the neighbourhood unit. The comprehension of integrated societies is sought on the basis of systems theory. Both of these ideas are derived from the selective use of American sociology, particularly represented by the Chicago School and Parsons.

There are serious deficiencies both in the work of the originators and in the application of their ideas by town planners. The main ones are that they fail to understand situations which are based on social conflict and alienation rather than on co-operation, and they do not explain either the nature of existing society nor what causes it to change. Alternative theories and practices are therefore required.

The rest of the book is devoted to the detailing of an alternative theory and to its application in society in general and town planning in particular. It is argued that society may be more accurately understood on the basis of conflict theory and that town planning policies and their effects should therefore be seen in relation to the struggles for the acquisition of scarce resources, political power and ideological conflict.

In this context, Chapter 3 develops a more detailed exposition of conflict theory and demonstrates its relevance by an historical analysis of the development of social and spatial conflict. The role of town planning in these conflicts is traced by comparing the effects of its statutory introduction in 1909 with the conditions prevailing in British cities during the reign of Queen Victoria. Thus the half century before 1909 is compared with the years up to the 1947 Town and Country Planning Act.

Chapter 4 concentrates on the contemporary conflicts over economic resources in Britain. Their current distribution is analysed and the spatial structure of cities is shown to depend partially on this aspect of the social structure. It is argued that to understand the spatial structure it is first necessary to comprehend the social structure. The effects of town planning on both are analysed.

Chapter 5 goes on to look at the relationships between power, politics and planners. These are examined by looking at some of the case studies of the political nature of town planning and comparing these both with the theoretical pursuit of the public interest by planners and also the equity of the effects of their actions. It is shown that, as with the distribution of economic resources, town planning tends to reflect rather than counteract the current distribution of political power.

The rationalisations of these states of affairs are examined in Chapter 6. There the relationships between ideology and social action are investigated. Two broad ideological positions are identified in British society and the stances adopted by town planners are argued to reflect one of them. It is maintained that the traditional stance of town planners concerned with the physical environment is derived from that of liberal ideology and serves primarily their own self interest.

The conclusions from these analyses are drawn together in Chapter 7. A series of related programmes are recommended concerned with the planning of the distribution of economic resources, the power structure and the ideologies of town planners. The primary immediate objective of social policy in general and town planning in particular is argued to be the eradication of the poverty cycle as represented by bad environment, poor schools, low income and mental strain. It is argued that without a multi-fronted attack on these issues the latent conflict between different social classes could well become a reality in the decades to come.

References

1 H. Orlans, *Stevenage: a sociological study of a new town*, Routledge & Kegan Paul (1952), p. 99

2 A. R. Radcliffe-Brown, *Structure and Function in Primitive Society* (London, 1952)

3 B. Malinowski, *A Scientific Theory of Culture and Other Essays*, Chapel Hill (1944)
4 T. Parsons, *The Social System*, Routledge & Kegan Paul (1951)
5 J. McLeish, *The Theory of Social Change*, Routledge & Kegan Paul (1969)
6 G. Herbert, 'The organic analogy in town planning', *Journal of the American Institute of Planners*, August (1963), 198–209
7 *ibid.*
8 *ibid.*
9 J. Vetch, Capt., *Poor Law Commissioners' Report on an Enquiry into the Sanitary Condition of the Labouring Population of Great Britain*, HMSO (1834), 382–94
10 C. Booth, *Life and Labour of the People of London*, 17 vols., Macmillan (1906)
11 E. W. Burgess, 'The growth of the city', in Park, R. E., Burgess, E. W. and McKenzie, R. D. (ed.) *The City, Chicago*, Chicago University Press (1925)
12 S. A. Quinn, *Human Ecology*, Prentice-Hall (New Jersey, 1950)
13 E. W. Burgess, 'Residential segregation in American cities', *Annals of the American Academy of Political and Social Science*, November (1928), 105–15
14 *ibid.*
15 *ibid.*
16 H. Hoyt, *The Structure and Growth of Residential Neighbourhoods in American Cities*, Washington D. C., Federal Housing Administration (1939)
17 C. D. Harris and E. L. Ullman, 'The nature of cities', *Annals of the American Academy of Political and Social Science*, **242** (1945), 7–17
18 R. J. Johnston, *Urban Residential Patterns: an introductory review*, Bell (1971)
19 P. Collison and J. Mogey, 'Residence and social class in Oxford', *American Journal of Sociology* (1959)
20 B. T. Robson, 'An ecological analysis of the evaluation of residential areas in Sunderland', *Urban Studies*, **3** (1966), 120–39
21 E. Jones, *The Social Geography of Belfast*, Oxford University Press (1960)
22 J. H. Westergaard, 'The structure of greater London', in *Centre for Urban Studies*, University College London (1964), 91–143
23 P. H. Mann, *An Approach to Urban Sociology*, Routledge & Kegan Paul (1970)
24 W. Firey, *Land Use in Central Boston*, Harvard University Press (1947)
25 *ibid.*
26 *ibid.*

27 J. M. Simmie, *The Sociology of Internal Migration*, C.E.S. University Working Paper 15 (Centre for Environmental Studies, London, 1972)
28 B. T. Robson (1966), *op. cit.*
29 G. Herbert, 'The neighbourhood unit principle and organic theory', *Sociological Review*, **XI**, July (1963), 165–213
30 *ibid.*
31 *ibid.*
32 The Community Centres and Associations Survey Group of the National Council of Social Service, *The Size and Structure of a Town*, Allen & Unwin (1943)
33 *Design of Dwellings*, HMSO, 1844, Section 2
34 National Council of Social Service, *op. cit.* (1943)
35 J. E. Barlow and G. I. Ramsdale, 'Balanced Population: an experiment at Silksworth, overspill township for Sunderland', *Journal of the Royal Town Planning Institute*, **52** (7), (1966), 265–69
36 *ibid.*
37 *ibid.*
38 *ibid.*
39 J. Rex, 'Economic Growth and Decline: their consequences for the sociology of planning', *Report of the Town and Country Planning Summer School*, Manchester (1968)
40 J. Klein, *Samples from English Cultures*, Routledge & Kegan Paul (1965), p. 128
41 *ibid.*, p. 223
42 *ibid.*, p. 226
43 J. Norris, *Human Aspects of Redevelopment*, Midlands (1966)
44 J. Rex, *op. cit.* (1968)
45 *ibid.*
46 H. Orlans, *op. cit.* (1952), p. 88
47 E. Hutchinson, *Willesden and the New Towns*, The Social Survey, (1947)
48 L. Kuper, 'Social science research and the planning of urban neighbourhoods', *Social Forces* (1951), 237–43
49 N. Dennis, 'The popularity of the neighbourhood community idea', *Sociological Review*, **6**, December (1968), 191–206
50 R. Glass, *Current Sociology*, **IV** (4), (1955)
51 H. Orlans, *op. cit.* (1952), 94
52 J. B. McLoughlin, *Urban and Regional Planning: a systems approach*, Faber & Faber (1969)
53 G. F. Chadwick, *A Systems View of Planning: towards a theory of the urban and regional planning process*, Pergamon Press (1971)
54 J. B. McLoughlin, 'A systems approach to planning', *Town and Country Planning Summer School*, Belfast (1967)

55 R. B. Mitchell, 'The new frontier in metropolitan planning', *Journal of the American Institute of Planners*, August (1961)
56 G. F. Chadwick, 'A systems view of planning', *Journal of the Royal Town Planning Institute*, 184–86
57 *ibid.*
58 *ibid.*
59 R. W. Morris, *Urban Sociology*, Routledge & Kegan Paul (1968)
60 L. Wirth, 'Urbanism as a way of life', *American Journal of Sociology*, **XLIV** (1), July (1938), 1–24
61 G. Simmel, *The Metropolis and Mental Life*, Chicago University Press (1936)
62 M. Weber, *The City*, New York Free Press (1958)
63 L. Wirth, *op. cit.* (1938)
64 *ibid.*
65 S. Lukes, 'Alienation and anomie', in P. Laslett and W. G. Runciman, (ed.), *Philosophy, Politics and Society* (Third Series), Blackwell (1969), p. 139
66 *ibid.*, p. 138
67 *ibid.*, p. 145
68 *ibid.*, p.137
69 *ibid.*, 140–41

3. A socio-political perspective on British town planning

The need for perspective

In order to understand the significance of town planning as it is practised now, it is first necessary to develop three converging perspectives. These are:

1. A theoretical perspective for understanding the nature of the social interactions which take place in the environing society of town planning.
2. An historical perspective tracing empirically these social interactions over time in the light of a preferred theoretical framework.
3. A second historical perspective tracing the role of town planning with respect to the significant social interactions which have been identified under (1) and (2) above.

These three perspectives may be interwoven to provide both a framework for the analysis of contemporary town planning and also an illustration of the likely outcomes of alternative policies in the light of past experience.

Such a perspective is necessary because it provides a way of continuously interpreting reality which is not dependent on the implicit assumptions of those who think that town planning can simply begin with a survey of today's conditions, which may then be analysed to produce tomorrow's plan in an entirely objective and scientific fashion. This perspective is also useful because a survey, analysis and plan technique cannot be applied to the identification of alternative future outcomes of plans. It is only on the basis of accurate historical experience and a satisfactory theoretical framework that some attempts can be made to predict the real effects of local, structure, corporate or policy plans.

A theoretical perspective

There are only a very limited number of useful theoretical perspectives in sociology. In the discussions concerning the nature of social interaction between groups and individuals, and hence the social characteristics of their respective societies, only four major explanatory propositions exist. While they all have a number of variations and different labels they basically boil down to the arguments that social interaction may be characterised by co-operation, anomie, alienation or conflict, and combinations of these forms.

In dealing with the social interactions which arise between individuals and groups in society, public agency policy makers in general and town planners in particular often assume that society is based on co-operation. This is partly because this makes their jobs much less impossible and partly because of their relationships with government and therefore the power structure. If one is able to assume that society is based on co-operation, then a comparatively limited range of policies will do for one situation. If society is based on conflict, however, then many situations will arise where only mutually inconsistent or self-defeating policies will satisfy all the parties to the conflict. Similarly, if society is based on co-operation, then public servants are only executing the 'general will' in obeying their political masters. Conversely, if society is based on conflict, then sensitive public servants might wonder at the morality of engineering policies according to the purposes of those groups who have acquired the most political power in society.

In contrast to public agency policy makers and planners with statutory executive responsibilities, academics do not have to concern themselves first with how to do things in practice and may therefore turn more readily to the less immediately practical pursuits of asking why they should be done at all. The results of asking this question are mainly significant in terms of tomorrow's rather than today's policies. But it does have the immediately practical result of exposing the paradoxes and inconsistencies that are glossed over and covered up by the search for unitary policies based on consensus and co-operation.

The theoretical perspective advanced here is based on conflict theory. It has a long tradition. Among the progenitors of the theory were Machiavelli,[1] Bodin[2] and Hobbes.[3] Among those who turned the analysis to empirical investigation were Hume[4] and Ferguson.[5] The idea of universal competition was also taken up as a central theme in the classical economic tradition exemplified by Smith[6] and in the demographic predictions of Malthus.[7] This line of thought was continued by social Darwinists like Spencer,[8] Ratzenhofer,[9] Gumplowitz[10] and Sumner,[11] and used as the ideological justification employed by business interests in modern society and also by various regimes seeking either to minimise the support given to the poorer members of communities or to assert the inherent inferiority of certain races. In its conservatism and lack of empirical support, social Darwinism is not unlike positivistic organicism in so far as it predisposes its adherents to admire the status quo, and is either not substantiated by such evidence as does exist or asserts relationships which cannot be quantified in a meaningful way. It is therefore to the second main branch of conflict theory that one must turn for a relatively thoroughgoing reformulation of the conceptual understanding of society in general and town planning in particular.

This second line of thought in conflict theory is derived primarily from Hegel.[12] The two major assumptions of his social philosophy were that:

1. Society is a moving balance of antithetical forces which generate social change by their tension and struggle.
2. Social history is an internal or quasi-logical evolution of the forces themselves.[13]

These themes were taken up and developed by Marx[14] who is, of course, the principal classical exponent of conflict theory. He argued that the history of humanity is explicable by the varying relations between men's bodily needs and the productive forces available for satisfying them. Accordingly,

> The totality of production relations constitutes the economic structure of society, the real basis upon which a legal and political superstructure arises and to which definite forms of social consciousness correspond. The mode of production of the material means of life determines, in general, the social, political, and intellectual processes of life.[15]

Consequently, the analysis of conflict in society begins with the mode of production. The mode of production consists of the machines, labour power, level of technical development and the prevailing form of distribution which are used to satisfy the physical needs of a given society. The relationships between these factors tend to operate independently of the human beings involved in them, but because all the members of a society must be caught up in its productive relationships, it is these which ultimately determine their other social, political and personal lives. The mode of production in society is said to lead to the productive relationships which the members of that society enter into in order to satisfy their material wants. Consequently the relations of production directly determine the economic organisation of men, and furthermore, indirectly, their social, legal, national and religious institutions and their moral and philosophical beliefs.

Marx goes on to argue that once the beliefs and ideologies of society have come into existence, they then influence and affect society in their own right. Thus, although they are based on the effects that the modes and relations of production have on the way groups perceive and understand society, they also have an existence of their own. They may be expounded both to support and to contradict the status quo.

The real force which drives society on, however, is, for Marx, the conflict arising from the inadequate social and economic organisation of the available productive forces for the supply of the needs of the whole of society. In modern society the determining factor in the outcome of conflict is economic power. The conflict over economic power is manifested in the struggle between different social classes. The main protagonists in this struggle were identified by Marx as the bourgeoisie who own and/or control the means of production and the proletariat who control only their labour. This they must sell in the market where the only obligation on the purchaser is to pay the current price. This reduces the human and moral significance of the relationships between employer and employee to one of power.

Marx also argued that the outcome of the struggle between social classes in modern industrial society would be the overthrow of the bourgeoisie and its replacement by a classless society. As this, he asserted, was the inevitable outcome of the dialectic conflict manifested by the class struggle, it became incumbent upon those with a similar ideology to try to bring about the classless society. This contention, together with his analysis of the driving force of society, were brought together to form a political programme for a new working-class revolution whose course and objectives were outlined in the *Manifesto of the Communist Party* written jointly by Marx and Engels.[16] In it they advocated:

1. The abolition of property in land and the application of all rents in land to public purposes.
2. A heavy progressive or graduated income tax.
3. The abolition of all right of inheritance.
4. The confiscation of the property of all emigrants and rebels.
5. The centralisation of credit in the hands of the state by means of a national bank with state capital and an exclusive monopoly.
6. The centralisation of the means of communication and transport in the hands of the state.
7. The extension of factories and instruments of production owned by the state and the bringing into cultivation of waste land and the improvement of the soil generally in accordance with a common plan.
8. The equal liability of all to labour, and the establishment of industrial armies especially for agriculture.
9. The combination of agriculture with manufacturing industries and the gradual abolition of the distinction between town and country by a more equable distribution of the population over the country.
10. Free education for all children in public schools, the abolition of children's factory labour and the combination of education with industrial production.

It will be seen that a number of these proposals have been met by the provisions of the 'welfare state' in Britain.

Marx's influence is spread beyond social policy and permeates a great deal of subsequent sociological thought. In particular, his introduction of the notion of class conflict based on the struggle for the use of productive resources as the dominant theme and driving force of modern industrial society; his analysis of the origins and uses of ideology; the significance he attached to power; and the idea of a ruling class are all recurring themes in subsequent sociology.

The investigation of the nature and power of ruling élites has, for example, formed a particularly fruitful strand in sociological thought. Mosca,[17] Pareto,[18] Michels,[19] Sorel,[20] Mills[21] and Bottomore[22] have all dwelt upon this theme. The first four of these (that is to say, Mosca, Pareto, Michels and Sorel) are critical of

Marx's contention that the necessary and inevitable outcome of social change will be a classless society. Mosca and Pareto argue, for example, that in every society a minority will be found which rules over the rest of society. This minority is said to consist primarily of those who acquire political power, and influence political decisions. Conflict between this group and others in society does not reach the revolutionary situation predicted by Marx mainly because it undergoes change in its membership over time. This involves either the recruitment of new individual members from the lower strata of society, or the incorporation of new social groups, or occasionally by the complete peaceful replacement of the established elite by a counter-élite.

Michels went so far as to formulate an 'iron law of oligarchy', whereby political power in any society is always eventually concentrated in a few hands. Although he argued that it may be wrested from them by force, he doubted that a classless society could ever be formed. For one thing, he suggested, those holding political power actually have qualities, such as superior knowledge, political skill and the ability to control the lines of communication and information, which make them superior to those who are not members of the ruling oligarchy.[23]

The burden of these critiques of Marx is therefore the contention that:

1. The Marxist conception of a ruling class is erroneous because the continual circulation of elites prevents the formation and continuation of one ruling class, and

2. a classless society is impossible because in every society there is and must be a minority which actually rules.[24] The merit of these arguments depends to a large extent on the degree of circulation and openness of elites and whether or not individuals and groups can determine the course of their own existence by using ruling minorities only to execute their wishes. Thus, in order for the criticisms of Marx to have much force, it would have to be shown that the nature, composition and origins of ruling elites actually did change significantly over a reasonably short period of time. It would also have to be shown that there is no way to organise a society without having a ruling minority.

Failing these demonstrations, Williams would be correct to point out that the main critical arguments against Marx 'are essentially a refinement of social laissez-faire'.[25]

The notion that ruling positions are open to acquisition by talent and the emphasis on the desirability of competition and getting-on are all familiar tenets of laissez-faire, utilitarian liberalism. They provide both a moral justification for those who currently hold power and an illusory avenue of change for those who do not. In an industrial society like Britain they serve to support the contention that those who hold power are necessarily worthy to do so and, following from this, that the system which brought such worthies to the fore should be maintained.

Mills has reformulated the notion of the power elite in contemporary terms. He says that 'we may define the power elite in terms of the means of power – as those who occupy the command posts'.[26] As Bottomore succinctly puts it, the themes of his book *The Power Elite: Military, Economic and Political* are:

1. The transformation of a society in which numerous small and autonomous groups had an effective say in the making of political decisions, into a mass society in which the power elite decides all important issues and keeps the masses quiet by flattery, deception and entertainment.

2. The corruption of the power elite itself, which he attributes primarily to a state of affairs in which it is not accountable for its decisions to any organised public and also to the dominant value of the acquisition of wealth.[27]

Here, the Marxist concern about the existence of a ruling elite, whose interests are not those of the masses, and its corruption to serve primarily the capitalist goal of the acquisition of wealth are reiterated. While such a debate continues, an examination of British town planning as a social institution must ask what its interrelationships with the power structure are and whether they support or question the values and aspirations of a limited controlling group or groups in society.

A second strand in the critiques of Marx which also requires further debate in the context of town planning is the analysis of the origins and uses of ideologies. This analysis was initiated by the debate about whether any of the principal types of society, identified by Marx, were caused by other than economic forces. Schumpeter, for example, 'drew attention to the difficulty of explaining the rise of European feudalism by economic factors, and to the tendency of social institutions to maintain their form in changed economic circumstances'.[28] Weber, Mannheim and Myrdal also drew attention to the importance of value systems in the way that, for example, sociologists see and define their subjects of study. Thus, as Rex has pointed out, Weber argued that:

> 1. the conceptual scheme of the sociologist might be affected by the particular value-standpoint which he himself adopts [and]
>
> 2. . . . activities might be judged according to the contribution which they make to the attainment of the participant actors.[29]

Again the same author says that,

> Mannheim, whose position owes much to Marx on the one hand, and to Weber and his predecessors on the other, saw the implications of this latter point. For if sociology is concerned with showing the relationship between activities and the purposes of actors in a social system, there is no such thing as objectivity in the sense of letting the facts speak for themselves. What were necessary facts depended upon from whose point of view you looked at them.[30]

It may well be true, as Weber argued in *The Protestant Ethic and the Spirit of Capitalism* that the rise of modern industrial capitalism required not only changes in the modes and relations of production and the formation of a new class, but also a change in men's attitudes to work and the accumulation of wealth, attitudes which were caused by the Protestant religion. But at the same time, the ideology supporting such a development of capitalism was clearly in the interests of those who accumulated wealth rather than those who did not. Consequently, although it may be necessary to modify the causal importance attached by Marx to ideologies, it is still true that they reflect the underlying conflicts of interest in society.

Accordingly, we may accept Myrdal's formulation of the place and importance of ideologies or values in society. His propositions are:

> 1. That there are conflicts of 'value-premises' or as we should say aspirations or aims between groups . . .
>
> 2. That these conflicts are sufficiently radical in scope to affect the structure of . . . society at almost any point at which we care to study it . . .
>
> 3. That the actual course of events is likely to be determined by the power at the disposal of groups and that the balance of power might change so that particular value premises might gain in social significance.[31]

As applied to town planning this raises the questions of what ideological conflicts exist within the society whose planning is being examined and how are these conflicts reflected in the ideologies of the planners themselves and in their recommended policies? It also means that the ideologies of the town planners need to be specified.

Contemporary formulations of conflict theory

During the 1950s there was a revival of interest in conflict theory largely as a result of the attempts of Coser in *The Functions of Social Conflict* and Dahrendorf in *Class and Class Conflict in an Industrial Society* to reformulate structural-functionalism particularly as represented by Parsons. The work of the German sociologist, Simmel, influenced this revival particularly in the work of Coser who based his own theories on those of the German. Simmel is also important because his 'approach to sociology can best be understood as a self-conscious attempt to reject the organicist theories of Comte and Spencer . . .'[32]

Simmel inherited the tradition of German scholarship and idealistic philosophy which vigorously opposed the organicist view of social life. He represents a point of departure in these streams of thought because he rejected both the organicist and the idealist schools. He argued that, as Coser points out, 'society consists of an intricate web of multiple relations between individuals who are in constant interaction with one another'.[33] Consequently, for Simmel, the legitimate subject matter for sociology lies in the description and analysis of particular forms of social interaction and their manifestation in group characteristics. Among the most important forms of social interaction between groups which require explanation are conflict and co-operation, subordination and superordination. The important thing to note about these forms of social interaction is that, as far as Simmel is concerned, different interests may be satisfied either by conflict or by planned co-operation and aggressive drives may be satisfied in forms of conflict varying from gang warfare to legal battles.

Simmel also differs from Marx in his analysis of the origins of different social types in society. In his view, the fact that, for example,

> someone is poor does not mean that he belongs to the specific social category of the 'poor' . . . It is only from the moment that (the poor) are assisted . . . that they become part of a group characterized by poverty.

This group does not remain united by interaction among its members, but by the collective attitude which society as a whole adopts toward it . . .[34]

In other words, although the poor are created by society they are not, for Simmel, primarily characterised by the lack of means of production but rather by the attitudes which other members of society have towards them. This seems, to say the least, a rather tenuous causal explanation of the existence of different social classes.

Those sociologists who tried to reformulate structural-functionalism found Simmel attractive particularly because of his assertion that social interaction, or sociation, involved co-operation as well as conflict. Structural-functionalism could be reformulated not by destroying its theoretical underpinnings but by merely adding the notion of conflict to that of co-operation as an additional basis for social interaction. It only remained then for Rex, in his book *Key Problems to Sociological Theory*, to note that anomie represents a third possible form of social interaction for a relatively comprehensive set of propositions to emerge without the necessity of having to refute a major school of sociological theory.

Indeed, far from refuting structural-functionalism, both Coser and Dahrendorf merely sought to include conflict as one of the forms of social interaction which could serve useful functions in society. Thus Coser analyses the functions of social conflict and Dahrendorf proposes a series of tenets which are the opposite mirror images of those of structural-functionalism.

Coser, for example, distinguishes between conflicts which 'do not contradict the basic assumptions upon which the relationship is founded' and those 'in which the contending parties no longer share the basic values upon which the legitimacy of the social system rests'.[35] While it is the latter type of conflict with which the mainstream of Marxist thought is concerned, it is the former which Coser regards as occurring more frequently and to which he therefore attaches greater importance.

He argues that 'one safeguard against conflict disrupting the consensual basis of the relationship is contained in the social structure itself: it is provided by the institutionalization and tolerance of conflict'.[36] This means that, within limits, society allows issues to be settled by conflict and that this tolerance is both one of the norms of society and a healthy way of ensuring its flexible adjustment to new conditions. But, as Rex argues,

In saying this, Coser seems to go far towards saying that the balance of power is the basic factor in social relationships and that the normative structure is a dependent variable. One might well ask, therefore, whether it would not be better to start one's analysis with the balance of power or the conflict of interests which this balance of power is supposed to settle, rather than beginning by assuming the existence of norms.[37]

This is what Marx proposes and would make either unnecessary or irrelevant Coser's distinction between conflicts which do not contradict the basis of social interaction and those where the contending parties do not share the same values on which the legitimacy of the social system rests.

In seeking to describe the positive functions of social conflict, Coser also argues that its disruptive effects are minimal in societies whose members have many roles and who participate only segmentally in the total relationships comprising those societies. Conversely, it is likely to be more disruptive in groups where interaction is frequent and personalised. The implication of this analysis is therefore that, in advanced industrial societies where inter-relationships are said to be generally segmental, conflict is neither likely to be significantly disruptive of those relationships nor focussed on the same issues by large conflicting groups. In other words, the polarisation of conflict into that between major social classes such as, for example, the bourgeoisie and the proletariat is not likely to occur because potential members of those groups do not have the same interests. Instead, they are likely to form different, smaller coalitions with different people over different issues. Thus conflict in a plural society is said to be a continuously changing process as coalitions composed of different members coalesce and disband as issues arise and are settled.

But, as Rex points out, 'the different segmental relationships may not be merely arbitrarily or randomly related to one another. There may be some sort of means-ends relationship between them. If this is so there may be a conflict in the dominant or ultimate segment which will spread all the way back along the means-end chain.'[38] Thus, 'the concept of randomly varying segments is as artificial as the concept of complete functional integration'.[39] It may therefore be argued against Coser that modern industrial societies are neither as segmented in practice as he implies nor are the conflicting coalitions arising from society unrelated and arbitrary. Indeed, an industrial society, characterised by a complex division of labour, must emphasise the inter-relationships of its parts if only in order to produce the goods and services it requires. Furthermore, although the Marxist two-class model is too simple to describe contemporary industrial society, whose increasing complexity leads to a structural division of labour. If this structure places certain groups in a continuous situation in relation to the production of goods and services and other groups in different positions, then it is most unlikely that their interests will be identical or that they will form part of the same coalition, particularly where it comes to decisions about the distribution of goods and services. It is, therefore, at least as likely that modern industrial societies will produce groups in continuous conflict over the distribution of power and resources as that they will be characterised by continuously changing coalitions or even the circulation of elites.

The last category of conflicts which Coser mentions are those of the safety-valve type. They are the kind that Parsons discusses in his analysis of deviant behaviour. Rex outlines their course as follows:

> the failure of 'alter' to conform to ego's expectations might lead to one or two alternatives. Either ego will learn to have new expectations and learn successfully without pathological complications, or he will develop an ambivalence so that behaviour indicative of various sorts of tension release will be evident, and even the process of bringing ego back into line with society's requirements has to make allowance for this letting off steam.[40]

It is not clear, however, what is supposed to happen if ego continues to press his original claims. While some conflicts may take this course, those between groups whose interests are irreconcilable or those where groups or individuals refuse to be subdued cannot be explained in this way.

Another critic of Marx and a reformulator of structural-functionalism is Dahrendorf. He argues that neither the homogeneous capitalist class predicted by Marx nor the working class have developed. The capitalist class, he says, has dissolved and given way to a plurality of partly competing and partly different groups. Similarly, the proletariat has dissolved into a plurality of roles endowed with diverging and often conflicting expectations. 'Thus, contrary to Marx's expectations, the increasing differentiation as well as homogeneity of classes was checked by the decomposition of labour and capital, the emergence of white-collar workers and bureaucrats, and the institutionalization of social mobility.'[41]

Dahrendorf also criticises structural-functionalism. As he says, this view of society based on the propositions that:

1. Every society is a relatively persisting configuration of elements.
2. Every society is a well-integrated configuration of elements.
3. Every element in a society contributes to its functioning.
4. Every society rests on the consensus of its members. He argues that such a set of propositions is incapable of explaining why social change takes place. Consequently, his reformulation of structural-functionalism simply proposes the addition of four diametrically opposed contentions to those of the original. Thus:

1. Every society is subjected at every moment to change; social change is ubiquitous.
2. Every society experiences at every moment social conflict; social conflict is ubiquitous.
3. Every element in society contributes to its change.
4. Every society rests on constraint of some of its members by others.

The result is that stability and change, integration and conflict, function and dysfunction, consensus and constraint, are two equally valid aspects of every imaginable society.[42] The questions which then arise in Dahrendorf's mind are:

1. How do conflicting groups arise from the structure of society?
2. What forms can the struggle among such groups assume?
3. How does the conflict among such groups effect a change in the social structures?[43]

These questions lead Dahrendorf to the argument that the structural origins of social conflict lie in the dominance relationships in society, as follows:

1. In every imperatively co-ordinated group, the carriers of positive and negative dominance roles determine two quasi-groups with opposite latent interests.
2. The bearers of positive and negative dominance roles, that is to say, the members of the opposing quasi-groups organise themselves into groups, such as parties and trade unions, with manifest interests.

3. Interest groups which originate in this manner are in constant conflict over the preservation or change of the status quo.

4. The conflict among interest groups in the sense of this model leads to changes in the structure of their social relations, through changes in the dominance relations.[44]

These arguments, however, pose as many questions as they answer. Foremost among these must be what constitutes the basis of dominance. If the basis is, as Marx argues, economic, then Dahrendorf treats only the symptoms of conflict rather than its causes. Even if the economic situation of the quasi-groups who are parties to the conflict are not all identical (as, for example, they are not in the distinction between property owners and non-owners), the underlying similarities could be greater than the visible differences. Conflict could be taking place between groups forming relatively large and homogeneous social classes. Even if conflict can only be identified as taking place between relatively small and localised groups it is still necessary to identify the basis of dominance. Finally, it could be argued that conflict between quasi-groups possessing different dominance characteristics, whatever their basis, is very much the struggle for power and resources identified by Marx as the manifest symptom of the dialectic in society. What Dahrendorf is therefore proposing is a theory which is close to that of Marx without having the same potential degree of explanatory power possessed by the original. Nevertheless, any adequate conflict theory must be concerned both with the power relations and changes in society. These Dahrendorf has highlighted.

Rex has produced the nearest thing to an adequate theory of conflict which may also be employed in the analysis of institutions, such as town planning, and their social contexts.[45] In his summary of this theory he first takes issue with the functionalist argument that society is organised around a common set of values. He argues that:

> [1.] Instead of being organized around a consensus of values, social systems may be thought of as involving conflict situations at central points. Such conflict situations may lie anywhere between the extremes of peaceful bargaining in the market place and open violence.[46]

Most conflict will not, of course, lead to open violence but rather to agreements and contracts. This should not disguise the fact that such accommodations are based not on mutual co-operation but the attempts of one group to achieve as many and as much of its aims as possible in the face of the same desires among other groups. In situations of scarce power and resources, therefore, one group's gain is almost certainly another group's loss.

Rex notes that:

> [2.] The existence of such a situation tends to produce not a unitary but a plural society, in which there are two or more classes, each of which provides a relatively self-contained social system for its members. The activities of the members take on sociological meaning and must be explained by reference to the group's interests in the conflict situation.[47]

It is argued that the sociological explanation of group or class activities, in a society not characterised by a commonly held set of values, lies partly in the analysis of their different values and aspirations. Hence, causal explanation of social phenomena lies not only in the analysis of social structure, as the structural-functionalists appear to argue, but also in the analysis of the aims, interests, values and aspirations of different structural situations.

Rex also argues that parties to conflict will not usually possess equal power, so that:

> [3.] In most cases the conflict situation will be marked by an unequal balance of power so that one of the classes emerges as the ruling class. Such a class will continually seek to gain recognition of the legitimacy of its position among the members of the subject class, and the leaders of the subject class will seek to deny this claim and to organize activities which demonstrate that it is denied.[48]

Among the activities that both parties will engage in is an ideological battle. The ruling class will attempt to persuade the ruled that the claims to authority by the ruling class are based on a valid set of propositions, and that the ruled should abandon some or all of its values and aspirations in favour of those held by and legitimising the position of the ruling class.

It should not be assumed, however, that any given set of power relations is fixed and immutable. As Rex says:

> [4.] The power-situation as between the ruling and subject classes may change as a result of changes in a number of variable factors which increase the possibility of successful resistance or actual revolution by the subject class . . . [and]

[5.] In the case of a dramatic change in the balance of power the subject-class may suddenly find itself in a situation in which it cannot merely impose its will on the former ruling-class, but can actually destroy the basis of that class's existence.[49]

Such violent and revolutionary changes in the power relations of society provide the most spectacular evidence of conflict and change. While modern Britain has not actually experienced such manifestations of the outcome of the aims and aspirations of different groups, it is interesting to speculate on how far the inter-war years represent a revolutionary situation, the outcome of which was not fully expressed until the establishment of the early post-war agencies of social welfare. These, largely the product of a Labour government, were, as Rex argues, in principle:

[6.] Justified and even affected by the morality of conflict and by pre-revolutionary charters and utopias.[50]

The same author also points out however that:

[7.] A change in the balance of power might lead not to complete revolution, but to compromise and reform. In this case, new institutions might arise which are not related simply to the prosecution of the conflict, but are recognised as legitimate by both sides. Such a truce-situation might in favourable circumstances give rise to a new unitary social order over a long period, in which limited property rights and limited political power are regarded as legitimately held by particular individuals.[51]

This would reflect the case, for example, of the institutions of social welfare comprising the welfare state in Britain. But, the important caveat to remember in their analysis is that their existence rests on a balance of power and if this should change, then it might be expected that this would be reflected in their administration. For example, should a group or coalition gain power and win support for an ideological position, then it would be expected to organise the institutions of social welfare more to suit its values and aspirations than those of other groups.

Taken together, the propositions provided by Rex provide a useful framework for the analysis of particular social institutions and their social context. As he says,

The classification of basic conflict situations, the study of the emergence and structure of conflict groups, the problem of the legitimation of power, the study of the agencies of indoctrination and socialization, the problem of the ideological conflicts in post-revolutionary situations and in situations of compromise and truce, the study of the relations between norms and systems of power – all these have their place within it.[52]

Such studies are relevant both to the analysis of total social systems and 'to the design of research into problems of particular institutions and social segments'.[53] In the case of town planning this means that conflict theory should be an applicable theoretical perspective both to the society in which the planning is taking place and to the effects and the relationships that society and planning have on one another.

Empirical evidence

In order to test the validity of conflict theory as applied to society and town planning, and to reach any real understanding of both, requires empathy and evidence. Empathy is required because most of what is to be analysed will be beyond the personal experience of the investigator or policy maker. At the same time, without a sympathetic feel of the irrational and emotional elements of social interaction, it is not possible to comprehend the real significance of evidence. It is also likely that irrelevant subjective analysis will be imposed on social interactions which have quite another meaning for the participants.

Empirical evidence is required as the raw material of both theory and its applicability. Without basic data it is all too easy for polemic and rhetoric to reign. Furthermore, if the real point of engaging in debate is to change things, then the best way to get people to change their minds is to show them evidence of where they are wrong. Nevertheless, there are limitations to empiricism.

In the first place, to demonstrate to a group that they have been exploiting another group may lead equally to their becoming more efficient exploiters or to a less predatory form of social interaction. In the second place, the more important the debate the less susceptible it becomes to empirical elucidation. Thus liberty, equality, fraternity and justice are very difficult to measure empirically but extremely important in the making of public policies. Third, the real significance of data can be just as much obscured as illuminated either by the techniques used for their collection or by the belief that somehow the facts may speak for themselves. Thus, while empirical evidence is important, one must beware of making banal, counter-productive or mystifying assertions purely because the data is available. One must also beware of not entering significant debates purely on the grounds that data is not available.

In attempting to build up a socio-political perspective on the interactions between British town planning and its environing society, one therefore needs a balanced mixture of theory, evidence and empathy. So far the theory has been outlined. It is now necessary to examine the available evidence in the light of conflict theory.

Three kinds of basic evidence are required. One needs to know the distribution of significant resources and power between different groups in society. One also needs to know what ideological propositions are advanced by the different groups to justify these distributions. These relationships need to be traced over time. If they showed, for example, that a particular group continuously acquires a disproportionate share of resources and power and that an ideology is promoted that seeks to justify this situation, then it may be inferred that conditions for social conflict exist. Furthermore, either such social interaction will arise or the balance of power is being maintained in such a way that relatively disadvantaged groups are unable to do much about the distribution of resources and power.

As far as town planning is concerned, one would need to know, in the light of such evidence, what effects the activity has on the distribution of resources and power. One would also need to understand the relationships that town planning has with different groups in society and the ideological stances it adopts with respect to these groups, their possession of scarce and desirable resources and power and their values and aspirations. The main question that would be asked when one considers such evidence is why such relationships do or don't change. Instead of asking why society continues to exist in the form that it does, and thus placing undue emphasis on the status quo, one is primarily interested in why society changes and what would constitute a 'better' set of social interactions.

Victorian Britain and the development of social and spatial conflict

In order to gauge the effects that town planning has had on the distribution of resources and power in British society, it is necessary to look back briefly to the era preceding its statutory introduction in 1909. This will provide a comparison of the kind of differences that town planning has made to the nature of social interaction in Britain. Such a comparison faces two major difficulties. In the first place, a continuous process of change is under way in society with or without the intervention of town planning, so it is necessary to try to unravel only those changes which may be attributed directly to the influence of town planning. In the second place, all sorts of public and private agencies contribute to changing even those factors which are the prime concern of town planners. Again the problem is to exclude those changes which have not been caused mainly by town planning.

If one turns first to the period preceding the introduction of town planning, one finds that during the half century preceding the commencement of the reign of Victoria in 1837, Britain was transformed from a country whose economy and living conditions were dominated by agriculture to one based on the factory and the town. Within a generation the most common life-style was changed from rural to urban. Economic change was expressed in social and spatial change. The processes of urbanisation which accompanied the industrial revolution radically altered the conditions of town life, the balance between town and country, and between different regions. The effects of the rapid change and increase in industrial production that reached its zenith in the years between 1821 and 1836 were compounded by an equally vigorous increase in the sheer size of the population. The population of England and Wales doubled in the first half of the nineteenth century and doubled again in the next sixty years. Furthermore, by the definition used in the Census of 1911 some 80 per cent of this population could be classified as urban and was increasingly concentrated in large cities.

These massive increases in industrial production and population were accompanied not only by urbanisation but also by vile living conditions for the working classes, the concentration of economic and political power and the ideology of laissez-faire. Thus, throughout the reign of Victoria there was a continued concentration of major areas of power in the hands of what Kitson-Clark calls the 'nobility gentry old style'.[54] Even in the early twentieth century, Laski[55] and Nightingale[56] were able to show that England's ruling class consisted of about a thousand families. At the same time, economic power became increasingly remote throughout the nineteenth century as workers had to deal with poker-faced men whose relations with them were dehumanised and strait-jacketed. Meanwhile their real employers became different types of people hedged around with considerations of education and class position. This social distance was further increased, and modern industrial social relations began to take shape, in the conditions of the joint-stock, impersonal financing of industrial developments.

At first, these economic relationships were not exactly reflected in politics. Contrary to popular belief, the 1832 Reform Act was not a symbolic arrival at the ultimate position of power by the bourgeoisie. Until new patterns of power began to emerge as a result of political pressures before and after the 1867 Reform Act, and the economic stagnation from the early 1870s, Parliament continued to be dominated by the old feudalism and landed interests.

By the last quarter of the nineteenth century, however, there was a conjunction of economic and political power which was reinforced by the ideology of laissez-faire. This bourgeois ideology, having emerged in legislative form with the repeal of the Corn Laws in 1846, was seen at its sharpest in 1884 when Herbert Spencer published *The Man Versus the State.* In it he viewed government interference with market mechanisms as misconceived on three counts:

1. In the belief that all suffering ought to be prevented, something which he thought not to be true as much suffering is creative.
2. In the belief that all evil should be removed, given the defects of human nature, a belief which he considered to be misplaced.
3. In the belief that evils of all kinds should be dealt with by the state; this, he thought, ignored the proper role of other agencies.

He concluded that such government interference was unnecessary because the industrious and talented individual could always, in a free society, be the agent of his own success.[57]

This was an ideology which not surprisingly appealed greatly to those already possessing economic resources and political power and also to those who could be persuaded that either or both of these could be theirs. The results of rapid industrial and commercial growth accompanied by a population explosion, in such a conjunction of circumstances and climate of opinion, were that while a relatively small number of people became extremely wealthy and others achieved a tolerable standard of living, for the masses, Victorian Britain meant living conditions characterised by overcrowding, congestion, poverty, crime, ill-health and heavy mortality.

These conditions were to be found in growing urban areas containing no supervisory authority. It was difficult, if not impossible, for their inhabitants to demand improvements. Even after the conditions were documented and recognised, the only significant responses arose as a result of the threat of heavy mortality and crime to bourgeois life and property. The concern with disease and criminality led to some interference with the private-enterprise market system in the last quarter of the nineteenth century.

Before this time, urban development clearly reflected the different access to economic resources possessed by different sections of British society. Comprehensive attempts to plan working-class towns did not influence the way other working-class towns were built. In contrast, the development of towns of conspicuous consumption for the bourgeoisie was emulated. The building, for example, of New Lanark (1800–24) by Robert Owen, and Saltaire (1851–71) by Titus Salt, had little noticeable effect on the growth of other working-class towns. Although no set of generalisations can be applied universally to the growth of British towns in the nineteenth century, it may be said that there was more forethought and regulation in the spa and seaside centres of conspicuous consumption for the bourgeoisie and more chaotic blind growth in the towns where production or distribution of material goods in large quantities preponderated. In towns concerned with more than just working and sleeping, more care was taken to provide for some of the social needs of the people. These towns were more thoroughly and comprehensively planned and less intensively developed because they served the bourgeoisie with their high incomes and expenditures. So it was that British society produced spatial distinctions reflecting its social differences, which were themselves based primarily on the access to and conflict over economic resources.

In such a society the revolt of the philanthropists against the industrial town, voiced by men like Cobbett and Shaftesbury, was doomed to fail. The combination of vested interests and the ideology of laissez-faire saw the existence of a class of city dwellers who had never known a decent environment as a necessary basis for the achievement of industrial and commercial productivity of which those vested interests were the beneficiaries.

This view of the overriding importance of productive expenditure was also characterised by a zeal for economy in public administration. This demanded that such expenditure be remunerative and that the profit must accrue to the expending agency in the form of measurable pounds, shillings and pence. Public administration during the reign of Victoria came to be 'the science [of] the guiding of the sewage of the country in the way it should go, it [was] the science of improving the architectural aspect of the city until it [took] the foremost rank in the notebook of the dilettante'.[58] In such a climate of opinion the most telling arguments for reversing the effects of market competition and conflict on the distribution of life-chances and conditions, were those which demonstrated the profitability of reform. Among the reformers, Thomas Beggs argued that sanitary improvements increased the stock of human capital and thus improved employment and investment opportunities.[59] Octavia Hill pointed to the common exaggeration of the cost of reforms because of the failure to deduct the compensating increase in rateable values which they brought about.[60] An attempt was also made by William Farr[61] to measure the pecuniary loss to the community as a result of avoidable mortality. He calculated that the mean English lifetime in 1876 was 40·86 years but in healthy districts it was 49·0. Bringing England up to the standard of the healthy districts would, he believed, have increased the economic value of the population by £1050 million. This point had been clearly illustrated when, in 1854, an epidemic of cholera killed 2000 people in Newcastle-upon-Tyne and Gateshead, while in Tynemouth, eight miles away, where sanitary regulations and drainage had been improved, there were only four deaths from the disease.

Not only were the inequitable results of the conflict over access to scarce resources to be seen in comparisons between different regions and towns of Britain, particularly between towns of conspicuous consumption and those of industry and commerce, but also, especially in the latter, between those areas inhabited by the bourgeoisie and those containing the proletariat. Although the recognition of the social segregation of cities is commonly attributed to Burgess[62] and Hoyt,[63] in fact Vetch[64] noticed, in the middle of the nineteenth century, that most British towns grew sectorially. This process was precipitated by the rapid growth and migration of the population. So, as people multiplied and swarmed into the industrial and commercial centres of Britain, the deterioration in living conditions, which was the result of high population densities, induced those who could command the resources to move further and further from the centre. In doing so they tended to establish gradients of command of access to communications, commerce and the more favoured locations. For many, however, there was no choice of locality. Large numbers of working people had to continue to live in the densely populated central areas in order to acquire casual employment and subsidiary earnings for women.

In so far as the agencies of government regulated the development of industrial and commercial towns, they tended to favour the bourgeoisie. Consequently, for most of the nineteenth century working-class areas developed physically and socially in the most haphazard ways, while the quarters organised by the wealthy classes were subject to more deliberate foresight. Similarly, it was these classes who benefited most from improvements in standards of health and environmental conditions; benefits illustrated by the longer fertility of mothers, better survival of children and the greater size of family. In London in 1912, for example, the average mortality was 91 per 1000 population. In rich Hampstead it was 62, while in poor Shoreditch it was 123.

Similarly, the very growth of industry and commerce in the centre of cities, from which the bourgeoisie drew their wealth, forced up the residential rents of the poor. At the same time the improvements in communications, which permitted the bourgeoisie improved access to industry and commerce from their homes increasingly situated further from the centre, were also effected at high cost to the poor. For example, in 1877 the London Metropolitan Board of Works proposed a bill to try to accommodate people displaced from the West End (by road and other 'improvements') in Grays Inn Road, a mile or two from their previous dwellings. This involved about one working hour a day lost in travelling time. The loss of this hour, at a wage rate of five pence per hour, meant a loss of two shillings and sixpence a week. This could be considered a tax upon the workmen for removing them. Small margins of extra cost like this are crucial to people on low wages. The prevailing bourgeois ideology in the agencies of government viewed all these phenomena in a different light. While, for example, the large working-class family represented improvidence in the eyes of the middle-class Malthusian, the large middle-class family was a symbol of success. While road improvements facilitated commercial communications for the bourgeoisie, the taxes they imposed on the poor were ignored.

So it was that Victorian Britain came to reflect in its spatial patterns and government 'policies' the underlying relationships to production and economic resources. By the last quarter of the nineteenth century, the interests of industrial and commercial capital were served not only by the factory system and its attendant commercial institutions but also by a coherent ideology and political power. This conjunction of economic and political power together with the pressing of its ideological justification ensured that the agencies of government, the only agencies with sufficient information and, albeit limited, power to ameliorate the effects of the market place on the lower social classes, failed to redress effectively the balance in living conditions between the rich and the poor.

While there may be some excuse for such inactivity before and during the documentation of such discrepancies, once they have been documented and deplored, their continued existence for generation after generation in one of the most affluent countries in the world begins to look increasingly like the maintenance of an economic and political system for the furtherance of narrow class-interests. Evidence, for example, of discrepancies between life-chances for different social classes became generally available when the decennial census was supplemented by the compulsory registration of births, marriages and deaths in 1837. Two years later, in 1839, Chadwick's report on the sanitary conditions of the labouring population showed the differences between life expectancy for different social classes in, for example, Bethnal Green. There the average age of death for gentlemen and persons engaged in professions and their families was 45; for tradesmen and their families 26; and for mechanics, servants and labourers and their families 16.[65] At the following census, in 1841, the Registrar General showed the geographic differences in life expectancy at birth. The average expectancy for England and Wales was 41 years. For rural Surrey it was 45, for commercial London 37 and for industrial Liverpool 26. Two years later, in 1843, it was shown that life expectancy in industrial Manchester was 24 years against 40 for England and Wales as a whole. The reaction on the part of the ruling class to such information varied from unconcern, through nothing can be done, to let us try to prevent their recurrence. Thirty years later, however, the figures were much the same and the economic and political system which generated such great capital wealth had not seen fit to use some of this wealth to ensure minimum standards of living for the lower social classes.

Not only did the economic and political institutions of Victorian Britain fail to benefit the whole of society equally, but also, under the guiding ideology of laissez-faire, the extension of government responsibility for living conditions was actively resisted. As early as 1840, a select committee suggested a general act to apply to all future building, a general sewerage act, the appointment of boards of health in all towns above a certain size, and inspection and supervision of crowded burials. The arguments for such measures were that existing conditions created an economic loss or that the state of towns fostered the anti-property activity of crime and threatened the social structure. These proposals were not accepted and the same unwanted characteristics of towns that were found in the 1830s and 1840s were still just as prevalent twenty or thirty years later.

One of the main contributing factors to this continuation was the resistance by the bourgeoisie to the extension of effective government machinery for the regulation of living conditions. Even the regulation of new development was exceptional before the general introduction of building by-laws under the provisions of the Public Health Act of 1875. The prevailing suspicion of government interference in the market place meant that the general result of changes in the mid-nineteenth century was the establishment of several networks of authorities, each responsible for only a very few functions and each with a different set of local boundaries. This fragmentation of authority and responsibility probably contributed as much as anything to the continuation of appalling living conditions for the lower social classes.

The underlying divergence of interests resulting from different relationships to the means of production, and hence to political power and authority, seldom erupted into violent conflict even during the nineteenth century. Apart from instances of machine breaking and the treatment meted out to the early trade unionists, conflict in the nineteenth and, indeed, twentieth centuries is generally represented by relatively institutionalised trials of strength and struggle. In so far as the protagonists in such struggles were frequently, if not always, drawn from different social classes with different interests, so conflict is manifested in class struggle. One of the serious drawbacks of non-violent institutionalised conflict for the under class is that the institutions or 'rules of the game' are usually those of the upper social classes. Nowhere was this more evident in Victorian Britain than in the treatment of poverty.

Poverty, or pauperism as it was then called, was endemic in British society. Nevertheless, by the Victorian era, the central aim of Poor Law administration was to stop outdoor relief to the able-bodied. In practice many Poor Law Unions refused relief to the aged and in some cases to all applicants. Across the whole field of relief spread the stigma of pauperisation. This unsympathetic view of poverty was brought to its study by Booth in the 1880s. He was so shocked by what he found in London, as to be converted to the view that, 'The individualist community on which we build our faith will find itself obliged for its own sake to take charge of the lives of those who, from whatever cause, are incapable of independent existence up to the required standard and will be fully able to do so.'[66] Nevertheless, the Poor Law Commission Reports of 1909 reflect the class struggle in their conflicting ideological approaches to poverty and its treatment during the Victorian era. The main ideological positions to be seen in conflict in the Poor Law Commission were those of laissez-faire and socialism. The former wished to retain the fundamental principles of 1834. The socialists, in contrast, were more concerned with efficient local government, specialised social services and the total abolition of the Poor Law and its agencies. Laissez-faire won the day and the workhouse remained a symbol of a basic continuity in the dominant forms of social action until after the First World War.

Victorian reluctance to share wealth and income throughout the community was also reflected in housing conditions. The underlying conflict between communal responsibility and the acquisition of private wealth and property was and is reflected in all legislation on housing. Thus, while industrial towns expanded and every scrap of land was built upon, there remained a permanent shortage of houses. The results were that in 1884 the population density in parts of Liverpool, for example, was estimated to be 1210 people per acre.

Politics and change

By the last quarter of the nineteenth century the seeds of change had been sown. A few examples of rehousing inside cities gave rise to slightly broader ideas of government regulation in the market. Between 1879 and 1895, for example, George Cadbury was responsible for the development of Bournville. This was influential because the architect was later involved in new town planning at Letchworth. Also, Seebohm Rowntree, on the basis of both his investigation of working-class conditions at York and his involvement in the New Earswick scheme, played a prominent part in the wartime planning of housing needs by helping to prepare the way for the Housing Act of 1919, which was the first of any major importance. Such manifest changes did not take place, however, until an organised labour movement joined the struggle for economic and political power and its ideologists elaborated alternative versions of the nature of society and the kind of role that might be expected from government. The sense of working-class identity and solidarity grew in the 1860s and 1870s. Central in working-class experience throughout the century, however, was an approach to society, to social organisation and purpose, and to concepts of democracy and community, fundamentally different from that which rested on the individualism of the wealthy classes. Chartism and suffrage agitation in the 1860s were forms of awareness of identity in action. The fight for reform of trade union legislation was another, and the successful campaign from 1867 to 1876 gave the movement a new unity expressed in the establishment of the Trade Union Congress. Working-class identity and the rejection of bourgeois organisations for the institutionalisation of conflict were signalled by the establishment of specifically working-class institutions such as the Trade Union Congress in 1868 and the working-men's clubs, most of which were combined in the Club and Institute Union founded in 1862. This growing unification embodied in working-class institutions, encompassing independent trade unions and co-operative political and educational activities, illustrated the emergence of institutions and ideologies which were to counter those of the bourgeoisie and laissez-faire during the twentieth century.

The struggle was to be a political one. The year before the end of Victoria's reign, the Labour Representative Committee was created.

This signalled the end of the unchallenged bourgeois dominance in politics and was confirmed when the Committee changed its name to the Labour Party after the election of 1906. From that time, government policy came to reflect more clearly the conflict over power and resources in British society.

The effects of the introduction of statutory town planning

The first decade of the twentieth century saw both the institutionalisation of conflicts between organised labour and capital marked by the emergence of the Labour Party, and the emergence of a kind of 'truce' marked by the introduction of an embryonic 'welfare' state. All these changes coming within such a comparatively short space of time make it particularly difficult to unravel the contribution made by the introduction of statutory town planning in 1909. One thing is clear. All the new institutions of welfare, including town planning, when taken together did not radically alter either the underlying conflicts in British society or the distribution of resources and power which generated this conflict. Indeed the conflicts between labour and capital were to reach their zenith during the inter-war depression and the general strike of 1926.

The three main contributions that the emergent statutory activity of town planning made to the allocation of scarce resources during the first half of the twentieth century were the new towns, development plans and their ramifications, and its influence on housing. These three contributions were both responsible for the allocation and location of some scarce resources and also were subject to the influence of political power.

The new towns idea propagated by Howard in his book *To-morrow* (later retitled *Garden Cities of To-morrow*), published in 1898, and by the Garden City Association, founded in 1899 (later becoming the Town and Country Planning Association), first bore fruits in 1904. Letchworth was started in that year, Hampstead Garden Suburb in 1905 and Welwyn Garden City in the 1920s. The idea achieved general legislative approval in the Town and Country Planning Act 1947 and the New Towns Act of 1946.

Although new towns were supposed to be one answer to the overcrowding, congestion and poor living conditions of the industrial and commercial centres of the nineteenth century, they have never provided accommodation and work for a significant proportion of those families who suffered most from these conditions. Mann, for example, points out that,

> Howard's idea of the Garden City as a place where people of all classes in the eighteen nineties would live seems to be somewhat out of touch with reality. Although poverty at this time was widespread, and drunkenness was a common phenomenon, Howard seemed to be able to ignore these aspects of working class life almost entirely.[67]

Thus the first town planning answer to the environmental conditions resulting from the inabilities of some groups to gain sufficient resources and power was produced by people with insufficient understanding, empathy and information about working-class life in Britain. Instead, the new towns movement was largely based on four essentially middle-class ideas. The first was the belief that towns have failed to produce satisfactory living conditions and life styles as the countryside had and that the solution to the problems of inner urban-areas was therefore to be found in planned suburbanisation and decentralisation. The second was the belief that there existed some mechanical link between the environment and human behaviour and that what was needed to produce happiness was 'good environment'. The third was that the old evils of inner urban-areas of poverty, ill-health, crime and congestion were so intractable as to be insoluble and that efforts should therefore mainly be directed to preventing their repetition elsewhere. The fourth was that happiness could be promoted by mixing all sections of the population together in socially balanced neighbourhood units, thus ameliorating the divisions in society which had arisen with the industrial revolution and which were reflected in the socio-spatial structure of cities.

The main attraction of these ideas is that they are platitudes which do not challenge the existing order. It is therefore possible for those with resources and power to espouse them either because they appear sufficient to assuage their social conscience or because they do not threaten to solve the problems which spawned them by redistributing either resources or power from the rich to the poor. While this may be 'practical politics', in the sense that it is possible to get some consensus on such ideas, it is not a practical way of resolving the underlying conflicts between different groups in society.

Right from their inception the new towns did not provide either housing that the poor could afford, appropriate employment to make them less poor, or a relevant location of either. The rents charged at Letchworth, for example, were too high for manual workers; the new towns have not encouraged unskilled and semi-skilled employment; they are too far away from such employment for workers to bear the commuting costs and, in any case, what such workers need immediately is work and housing in existing urban centres. Instead, the new towns have benefited organised, skilled or white-collar workers. But it should be remembered that governments need the votes of such groups in order to acquire political power and they tend to be the sort of groups who can compete competently for economic resources anyway. Thus the main effect of the new towns policy during the first half of the twentieth century was to allocate more resources to affluent members of society than to the poor. This allocation reflected their relative political power.

The second main contribution to allocation made by town planning up to the end of the 1940s was the regulation of land use. The Housing, Town Planning Etc. Act of 1909 and its early successors were concerned with providing discretionary powers that enabled local authorities to regulate new development in such a way as to secure 'proper sanitary conditions, amenity and convenience'. By the Second World War it was clear that insufficient use was being made of these discretionary powers even to achieve such limited objectives. Consequently, the Town and Country Planning Act of 1947 made the production of a development plan mandatory. Such plans embodied a number of functions. They were broadly:

1. The assertion of the regulation of land use.
2. The instruction of developers on the shape and requirements of the plan.
3. A way of allowing the planning authority to implement parts of the plan.
4. A way of communicating the ideas of the plan to the public.

The most obvious physical results of such plans have been the establishment of green belts, roads, the segregation of land uses and the kinds of distributing and commercial centres characteristic of British cities.

The main beneficiaries of this artificial regulation of the use of land were the owners of land and property. In outline, this is because regulation reduces the supply of land in general and land for particular uses at the margin. A reduction in supply may increase price and any reduction in the supply of such an inelastic commodity as land makes larger rather than smaller differences to its price.

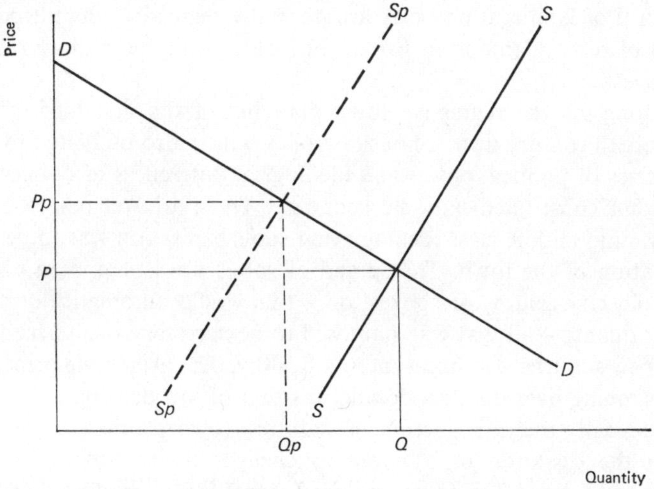

Figure 2. Effect of town planning on the price of land: ***D****, demand for land;* ***S****, supply of land;* ***Sp****, supply of land with planning;* ***Q****, quantity of land;* ***QP****, quantity of land available with planning;* ***P****, price of land;* ***Pp****, price of land with planning*

Figure 2 outlines this process in a highly simplified way. It illustrates the supply schedule *SS* and the demand schedule for land *DD* before the introduction of the regulation of its use. This results in the quantity *Q* of land being used at price *P*, perhaps for housing. With the introduction of the regulation of land use, the quantity available at the margin is reduced, thus shifting the supply schedule to *SpSp*. If other things remain equal the price of land available, again for perhaps housing, is raised from *P* to *Pp*.

The main beneficiaries of such a change must be those who own land and property because, other things being equal, a change in the supply of an inelastic commodity leads to a steeply linear increase in its value. They are therefore able to improve their competitive position despite the rapid increase in prices. A second point to note is that the greatest increases must also go to those who possessed the most land and property before the introduction of town planning. Thus the regulation of land use can have strongly regressive effects in ownership and control of scarce resources. The result can be that, although the benefits accruing from the ownership and control of land and property are normally regressive, the introduction of town planning in Britain probably made them more rather than less so.

Alongside the regressive town planning of the first half of the twentieth century went a housing policy which also oscillated to the vagaries of political power and ideological differences of opinion as to what constituted national economy. The 1909 Act reflected the prevailing middle-class ideology that suburbanisation was to be the salvation of the town. The spread of suburbs was supposed to rid the old city centres of congestion – this would automatically raise their quality – all that was supposed to be necessary was to see that the new suburbs were pleasant and healthy. The overriding principle of planning over the next decade was that of low density.

Ironically the introduction of statutory town planning coincided with the cessation of a boom in cheaper houses owing to the threatened Land Tax clauses in the Liberal Party's budget that was presented to the House of Lords by Lloyd George in 1909. These clauses, together with proposals for heavy increases in direct taxation on the wealthier social classes, were designed to pay for social reforms which more immediately benefited other sections of the community and, therefore, they provoked a constitutional crisis when they were rejected by the Lords. Here again the underlying conflicts in British society rose to the surface and were only overcome by a political alliance between the Liberals, Labour and the Irish. They were overcome, however, not because the wealthier classes accepted the values and merits of their opponents' case but because they were forced to retreat a little by superior political power.

After the First World War, housing policy changed direction under a Conservative government. In 1923 Chamberlain, Minister of Health, introduced a comprehensive housing bill. In the words of the Fifth Annual Report of the Ministry of Health 1923, 'The main objects of this act were the encouragement of private enterprise in the erection of working-class houses by the grant of subsidies and by the provision of facilities for obtaining capital for the erection and purchase of houses.' But, subsidies were only made available if it could be shown that private enterprise was unable to cope with the demand for housing. It is now clear, however, that the lower social classes cannot generate effective demand for housing in the market place and then, as now, a Labour government returned responsibility for working-class houses to local authorities by the Wheatley Housing Act of 1924.

The combination of Chamberlain's and Wheatley's subsidies produced 400 000 houses in three years, and production reached a peak in 1927 when some 273 000 houses were completed. It should be noted however that it required considerable interference with free market mechanisms to achieve this figure and, even so, the Wheatley Act failed to produce houses within the means of the lower paid. It was only towards the end of its existence in 1932, and owing to falls in building costs and interest rates, that the Act produced the 'nine shilling house'. At the very moment that houses were being produced at rents that the working classes could afford, the Act mainly responsible for this divergence from 'normal' market forces was repealed by a Conservative government. The same Administration also put paid to the Greenwood Slum Clearance Act of 1930. Again a product of the second Labour government it was designed to clear and build in parallel with the Wheatley Act and improving on the provisions introduced in 1924. The inter-war period was therefore one which illustrated most clearly the basic conflicts in British society. On the one hand the working classes found themselves both new forms of economic and political organisation, but on the other they learnt to their cost that the class struggle was a continuous one and temporary victories were gained only as government succeeded government. They also found the depths of despair into which a capitalist system could plunge them together with the willingness of members of the wealthier social classes to break the effectiveness of collective strike action. Thus at no time have the conflicts underlying British society and their economic, political and ideological manifestations been more sharply brought into focus than between the two World Wars.

Wartime change and the Welfare State

For a time, internal conflict was subsumed in the unity of purpose brought about by the need to fight a common enemy. This period of unity following social, economic and political struggle gave birth to some new institutions of truce. For example, the Barlow Commission did much to crystallise opinion about what town planning could or ought to do and what powers would be required. It recognised that existing power to regulate the market was inadequate and could not cope with the problems confronting the Commission. On the other hand it failed to realise or admit that it was not facing finite, static problems but dynamic tension and struggle between organised labour and capital. Consequent legislation simply encouraged more semi- or sub-urban development and sops for the underprivileged regions of Britain.

So it fell to the Labour government of 1945 to create the institutions of welfare designed to arrest the effects of the market on life in Britain. The Bank of England, coal, gas, electricity, airlines, railways and medical services were taken into public ownership. From August 1947 to June 1948 all private house construction was stopped and subsequently continued in the ratio of one to four local authority houses.[68] The early hopes for the Welfare State were short lived. Titmuss argues that the Welfare State was established too quickly and on too broad a scale.[69] It may well be, however, that the institutions of welfare needed to maintain an effective and just truce between capital and labour need to be stronger and more independent if they are indeed to prove lasting and effective.

Conclusions

It has been argued that post-industrial British society is based primarily on conflict. This varies from violent clashes to trials of strength and continuous struggle. It is the latter more often than it is the former. Conflict arises as a result of different relations and access to the means of production on the part of different groups in society. It is most often manifested in the struggles for economic or political power. Strangely enough it is spurred on both by the ideology of laissez-faire and by socialism. The former tells a man that he is inferior if he acquires less wealth and property or consumes less than other men. It therefore encourages him to compete with other men and groups for such desirable resources. Socialism, on the other hand, tells a man that the community has some responsibility for all of its members and that therefore if some have cake while others lack bread, there is something fundamentally wrong with this state of affairs. Again, the answer is change. Thus, the conflict model of society also comes to be associated with ideas of dynamic tension and change. As applied to Britain, it may be argued that the history of that society is explicable in terms of the continuous struggle between capital and labour.

The preceding evidence may be argued to show that the rise which took place during the nineteenth century, of a wealthy commercial, manufacturing, property and capital-owning class was reflected both in parliament, in the ideology of laissez-faire, and the kind of manufacturing, commercial and financial institutions which grew with its rise to social hegemony. The interests of this class were reflected in the proposals, or lack of them, for altering the living conditions of the labouring classes while at the same time centres of conspicuous consumption were established enabling the former to display their wealth.

The power of the motive of self-interest among the wealthy classes was also illustrated by the comparative failure of the utopians, philanthropists and reformers to effect any significant change in the predominant nature of society by strength of argument and example alone. Such significant change was not forthcoming until labour organised and united in economic centres and forced its way into the power structure. Such an interpretation of British social history relies heavily on the simple chronology of events. Nevertheless, it is held to be evident that although the problems of heavy mortality, poverty, poor housing and the rest were documented fairly early in the nineteenth century, almost nothing was done to combat these evils until the Labour Party posed an increasing threat to the political power of the Liberals during the early part of the twentieth century. It is also a fact that it was not until the Labour Party was actually able to form a government that such issues were regularly confronted and became central to party manifestos.

It is also interesting to note that the institutions of truce or welfare that were created during the first half of the twentieth century, of which town planning was one, did not radically alter the structural conditions for social conflict. Town planning, for example, did not contribute to a more equal society. On the contrary, the new towns and the regulation of land use and housing policy may have been marginally regressive in the way they contributed to the allocation of scarce resources. This also reflects the unequal distribution of political power. Much of the allocative effects of town planning and the other institutions of welfare have been hidden by the slow but continued rise in average standards. So that in order to trace their 'real' contribution to distribution, relative differences need to be traced over time. Should these relative differences prove to be regressive, then this would be the sort of evidence that would support an understanding of society based on conflict theory and create some considerable doubt about the position of town planning and other institutions of welfare in such a society.

References

1 N. Machiavelli, *The Prince*, Penguin (1970)
2 J. Bodin, *Six Books of the Commonwealth*, Blackwell (1955)
3 T. Hobbes, *Leviathan*, Penguin (1966)
4 D. Hume, *Enquiries Concerning Human Understanding*, Oxford University Press (1966)
5 A. Ferguson, *Essay on the History of Civil Society*, Edinburgh University Press (1966)
6 A. Smith, *Wealth of Nations*, Penguin (1970)
7 T. Malthus, *First Essay on Population 1798*, Kelley, (USA, 1926)
8 H. Spencer, *Sociology*, Appleton-Century Croft (New York, 1892)
9 Ratzenhofer, G. *Wesen und Zweck der Politik als Teil der Soziologie and Grundlage der Staatswissenschaften*, Aalen, Verlag Schilling (1967)
10 G. Gumplowitz, 'Grundriss der soziologie', in *Ausgewahlte Werke II*, G. Galomon (ed)., (Innsbruck, 1926)
11 W. G. Sumner, *Social Darwinism*, Prentice-Hall (1963)
12 F. Hegel, *Political Writings*, Oxford University Press (1964)
13 G. H. Sabine, *History of Political Theory*, Harrap (1963)
14 K. Marx, *Capital*, Allen & Unwin (1946)
15 *ibid.*
16 K. Marx and T. Engels, *Manifesto of the Communist Party*, International Publishers (New York, 1932)
17 G. Mosca, *The Ruling Class*, McGraw-Hill (1960)
18 V. Pareto, *Mind and Society*: *Treatise on General Sociology*, Tiptree Book Services (1963)
19 R. Michels, *Political Parties*, Collier-Macmillan (1966)

20 G. Sorel, *Reflections on Violence*, The Free Press (Illinois, 1950)
21 C. W. Mills, *The Power Elite*, Oxford University Press (1971)
22 T. B. Bottomore, *Elites and Society*, Penguin (1970)
23 R. Michels, *op. cit.* (1966)
24 T. B. Bottomore, *op. cit.* (1970)
25 R. M. Williams, *The Reduction of Intergroup Tensions* (SSRC Bulletin No. 57), (New York, 1947)
26 C. W. Mills, *op. cit.* (1971)
27 T. B. Bottomore, *op. cit.* (1970)
28 J. A. Schumpeter, *Capitalism, Socialism and Democracy*, Allen & Unwin (1950)
29 J. Rex, *Key Problems of Sociological Theory*, Routledge & Kegan Paul (1970) p. 121
30 *ibid.*
31 *ibid.*, p. 122
32 L. Coser, *The Functions of Social Conflict*, The Free Press (New York, 1956)
33 *ibid.*
34 G. Simmel, *Sociology of Georg Simmel*, Collier-Macmillan (1964)
35 L. Coser, *op. cit.* (1956), p. 151
36 *ibid.*, p. 152
37 J. Rex, *op. cit.*, p. 116
38 *ibid.*, p. 117
39 *ibid.*
40 *ibid.*, p. 119
41 R. Dahrendorf, *Class and Class Conflict in Industrial Society*, Routledge & Kegan Paul (1969)
42 R. Dahrendorf, 'Toward a theory of social conflict', *The Journal of Conflict Resolution*, **XI** (2), (1958), 170–83
43 *ibid.*
44 *ibid.*
45 J. Rex, *op. cit.* (1970), 122–31
46 *ibid.*, p. 129
47 *ibid.*
48 *ibid.*
49 *ibid.*, 129–30
50 *ibid.*, p. 130
51 *ibid.*
52 *ibid.*
53 *ibid.*
54 G. Kitson-Clark, *The Making of Victorian England* (London, 1962)
55 H. J. Laski, *The British Cabinet, A Study of Its Personnel*, Fabian Tract No. 223 (1928)

56 R. T. Nightingale, *The Personnel of the British Foreign Office and Diplomatic Service 1857–1929*, Fabian Tract No. 232 (1930)
57 H. Spencer, *The Man versus the State* (London, 1950), pp. 16 and 34
58 *The Financial Reformer*, August 1858
59 T. Beggs, 'A review of sanitary legislation in its economical aspects', in *Sessional Proceedings of the National Association for the Promotion of Social Science*, Vol. IX (no date), p. 36
60 O. Hill, *Royal Commission on Housing of the Working Classes Report*, Vol. II (no date), p. 288
61 W. Farr, *Vital Statistics*, in 'Selected Writings', N. A. Humphreys (ed.), (London, 1885), p. 467
62 W. Burgess and R. Park, *The Growth of the City: An Introduction to a Research Project*, American Sociological Society (1924)
63 H. Hoyt, *The Structure and Growth of Residential Neighbourhoods in American Cities*, Federal Housing Authority (Washington, 1939)
64 J. Vetch, Capt., *Poor Law Commissioners' Report on an Inquiry into the Sanitary Condition of the Labouring Population of Great Britain* (1834), 382–94
65 E. Chadwick, *Report on the Sanitary Conditions of the Labouring Population* (London, 1842)
66 C. Booth, *Life and Labour of the People of London*, 17 vols., Macmillan (1906)
67 P. H. Mann, *An Approach to Urban Sociology*, Routledge & Kegan Paul (1965), p. 124
68 H. Orlans, *Stevenage: a sociological study of a new town*, Routledge & Kegan Paul (1952)
69 R. M. Titmuss, *Essays on the Welfare State*, Unwin University Book (1963)

4. Social conflict and spatial inequality

Conflict and the structure of society

The distribution of scarce and desirable resources in British society is structured in such a way as to produce varying degrees of conflict between groups in different situations, and not only over their current distribution but also over the dynamic mechanisms maintaining and changing that distribution. The distribution of resources such as property, wealth and special skills determines the structure of society which in turn is both reflected in and reinforced by the distribution of status and political power. Conflict over these desirable resources and attributes is therefore a product of the relationships between the structure of society, its underlying distribution of resources and the different interests of groups found in different parts of the social structure. These are not static relationships. They exist in a continuous state of dynamic tension in which different groups, seeking to further their interests, are constantly competing, either overtly or covertly and with different degrees of energy, to improve their portions of scarce resources and hence alter their situation in the social structure.

The social structure itself consists of those regulating mechanisms and recurring patterns of social interaction which continue to exist over time, to the extent that they become characteristics of a particular stage in the development of society. The social structure is therefore the relatively regular but intangible patterns of social interaction found in society, together with the values and beliefs which give meaning to that interaction and which also embody a relatively consistent body of normative propositions on the basis of which society is regulated both formally and informally. The basis of the social structure is the distribution of scarce and desired resources and its existence is manifested by the relations of social groups to this distribution.

The relations of groups to the distribution of resources are manifested both socially and spatially. As Pahl says, 'The built environment is the result of conflicts, in the past and present, between those with different degrees of power in society – landowners, planners, developers, estate agents, local authorities . . . [and] . . . The Social structure is the key to the spatial structure.'[1] If town planners are to understand the spatial structure, they must therefore first understand the social structure. The social structure may be analysed according to the differential possession of scarce resources by different groups. These groups may be conveniently labelled social classes. To reach an approximate understanding of why social structure takes a particular form, town planners may find it particularly appropriate to investigate the relationships between social class and the possession of economic resources such as income and wealth together with the access which these resources provide to property. The resulting differential access to property should then illuminate the causes of the spatial structure of cities, which is the principal concern of town planners.

Social structure and social class

For Marx, the social structure was manifested in the social class system prevailing in society because 'a group of people share a common relationship to property, perform the same function in the organisation of production, have similar relations to power in society, and have a tendency to common behaviour patterns, as determined by their objective behaviour'.[2] It was, for him, on the basis of these relationships that the regulating ideas and power of the social structure rested. To these notions he added the more contentious idea that social classes, as such, did not really come into existence until different groups became manifestly conscious of their different interests and acted accordingly. In this process covert becomes overt conflict. Common sense suggests, however, that groups do not always clearly recognise and articulate their interests vis-a-vis other groups nor are they always in a position to do so without prompting from those outside the group. This does not, however, alter their situation in the social structure nor their social class-position. It is therefore possible to speak of the existence of a social class without it necessarily being accompanied by a manifest and coherent class consciousness.

As Weber argued, although a social class has an economic base it is not necessarily an action group, although it may develop into one under certain circumstances. He also argued that it is useful to identify not only the economic differences distinguishing social classes but also the social distinctions of status and the political differences giving rise to phenomena such as political parties. All the same, the primary determinant of the social structure remained, for Weber, the economic forces of society to the extent that he argued:

We may speak of a class when

1. a number of people have in common a specific causal component of their life chances in so far as
2. this component is represented exclusively by economic interests in the possession of goods and opportunities for income
3. and is represented under the conditions of the commodity or labour markets.[3]

Class situation is therefore ultimately market situation.

The Registrar General distinguishes five main social classes in Britain. They are termed professional, intermediate, skilled manual, semi-skilled manual and unskilled manual workers. In general each successively lower social class position represents a weaker market situation. Table 1 shows the proportions of economically active individuals found in each of the five social classes at the time of the 1966 Sample Census. It may be seen that the social class structure in Britain, like most advanced industrial nations, takes the form of a

Table 1. Great Britain 1966, social class structure

Social class	*Percentage of economically active individuals*
Professional	2·9
Intermediate	14·6
Skilled manual	49·1
Semi-skilled manual	22·3
Unskilled manual	8·0
Not classified	3·0

$N = 24\,857$. Source: *Social Trends*, HMSO, (1971), p. 59

diamond. At the top just under a fifth are non-manual workers whose market situation is based on their possession of wealth, property, size and security of income. In the middle half, the economically active population are skilled manual workers whose market situation depends largely on the size of their incomes and organised collective action usually based in the trade union movement. To be strictly accurate the term 'middle class' should be reserved for this group rather than the non-manual workers to whom the label is usually attached. At the bottom of the social class structure and usually in the weakest market situation are nearly one third of the work force who are semi- or unskilled manual workers.

This hierarchy of economic power when brought to the market place determines, other things being equal, the amounts of property, goods and services that individuals may secure and also their potential for acquiring more of these scarce and desirable things in the future. The simplest measure of this power is money, and hence it is possible to trace the relationships between, for example, income, wealth and property in order to produce a rough picture of the effects of the social structure on the life-chances of groups in terms of access to property and hence on the spatial structure.

Economic resources and social class

With respect to the relationships between economic resources and social class, the first striking feature of the distribution of income and wealth in Britain is inequality. One measure of income inequality is the relationship between the proportion of income units in a given category and the proportion of total available income they receive. The greater the discrepancy between these two proportions, the greater the degree of inequality. According to Lloyd's Bank, in 1968 those in the income range £275–599 represented 19·6 per cent of income units in Britain but received only 8·1 per cent of incomes after tax. Conversely those in the £2000 and over range represented 8·9 per cent of income units but received 20·4 per cent of income after tax. In more general terms, the top third of income units shared about half the total post-tax income while the bottom two thirds divided the remaining half between them.

The inequalities of income distribution are surpassed, however, by inequalities in the distribution of wealth, particularly in the form of property and capital. Thus Meade[4] estimated that in 1960 the top 1 per cent of the adult population in Britain owned 42 per cent of the total net private capital, whereas the top 5 per cent owned 75 per cent of it. Similarly, Atkinson[5] shows that by the end of the decade 90 per cent of the population owned less than half of the total personal wealth in the country while at the other extreme 92 people were each worth at least £2½ million pounds – a sum it would take the average working man 2000 years to earn.

The unequal distribution of wealth is specified more precisely in Table 2. The table is notable first for its description of the distribution

Table 2. United Kingdom 1961 and 1969, distribution of wealth by groups of owners

Percentage of wealth owned by	1961	1969
Most wealthy 1%	28·4	21·4
Most wealthy 5%	50·6	41·3
Most wealthy 10%	62·5	52·7
Most wealthy 50%	92·5	90·2
Bottom 50%	7·5	9·8

Source: *Social Trends*, HMSO, (1971), p. 81

of wealth and second for portraying how far that distribution changed during the 1960s. It may be seen that in 1969 the top 1 per cent owned 21·4 per cent of wealth as opposed to 28·4 per cent in 1961. Nevertheless, the bottom half only increased their share of wealth from 7·5 per cent to 9·8 per cent during the period. These figures illustrate the unequal distribution of wealth. They also show that when redistribution takes place it tends to filter down the distribution structure rather than go directly from those at the top to those at the bottom. This reflects the increased use of 'tax planning', whereby the incidence of tax can be minimised by spreading an individual's wealth around other members of his family, and the use of trust funds. Thus, although some redistribution of wealth took place during the 1960s, very little of it went to the lower half of the population and most filtered around the members of already wealthy families rather than improved the lot of those most in need.

When the significance of the distribution of wealth is discussed, it is necessary to define the term as precisely as possible. This is done in Table 3, which shows both the different categories of wealth and also how they changed during the 1960s.

Table 3. United Kingdom 1961 and 1969, change in categories of wealth (in £ thousand million)

Distribution of wealth by type	1961	1969
Company shares and debentures	12·7	19·8
Securities, mortgages, building society shares and deposits	10·5	13·9
Life assurance policies	6·5	15·5
Cash at the bank	7·4	9·5
Household goods, pictures, china, etc.	1·9	3·3
Land and buildings	12·5	29·8
Other assets	7·4	9·8
Total gross wealth	58·9	101·6

Source: *Social Trends*, HMSO, (1971), p. 81

Wealth may be defined as consisting of the following: company shares and debentures; securities, mortgages, building society shares and deposits; life assurance policies; cash at the bank; household goods, pictures, china etc.; land and buildings. It is interesting to note that three of the most significant categories of wealth, mortgages, life assurance and land and property can be directly or indirectly linked to the spatial structure. This means that the unequal distribution of wealth is reflected in the properties of the spatial structure.

Table 3 shows that the greatest increase in wealth during the 1960s took place in land and buildings. This category more than doubled during the period. It rose from £12·5 thousand million to £29·8 thousand million in eight years. The value of life assurance policies also more than doubled from £6·5 to £15·5 thousand million. Mortgages and related assets, on the other hand, only went up from

£10·5 to £13·9 thousand million and company shares and debentures from £12·7 to £19·8 thousand million.

Marx argues that the ownership and control of such wealth in capitalist society gives rise to a hegemonic class which rules not only by virtue of its ownership and control of wealth but also because it controls the major channels of education and communication. It has been argued, however, that this situation is declining because of an increase in the separation of ownership and control. This view has been contradicted by Florence, who has shown that,

> The controllers – directors and top executives, in whose hands the major strategic policy decisions lie – are, in fact, owners of large stockholdings themselves: the wealthiest shareholders of any identifiable group in society . . . For an inherent conflict of interest between large shareholders and controllers there is no plausible case on the evidence. In societal perspective, the two overlap, to the point of near-identity: private wealth is not divorced from private corporate power.[6]

Members of this ruling class tend to be self-recruiting and to come from similar and restricted backgrounds. Guttsman showed that, in the 1950s, 31 per cent of the directors of large insurance companies and 50 per cent of the directors of large banks were recruited from Eton alone.[7] Both these groups of institutions are among the largest investors in property and hence exercise a considerable degree of control over the spatial structure.

The other direct link between the ownership and control of wealth and the spatial structure is the property companies. A report from Counter Information Services says that '100 men have shared over £400 million between them from the property market over the past 20 years'.[8] The concentration of wealth and power in the spatial structure has now reached the stage where 'The ten largest property companies control assets approaching £3000 million, larger than the entire gold and dollar reserves of the U.K. Nearly all of these companies are de facto controlled by one or two men.'[9] The most notorious of them in London is Stock Conversion and Investment Trust. Over the fifteen years preceding 1972, £40 million of the profits of this firm have accrued to only two men called Clark and Levy. Their most infamous monument, the Euston Centre, netted a £64 million profit for the nominal equity interest of £1000.

At about the same time that Clark and Levy were making £40

million, 14 per cent of the population of Britain were living in poverty, 1·8 million homes were officially declared unfit for human habitation, and the number of homeless people doubled. While Levy lives in a seven storey house in Grosvenor Square,

many of the poor live in twilight areas which, in contrast with average areas, have more overcrowding, crime, rent arrears, debt, unskilled manual workers, infant deaths, problem families, unemployment, juvenile delinquents, youth unemployment, free school meals, educationally subnormal children, children in special schools, lack of standard housing amenities, children in care, people living in one or two rooms, people per acre, mental illness, scabies, bronchitis, dysentery, gastro-enteritis, infestation, and referrals to social service departments.[10]

The first attempts to measure accurately the amount of poverty in Britain were those of Booth and Rowntree around the turn of the century. Their concept of minimum necessary standards was incorporated in the Beveridge report which formed the basis of the post-World War II National Insurance scheme. As envisaged by Beveridge this minimum was to be guaranteed by social insurance with National Assistance providing for only a small (and diminishing) number of people. This, however, has never been the case and National Insurance benefits (see Table 4) have always been below

Table 4. Great Britain 1961 and 1970, persons receiving national insurance benefits

National Insurance benefit categories	*No. of recipients (thousands)* 1961	1970
Unemployment benefit	202	302
Sickness benefit	931	1060
Retirement pensions and widows' benefit (age 60–64)	5821	7693
Guardians' allowances, orphans' pensions and individual children's allowances	6	5
Maternity allowance	70	80
Injury benefit	61	66
Industrial disablement benefit	180	207
Industrial death benefit	21	29

Source: *Social Trends*, HMSO, (1971), p. 89

the assistance scale and governments have relied on National Assistance or Supplementary Benefits, as they are now called, to fulfil the role of a national minimum. Furthermore, their importance has increased rather than diminished. This is shown by Table 5. It

Table 5. Great Britain 1961 and 1970, percentages of national insurance beneficiaries (see Table 4) also receiving national assistance/ supplementary benefit

Benefit categories	1961	1970
	Per cent	
Unemployment benefit	14	19
Sickness benefit	13	15
Retirement pensions and widows' benefit (age 60–64)	22	27

Source: *Social Trends*, HMSO, (1971), p. 89

may be seen that the numbers receiving unemployment benefit, sickness benefit and retirement pensions during the 1960s all increased. At the same time, the proportions receiving these national insurance benefits and who needed to have them augmented by national assistance/supplementary benefits also increased. Unfortunately for those in poverty, Rowntree and Lavers, not surprisingly, were able to show that there was less poverty in York in 1950 than there had been at the time of Rowntree's last survey in 1936. This contributed to the common misconceptions of the 1950s that poverty had been abolished by the Welfare State and that Britain was a more equal society. Such beliefs lead to political slogans like 'you have never had it so good', to much discussion of the idea of an affluent society and to arguments about the withering away of the Welfare State and the right of affluent individuals to fend for themselves and to contract out of involvement in state-sponsored schemes.

This whole philosophy was called into question by Abel-Smith and Townsend in 1958 in their classic pamphlet, the *Poor and the Poorest*.[11] They questioned the validity of Rowntree and Lavers' conclusions and drew attention to large groups such as the old, widowed, disabled and sick who could not compete successfully in a market economy. On the basis of their work it is now realised that throughout the fifties the numbers and problems of these groups, together with those of low wage earners and large families, were substantial. Their numbers could be counted in millions and were growing, not shrinking. It was more likely that the distribution of economic resources was becoming less and not more equitable. Finally, it was apparent the equality of opportunity vaunted by the Government was a tawdry fabrication to the extent that, between 1950 and 1960, sections of the population had diets which were actually below medically recommended scales.

Symptomatic of this situation was the increasing number of people receiving national assistance rather than a decreasing number as envisaged by Beveridge. This was reflected in the estimates of Abel-Smith and Townsend that during the 1950s the number of households in poverty rose from 10·1 to 17·9 per cent, or that by 1960 some 14 per cent of the population of Britain was living in poverty. Although part of the increase may be explained by the fact that they defined poverty according to the national assistance scales and these increased during the period, nevertheless it is incontrovertible evidence that large and probably increasing numbers of people were living in poverty.

One of the main problems in discovering how many people are living in poverty and who they are, as with the difficulty of identifying the members of a hegemonic class, is that of definition. It is difficult to produce an objective definition of either which does not unduly prescribe what subsequently emerges as empirical verification. For example, the numbers and nature of those in poverty depends to a large extent on how the concept is defined.

In practice there is no absolute and objective definition of poverty which is valid in all countries at all times. It is a relative concept and can only be defined in relation to the living standards of a particular society at a particular date. Marx, for example, argues in *Wage, Labour and Capital* that 'Our needs and enjoyment spring from society; we measure them therefore by society and not by the objects of their satisfaction. Because they are of a social nature, they are of a relative nature.' Galbraith has also made the same point in his discourse on the *Affluent Society* where he argues that 'People are poverty-stricken when their income, even if it is adequate for survival, falls markedly below that of the community.' Also, as Durkheim had perceptively pointed out earlier, 'What is needed if (this) social order is to reign is that the mass of men be content with their lot. But what is needed for them to be content, is not that they have more or less but that they are convinced that they have no right to more.'[12] This last point has been clearly illustrated by Runciman in his book *Relative Deprivation and Social Justice*. There he shows that those possessing different amounts of economic resources tend to compare themselves with those around them or in closely related situations in the social structure. Those in poverty have little or no conception of the real differences between themselves and the affluent and consequently make few comparisons or demands for radical changes in their circumstances.

In Britain, however, the operational definitions of poverty used in research have not taken account of these more intangible aspects and have concentrated on practical and quantifiable concepts. Rowntree, the first to attempt a precise definition, considered that a family was in poverty if its earnings were insufficient to obtain the minimum necessary for the maintenance of physical efficiency. In effect this defined poverty as an inadequate level of food, clothing and fuel translated into money terms and adjusted for different sizes of household.

An alternative definition is to regard poverty as a continually moving average standard based on the actual distribution of income within a society. This has the advantage of demonstrating that poverty is concerned with economic equality as well as with survival. Operationally it may be used, as it was by Abel-Smith and Townsend, to examine how far household expenditure falls below the mean for the type of household.

The most commonly used definition of a poverty line, however, is that of the National Assistance or Supplementary Benefit scales which, although woefully inadequate to support families in acceptable circumstances in an affluent society, at least represent the Government's official operational definition of poverty. As the Government's own minimum standard, it is axiomatically scandalous if numbers of people are found to be living below this level.

In a discussion of the relationships between the structure of society, poverty and town planning, however, given the difficulties of defining either a hegemonic class or those in poverty, the most important issue is whether these respective conditions are the result of individual volition and ability or an inevitable consequence of the structure of society. And, if it is the latter, what effects does town planning have on the situation?

In this debate one may paraphrase Mills[13] to the effect that if one man is found, for example, in poverty, then this could be the result of his lack of motivation and ability. If seven and a half million people are found in poverty, then one must suspect that the causes lie elsewhere and probably in the structure of society itself. Nevertheless, as Coates and Silburn point out,

> The belief that the poor have only themselves to blame for their condition is a time honoured one . . . Critics seem to assume that primary poverty, a sheer shortage of money, cannot exist, but that secondary poverty, especially that proportion of secondary poverty which is caused by foolish and wasteful expenditure, can.[14]

A cursory glance at the immediate causes of poverty soon dispels these erroneous impressions. Rowntree found that, in 1899, the causes of poverty were:

1. Death of the chief wage earner.
2. Incapacity of the chief wage earner through accident, illness or old age.
3. Chief wage earner out of work.
4. Chronic irregularity of work.
5. Size of family.
6. Lowness of wage.

In 1960, Abel-Smith and Townsend found that the immediate causes of poverty were:

1. Unemployment	7%
2. Inadequate wages	40%
3. Old age	33%
4. Sickness	10%
5. Death of the chief wage earner	10%

Thus, the most important immediate causes of poverty are not, as the unsympathetic suppose, indolence, fecundity etc., but low wages or inadequate national insurance benefits. These are primarily the result of the economic structure of society together with the prevailing values, particularly with respect to welfare expenditure on the part of the Government.

Low pay, for example, is a continuous problem for those who work in the less prosperous regions or the more inefficient industries or, worse still, both. It is not a direct result of the personal characteristics of the recipients. It is neither a temporary phenomenon for a particular worker nor a result of working short hours. More often it is the result of ill-health or the special characteristics of the industry concerned. Thus, some industries have more than average numbers of low paid workers while others are saddled with wage councils or employment contraction. Regional differences are important in low income as is old age. Nearly half the workers, for example, with low incomes are over fifty years of age. As a result of these structural factors 2·5 million males and 5 million females earned, on average, less than £15 per week in 1968. When such meagre economic resources are brought to the market place they usually prove inadequate to acquire even basic necessities such as housing, fuel and food. The 1971 Family Expenditure Survey[15] shows that for those households expending less than £25 per week over half went on housing, fuel and food, while for those in the £60–80 category only one third of their expenditure was devoted to these three items. In other words, the poor have to spend proportionately more for probably worse necessities while the rich spend proportionately less of their incomes on basic necessities and probably get better quality for their money as well.

In response to these phenomena the institutions of welfare have failed to resist adequately the results of the social structure. In 1960, for example, national insurance benefits failed to reach all those in poverty in 5–6 per cent of instances because even wages plus family allowances were insufficient; in 3–4 per cent of cases because social insurance benefits were inadequate anyway; and in 4–5 per cent of examples because families were not even entitled to the full scale of benefits.[16] Furthermore, as Harrington[17] has argued in the United States and Titmuss[18] has pointed out in Britain, the social services, taken together, do not benefit the poor as much as the middle income population.

The result is that successive generations of the poor get caught in what has come to be known as the poverty cycle. This cycle is illustrated in Figure 3.

In general whatever point one enters the poverty cycle the eventual results are always roughly the same both in terms of the life-cycle of

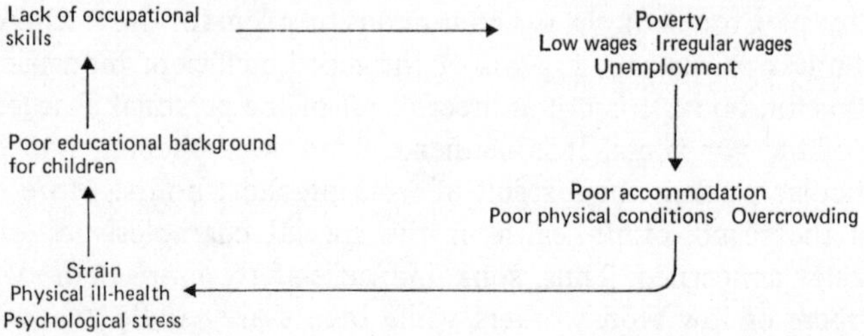

Figure 3. The poverty cycle (Source: SNAP 69/72, Shelter (1973), *p. 150)*

individual families or the life chances of successive generations. Poverty leads to poor accommodation which involves strain which makes for a poor educational background for children which leads to lack of occupational skills which leads to more poverty, and so on. The orientations of welfare services such as town planning have done little or nothing to break this cycle during the last twenty-five years. The social class structure of Britain may therefore be characterised as consisting of three main social groupings with two intermediate groups in the interstices. Although the two class model predicted by Marx has not yet developed, the social classes are marked off by their ownership and control of economic resources. At the top, less than 10 per cent own over half the total wealth, receive over a fifth of total incomes even after tax and control a great deal of the capital of the large insurance and banking institutions. A significant proportion of this group passes through one of the six major public schools. The basis of this ruling class is therefore its ownership or control of capital and a common, restricted educational or cultural background.

In the middle of the social class structure some 50 per cent of those who are economically active are defined by the fact that they sell their skilled labour in the market place. Skilled manual workers, in general, do not directly own or control large amounts of capital, although via increases in home ownership, life assurance, pensions and their trade unions, some small degree of fragmented or indirect ownership or control of capital is passing to this group.

At the bottom of the social class structure about 20 per cent of the population may be defined not only by their lack of capital but also by the fact that many of them are wholly or partly dependent upon the state for their very existence. This is because they are unemployed, old, sick, widowed, children, or lack occupational skills thought to be relevant in the market place.

These three main social classes may be called the upper or ruling class, the middle class and the lowest class, respectively. In the interstices between them may be found the lower middle class composed mainly of partly skilled manual workers and the upper middle class composed mainly of non-manual employees on salaries. To some extent the ownership and control of capital is spread through a majority of these social classes but decreases sharply with each successively lower division in the social structure. It should be remembered, however, that as with private corporations, it is not necessary to own all their capital in order to control or rule them.

Social class and spatial structure

It is now necessary to show how these social classes are related to the spatial structure. As far as the latter is concerned, the social class structure is directly linked to what happens on the ground first by the actions of those who own or control capital in respect of their use of land and property. Second, the social class structure is reflected in the spatial structure via the market place and the relative economic resources that different social classes bring to bear in their attempts to gain access to accommodation.

As far as the upper or ruling class is concerned, their primary effects on the spatial structure are to be seen in the commercial and industrial property and the price of land in cities. Their secondary effects may be traced through the price of land to the cost of its use for things like housing and consequently to bad housing and homelessness among the lowest social class. In 1958, property companies were quoted for the first time as a separate section on the London Stock Exchange. At that time the market value of the companies listed was £103 million. By 1972 their market value was £2644 million. The Counter Information Services Report points out that 'During this period of phenomenal growth it has been the institutions – the banks, insurance companies, pension funds, etc. – that have supplied the bulk of the finance needed.'[19] This inflow of capital has been controlled in such a way that only half of the permitted office space in London has actually been built, and at the same time office rents in the City of London are about twice what they are in New York. Also, men like Hyams still gain huge capital sums by leaving completed office blocks like Centre Point empty.

Some of those responsible for town planning have been the willing agents of the owners and controllers of capital in these developments. The chairman of Southwark's planning committee is quoted as saying of the developers that 'These people have made London the commercial capital of the world. You may not agree with the distribution of that wealth, but where would we be without them?'[20] Similarly, one of the residents in the £1000 per annum flats in Levy's Euston Centre is a man called Sames who is also the developer's planning consultant. He was chief planning officer with the London County Council, the planning authority responsible for the permission to build the Euston Centre. The Greater London Council's view on the redevelopment of Covent Garden was 'based on the fact that the maximisation of the return on the investment was the criterion for obsolescence . . . [they] were in accord with those of any property developer.'[21]

The first effect of commercial and industrial developments in cities, where the use of land is regulated by town planners and constrained by green belts, is to reduce the number of houses available. Between 1961 and 1966, for example, the number of dwellings in the City of Westminster fell by 7 per cent. A hundred years ago Godwin wrote 'our street makers when they are asked where the displaced occupants of the garrets and cellars are to go, shout without thought – "go to?" – "Anywhere"'.[22] There are very few places for the lowest social class to go. Those unskilled workers living in inner areas of cities have to live close to their work and cannot afford to move far either because of low wages or because they are dependent on inadequate state benefits. Many do not want to move from familiar districts, relatives and friends. So, as in places like Manchester and London a century ago, capital developments push them into the nearest slum. As Engels said in 1872, 'This is how the bourgeoisie settles the question in practice. The infamous holes and cellars in which the capitalist mode of production confines our workers are not abolished; they are merely shifted elsewhere.'[23] This process sets in motion a Giffin Paradox where those who can least afford it pay more for worse accommodation. In such circumstances the price of a basic necessity of life rises and, as there is no cheaper substitute for this necessity, as the price rises the poorer people must paradoxically spend more of their income on it. The result is that the poor must pay a higher proportion of their income for housing and, consequently, less on other essentials such as food, fuel and clothing. At the same time the kind of employment that active but unskilled workers can do tends to decline in inner cities while office employment for the upper and upper-middle social classes increases. This produces a further turn of the screw whereby the lowest social class is economically and socially trapped by the poverty cycle and physically trapped in inner areas of cities. The result is that increasing numbers of people in those areas are becoming wholly dependent on state support for their very existence.

The second effect of commercial and industrial developments in cities where land scarcity is statutorily maintained is to increase the demand for land. As the supply of land is inelastic anyway and is rendered more inelastic by town planning regulation, these forces result in a sharp increase in its price. The high price of land forces up the cost of housing. Table 6, for example, shows that while

Table 6. England and Wales/Great Britain 1963–70, housebuilding costs and prices

1963 = 100	1970
Cost of local authority houses (England & Wales)	163
Prices of new houses (Great Britain)	160
Prices of house-building materials (Great Britain)	131
Private sector housing land per plot (England & Wales)	204

Source: *Social Trends*, HMSO, (1971), p. 131

between 1963 and 1970 the cost of building materials only went up by 31 per cent, the cost of a private sector house plot went up by 104 per cent. This rate of increase accelerated during the early part of the 1970s as increased availability of mortgage funds increased the demand for the inadequate supply of building land and houses. The Nationwide Building Society estimated that average house prices rose by 31 per cent between July 1971 and July 1972. In London and the South East, 40 per cent of purchasers had to find deposits of more than £3000 in 1972. Not surprisingly, manual workers, representing some two-thirds of the work force, accounted for only 38·1 per cent of the borrowers from Nationwide.

Similar effects have been felt in the public sector of housing. 'In 1971, for example, Sir Desmond Plummer said – the GLC's programme this year for new housing contracts had almost been brought to a standstill because of the low level of London yardstick.'[24] This is the government housing cost yardstick which determines the amount of money that local authorities may spend on individual housing units. At the same time:

In the London Borough of Camden, the situation was even more serious; in each year from 1970 interest repayments have taken around 30 per cent more than the total income from rents. Camden is therefore in the position of those Latin American republics and others in the Third World, whose annual repayments on overseas loans exceed the volume of new aid.'[25]

The net result of these increases in house prices and rents is that the numbers of homeless people in temporary accommodation rose, between 1966 and 1970, from 7723 to 12 970 in Greater London and from 5308 to 11 313 in the rest of England and Wales. These figures only reflect the amount of such accommodation that is available. In London, for example, nearly three-quarters of all the people who apply for it are rejected. The amount of real homelessness is underestimated. The figures exclude:

1. Families 'on the streets' sleeping in an abandoned car or in the open.
2. Families living in squalor.
3. Families hopelessly overcrowded.
4. Families split up.
5. Families taken under stress by in-laws and friends.
6. Families in physical danger because of the unfitness of their property.
7. Families lacking many or all of the basic facilities. Thus there could be anything up to 50 000 people in Greater London alone who are officially or unofficially homeless.

Other forces are also at play in the spatial structure which reduce the amount of housing available for the lowest social class, increase its cost and benefit mostly the upper and upper-middle social classes. Table 7, for example, shows that new dwelling construction in

Table 7. England and Wales 1966–70, dwellings completed

	Number of dwellings (in thousands)	
Year dwellings completed	*Local authorities and new towns*	*Private owners*
1966	69	180
1967	82	178
1968	76	198
1969	68	160
1970	63	148

Source: *Social Trends*, HMSO, (1971), p. 127

England and Wales fell between 1966 and 1970. Even so, by 1970, more than twice as many new dwellings were being constructed in the private sector as by local authorities and new town corporations. In the same year, while the total increase in new dwellings was 211 000, the number of grants for home improvement totalled 180 000. More than half of these went to private owners and housing associations. Often such grants contribute to the process of gentrification where upper- and upper-middle-class families invade traditional working-class areas forcing out, on average, about two lower-class families and putting the cost of housing in the area beyond their reach. In Barnsbury, for example, a house was sold for £7000 in 1966 and, after improvement, for £22 500 in 1972. In something like a third to a half of such cases the improvement grant simply goes straight into the pockets of developers.

A number of government housing and town planning policies serve to reinforce and reflect the social class structure. The *Committee on Housing in Greater London (1965) Report* showed that the most expensive form of tenure is that into which many of the lowest social class gravitate (Table 8). Thus renting from a private landlord proved to be more expensive than owner-occupation, especially after tax relief on the interest paid on mortgages. Although local authority housing was the cheapest form of tenure, it is in fact largely reserved for the middle- and lower-middle sections of the manual working classes.

This situation is partly maintained by government policy on the

Table 8. Weekly costs of accommodation under different types of tenure

Dwelling cost (including land)	*Local authority*	*Housing association*	*Private landlord*	*Owner Occupation*	
				Before tax relief	*After tax relief*
£5500	£3.3.8	£7.14.1	£10.1.8	£8.13.1	£6.7.6

Source: *Committee on Housing in Greater London* (1965), Chairman Sir Milner Holland, HMSO, London

financing of houses. In 1969 and 1970, for example, the average government contribution to new permanent local authority dwellings was £26 per dwelling to which may be added £18 from local authority rate funds thereby making an average total contribution of £44 per dwelling. The average benefit to house mortgagors in the form of tax relief on mortgages was £45 per dwelling. Thus the main benefits in the spatial structure go to owner-occupiers, who normally come from the top half of the social class structure. The next best benefits go to the tenants of local authority or new town houses who usually come from the middle half of the social class structure. The Conservative government's Housing Finance Act of 1972 is designed to reduce these benefits.

Under this Act new rents are to be fixed for local authority and privately rented unfurnished accommodation and are to take into account the size, age, condition, amenities and neighbourhood of the dwelling, but exclude its scarcity value. In practice this means that the rents are increased by £1 per week in 1972–3 and by 50p a week in succeeding years. These rises will allow the Exchequer to withdraw subsidies to local authorities over the ensuing four years. Instead, the Exchequer is to pay 75 per cent of the deficit between the local authority's rent income and its expenditure on housing. The Exchequer will also pay 80 per cent of the cost of rent allowances for private tenancies. The remainder in each case will be met from the rates. If there is a surplus on the local authority's housing revenue account, it goes to the Exchequer to help pay for the rent allowances. In general, these provisions together with exhortations to local authorities to sell their houses are designed to reduce the amount of subsidy given to families in the rented sector of the market and at the same time to switch some of the source of this subsidy from property owners to non-property owners.

Meanwhile, in the private rented sector of the housing market, the sector in which most of the lowest social class is to be found, 'A *Guardian* inquiry into the rented flat market in London has revealed that thousands [of] tenants could be entitled to back payments because their landlords have been charging them more than they need pay.'[26] This, under the 1968 Rent Act, was supposed to be a 'tenants' Magna Carta'. Under this Act landlords have been increasing rents by 50 to 100 per cent as tenancies change hands. An architect of such policies, Stern, at one time a managing director of the Freshwater group that controlled more rented accommodation than anyone else, is responsible for some of the ideas contained in the Conservative Government's Housing Finance Act of 1972.

The take-up rate for rent and rate rebates in this sector is below 50 per cent of those entitled to claim. Apart from the stigma attached to making such claims:

> The disincentives to claim are considerable. A statement of earnings, capital resources, family situation, etc. must be submitted every six months, and any changes in circumstances reported immediately under pain of prosecution under the 1968 Thefts Act. Workers in lower income brackets may lose 85 per cent of wage increases through loss of benefits on rebates; an obvious weapon in the armoury of employers paying low wages.[27]

Nevitt has shown that there can be 'a marginal rate loss equal to 95 per cent on the £4 earned between £16 and £20'.[28] This of course is a much higher rate than even surtax.

All these factors combine to relate social class to the spatial structure in terms of the quality, cost and condition of their housing. Cullingworth[29] has shown, for example, that in England, in 1962, professional workers were nearly three times as likely to own their homes as other manual workers, while the latter were more than twice as likely to rent their homes in the private unfurnished sector as the former. Such differences confer not only relatively different degrees of security and prestige but also materially different living conditions and financial gains. Thus, while only 1 per cent of professional workers were living at densities of 1·5 or more per room, 7 per cent of other manual workers were living in such crowded conditions. Similarly, while 92 per cent of professional workers had the exclusive use of a fixed bath only 60 per cent of other manual workers had such a facility (Table 9).

All this is taking place within the context where, in 1972, the Government spent less on housing than any other of its major items of expenditure. Indeed, successive governments have spent proportionately less on housing over the last few years than any other of the fourteen Western European nations. At the same time, in 1972, the Minister for Housing and Construction admitted that there were 1·2 million houses in England and Wales representing 7·3 per cent of homes which were officially described as unfit for human habitation.[30]

Inequalities in the distribution of economic resources manifested in the social structure of Britain are reflected in the distribution of different kinds of property in the spatial structure. Here, as in the social structure, there is competition and conflict over access to property. As with the distribution of income, one group is favoured above all others and the elite members of that group derive the greatest benefits of all from property ownership. This situation is reinforced by the political system in so far as government policy towards alleviating the hazards of the market place in property are both regressive and inadequate.

The spatial structure, however, is composed not only of dynamic mechanisms allocating and distributing the use of different kinds of property but also of the processes which locate that property in space. The location of different kinds of property in different places determines the proximity of, and access to, other property and facilities on the part of those who acquire the use of that property. Hence the spatial structure reflects not only the distribution of resources in the social structure but also the manifest and physical location of the use of some of those resources.

These relationships are extremely complex and not fully understood. Simplified descriptions of them have been produced by the social ecologists. These show that there are general patterns in the social ecology of cities to the extent that, during the processes of urbanisation, different areas come to be associated at different times with different social classes. While it should again be stressed that

	Professional	*Small employers*	*Clerical*	*Foremen and Skilled*	*Other manual*	*Retired and Unoccupied*	*All households*
Number of households in sample	353	172	248	1119	554	229	3231
	Per cent of above households						
Tenure:							
Owns/is buying	71	66	50	39	26	43	43
Rents from Council	6	3	18	27	29	18	21
Rents privately unfurnished	16	28	25	31	39	36	32
Rents furnished	4	1	6	3	2	1	2
Has rent free, etc.	3	2	2	1	5	2	2
Persons per room ratio:							
Up to 0·33	13	14	12	5	9	41	16
0·34–1·49	86	86	86	90	84	57	80
1·50 or more	1	—	2	5	7	2	4
Households having exclusive use of:							
Fixed bath	92	90	77	72	60	62	71
Flush toilet	96	94	90	91	83	85	89
Hot water from tap	96	94	84	80	68	67	77
Garden	83	80	70	68	63	67	69
Garage	47	47	24	14	7	13	19

Source: Cullingworth, J. B., *English Housing Trends*, Occasional Papers on Social Administration No. 13, Bell (1965), pp. 32 and 33

these processes are in a continual state of change, nevertheless, analyses of the distribution of different social classes at any given point of time usually show that social distance is mirrored by spatial segregation.

The reasons for this spatial segregation have been noted by the author.[31] Thus, residential location is the result of the interaction between the independent, social, structural variables of age and household structure within specific social classes and a set of intervening variables represented by a family's values and aspirations. These lead it to locate residentially within its market constraints according to the balance it wishes to strike between the satisfactions derived from housing, employment, location and social intercourse. The connection between social class and residential location is that a household's source and size of income, the degree of job security enjoyed by its working members and their opportunities for occupational mobility combined with the style of life they wish to lead determines, to a large extent, the kind of accommodation they may live in, the nature and remuneration of present and possible future employment, the locations they can afford and the aspirations that they will be seeking to satisfy.

As a rule, the lower the social class, the more restricted is the supply of acceptable housing which they can afford. This is the result of the structure of the housing market and lower incomes. As far as the former is concerned, decreases in the supply of appropriate housing in the private sector have not been sufficiently multiplied by increases in the public sector. Private ownership is beyond the pockets of many and does not feature strongly in the aspirations of some, particularly the older manual workers. Higher in their priorities are the creation of a 'home' centred around suitable physical accommodation, located within easy reach of work and often enmeshed in extended kinship and friendship networks. As a result of these priorities there are marked tendencies among members of the lower social classes to emphasise the location of work, relatives or friends in their residential choices.

In contrast, the job density, that is to say the number of employment opportunities in any given occupational category tends to decrease for non-manual workers as they spiral up their occupational hierarchies. Consequently, the supply of opportunities and particularly those representing a promotion is more restricted. This, combined with the concept of work as a career rather than a job and the search for promotion, ensures that a substantial proportion of the higher social classes experience a peculiar type of employment scarcity. This often leads them to spiral from one job to a better one, often in different locations. The income and wealth generated from this type of employment, however, permits greater choice in the matter of housing and its location. This is because of the stronger market position of families of this type who are thus able to locate with better proximity and access to those facilities they value most highly.

Social distance is reflected in spatial segregation because of the differences in the abilities of families in different situations in the social structure to compete for those locations and physical facilities to which they accord priority in their scale of values. So, families lower in the social class structure have greater difficulty in competing for housing and tend to place greater value on this and local social networks. On the other hand, the higher a family is in the social class structure the greater and fiercer becomes the competition for better employment and locations, as these two factors are highly valued.

The manifest spatial structure is therefore the result of a very complex set of dynamic interactions between people, economic resources, values and places. All the factors are in a continuous state of competitive tension and change. For example, in any one year about a tenth of the population of Britain changes its accommodation. Over time, these changes are enough to change the social composition of particular spatial locations quite rapidly and radically. One school of thought uses the existence of such movement and change to argue that inequalities in the distribution of resources, access to property and the use of space are, in fact, justified on the grounds that the openness of this arrangement allows individuals to find a niche, in both social and spatial structures, which is both appropriate and a measure of their relative worth in society.

Social and physical mobility

The notion of social and spatial laissez-faire rests on the assumption 'that material riches and spiritual grace are firmly interconnected and that, if a man is poor, it is a sign that he has fallen from grace and no will on earth can save him'.[32] Such a market view of the distribution of desirable goods and services in society assumes that all individuals have an equal chance to compete in the market and that the undisputed inequalities that result are equitable expressions of the different possession of qualities required by society from individuals. Thus, differences in the social structure rest not on the relative power of individuals in the struggle for resources but rather on their particular qualities as individuals.

This school of thought is exemplified by functionalists such as Parsons, Davis and Moore. They argue that the social class systems found in advanced industrial nations reflect different distributions of desirable attributes and rewards, and are equitable because they are relatively open and therefore a just equation of reward with talent exists. The key assertions here are:

1. That social class is related to merit.
2. The mechanism ensuring this relationship is social mobility.

The case for these assertions may be argued historically. Thus, at birth every child acquires the position of his family in the existing rank hierarchy. This rank hierarchy is the result of the fact that:

1. Certain positions are functionally more important than others and require special skills for their performance.
2. Only a limited number of individuals in any society have the talents which can be trained to the skills appropriate to those positions.
3. The conversion of talents into skills involves a training period that necessitates the making of sacrifices.
4. In order to induce talented persons to make these sacrifices, future positions must carry an inducement in the form of differential access to the scarce rewards that society has to offer.
5. These scarce and desired goods are attached to certain positions.
6. Differential access to rewards has as a consequence the differentiation of prestige and esteem which leads to the institutionalisation of social inequality and hence social stratification.
7. Therefore social inequality is both functional and inevitable in any society.

The main characteristic of social laissez-faire is, therefore, that during an individual's lifetime his acquisition of resources and his power and prestige come to rest upon achievement rather than being ascribed to him by birth and privilege.

This view of the efficacy and equity of social laissez-faire may be challenged. In the first place, as Coser and Rosenberg[33] point out, social class may not be so much a functional necessity as a dysfunctional phenomenon limiting the optimum size of the social product. Thus it:

1. Limits the possibility of discovering talent because of unequal access to appropriate motivation, recruitment and training.
2. In limiting the search for talent it sets limits on the possibility for expanding productive resources.
3. Stratification functions to provide elites with political power necessary to procure the acceptance and dominance of an ideology and tends therefore to be conservative.
4. Social-stratification systems function to distribute favourable self-images unequally through a population. To the extent that these are necessary to the development of potential, they limit potential.
5. To the extent that inequalities in social rewards cannot be made fully acceptable to the less privileged in a society, social-stratification systems function to encourage hostility.
6. Stratification functions to distribute unequally the sense of significant membership in the population.
7. Unequal significant membership leads to unequal loyalty.
8. To the extent that participation and apathy depend upon a sense of significant membership in a society, social-stratification systems function to distribute, unequally in a population, the motivation to participate.

Therefore social inequality is not an unconsciously evolved device by which societies ensure that the most important positions are conscientiously filled by the most qualified persons. Indeed, the whole functionalist argument is circular, for it asserts that the most important positions are the most highly rewarded because they are the most important.

Not only is social inequality not a reflection of social merit but also serious doubt must be cast on the contention that the social class system is open enough to allow the amount of social mobility that would be necessary to continuously arrive at such a relationship. On the contrary, the British class structure is marked by restricted mobility which, at the very least, facilitates the protection of privileges. Nor is it true that the processes generating social mobility necessarily favour industrious and talented individuals. According to Lockwood,[34] who moves where and how is reducible to the operation of seven factors:

1. The ratio of higher to lower jobs in the occupational structure.
2. The degree to which occupations call for highly specific skills or for the acquisition of more diffuse criteria of ability.
3. Differential fertility.
4. The structure of educational opportunities and institutions.
5. The distribution of innate abilities in the different occupational strata.
6. The distribution of information and influence both in connection with education and jobs.
7. The distribution of the motivation to achieve.

Only the motivation to achieve is directly under the control of the individual and even this may be severely curtailed by such structural factors as unemployment and poor housing, both of which tend to result in apathy or deviance rather than high achievement motivation.

Social mobility is generally determined by structural factors beyond the control of the individual and such mobility as does occur is not necessarily related to merit. In Russia, for example, the period of greatest social mobility occurred in the decades around the Second World War. This coincided both with the period of the greatest proportionate increase in her industrial, governmental and educational systems and the disruption of her existing social structure by war. In more normal times, avenues of opportunity for social mobility are closely related to such factors as growth in the number of occupations requiring educational qualifications and particularly those associated with bureaucratic expansion in both the public and private sectors of the economy.

British education, however, has not provided avenues of opportunity for social mobility to a sufficient extent – rather the reverse. The institution of free education up to and including university education has, if anything, exposed the avenues of privilege rather than opened those of opportunity. Thus, while in 1968 the so-called 'public' schools took 2·5 per cent of the nation's children, the schools' products took 35 per cent of the places at Oxbridge, 42 per cent of Wilson's cabinet in 1967, 71 per cent of the directorships of Britain's most prominent firms and 91 per cent of Lord Home's cabinet places in 1963. In contrast, the lower the social class the less use is made of educational opportunities. Bernstein[35] has shown that children from working-class homes suffer from poor verbal ability and Jackson[36] has shown that both in the poorer schools and among the children selected for C streams, performance deteriorates between the ages of seven and eleven. The result is that by the time children are eligible for university less than 1 per cent of those from working-class homes and in the relevant age group actually receive a university education.

Basically, as Jackson points out,

> School can do hardly anything to alter the lack of money and power which makes the poor, poor. Every survey since the war has shown that our education system is biased against the working class, and especially against its poorest members . . . school legitimates the society of yesterday; celebrates a middle-aged, middle-class style of life.[37]

Thus, as with the distribution of income, wealth, property and accommodation, not only do the upper social classes have most to start with but they also derive the greatest benefit from the activities of the state. This is reflected in the fact that 'A university student costs the state £1000 a year or more – more than the total pre-tax annual wage, plus family allowances, of a farm worker with three children.'[38]

Not surprisingly, therefore, an analysis of social mobility in Britain undertaken by Glass and Hall[39] in the early 1950s, and not substantially modified by subsequent research, shows a rather modest amount of movement between social classes. In Britain:

1. Over the past 50 years much social mobility has been the result of changes in the occupational structure on to close levels.
2. Despite overall improvements the relative positions of the social classes have remained substantially unchanged.
3. Those already most favoured have made the most use of educational gateways to developing occupations.
4. There is not much evidence of the widespread adoption of middle-class values and aspirations among the working classes.[40]

Even Goldthorpe, talking of the preliminary findings of recent research in social mobility, conducted at Nuffield College, concluded that, 'There is still no basis for saying we have a truly open society. There are marked inequalities and opportunity is still associated with social origins.'[41]

Such restricted mobility in the social structure is reflected in restricted physical mobility particularly between different tenure classes in the housing market.

The movement between tenure classes has been outlined by Donnison.[42] Thus, in England in 1960–2,

> nearly half the newly formed (or reformed) households entered private rented property, and most of the rest started buying homes of their own. Very few went into council housing. In the few places where furnished accommodation was available, new households often began in furnished flats and rooms.

He goes on to say that,

> Subsequent moves among existing households followed a well marked pattern repeatedly found. More than half the movers went to property of the same tenure as that which they occupied before – about half the private tenants, the majority of council tenants and nearly all the owner occupiers who moved stayed within the same sectors of the market. Most of those who changed their tenures came from private rented property and followed two well marked routes leading to owner occupation and to council housing. These patterns of moves accounted for nine out of ten moves among existing households.

Thus, a family's physical mobility between tenure classes is restricted both by its market situation and by the structure of tenure categories and the supply of different types of accommodation in different locations.

Again, the most important mechanisms for housing mobility, like those of social mobility, are largely structural factors beyond the control of the individual.

Table 10 shows, for example, that the two growing sectors of the housing market are public and private ownership. The division between property owners and non-property owners is increasingly coming to reflect the division between those dependent on important elements of the welfare state and those whose dependence is less of necessity and more of selective choice. In contrast, those in the

Table 10. Great Britain 1960 and 1970, stock of dwellings by tenure

Tenure	1960	1970
	Per cent	
Owner occupied	42·0	49·5
Rented from local authorities or new town corporations	26·6	30·5
Rented from private owners	25·7	14·9
Other tenures	5·7	5·1

Source: *Social Trends*, HMSO, (1971), p. 125

private renting sector are slowly being squeezed so that sooner or later many will be faced with the dilemma of their inability to afford private ownership, while at the same time being unable to acquire local authority accommodation. This dilemma is exacerbated by the fact that the number of housing completions in the public sector in Great Britain has fallen since 1967 while the cost of housing has risen faster than any other major item of personal expenditure since 1962. At the same time, although rises in wages and salaries kept pace with rises in the cost of houses during the 1960s, they have not done so during the 1970s. This means that, at the margin, fewer people are now able to enter private ownership, while at the same time it is becoming more difficult to gain local authority accommodation because the number of completions has fallen.

The lowest social class is therefore increasingly trapped in the inner areas of cities in conditions of multi-deprivation and with little hope of improving its situation either by social or physical mobility. Instead, residential moves are often forced upon such people by the activities of property developers and town planners alike. For many this means moving from one slum to the next nearest poor accommodation, and experiencing increased rents and still more overcrowding. In contrast, subsidised commuter travel, urban motorways and urban renewal confer most of their benefits on the higher social classes, frequently at the direct expense of the poor as their slums are pulled down to make way for new lines of communication. This has been going on for nearly a century. Chapman, describing Central London in the 1880s, says,

The second factor complicating the housing problem in central London was the continual dislocation caused by street, commercial and railway buildings . . . Railway construction wrought such havoc that one must conclude that in human costs the railways were responsible for as much harm as good . . . In the 1870s, for example, the whole of Somers Town, a densely populated working class district, was torn down to make way for the railway construction north of St Pancras. Despite the protests of such groups as the Somers Town Defence League, the working classes were helpless in the face of the onslaught.'[43]

So, as Engels remarks, 'The capitalist order of society reproduces again and again the evils to be remedied.'[44]

Conclusions

The spatial structure, the primary concern of town planners, stands in a complex relationship to the social structure. Both the causal explanation of the social structure and its relationships to the spatial structure are imperfectly understood. Nevertheless, the distribution of economic resources which forms the basis of the social structure is manifested in the distribution of the use of different types of facilities and the conflicts over location, proximity and accessibility.

The main characteristic of these different forms of distribution is inequality. There is inequality both in the current distribution of land uses and in the mechanisms permitting individuals to alter their position in the structure of land uses. This structure, like that of the social structure, is largely determined by the decisions of corporations, financial institutions and government. Its dynamic relationships also tend to favour the privilege that is increasingly the preserve of those best situated with respect to these decision-making areas.

References

1 R. Pahl, *Whose City?*, Longmore, p. 191
2 D. Marquand and I. Clegg, *Class and Power*, Sheed & Ward (1969), p. 6
3 H. H. Gerth and C. W. Mills, *From Max Weber: Essays in Sociology*, Routledge & Kegan Paul (1967), p. 181
4 J. E. Meade, *Efficiency, Equality and the Ownership of Property*, Allen & Unwin (1964)
5 A. B. Atkinson, *Unequal Shares: wealth in Britain*, Allen Lane (1972)
6 P. S. Florence, *The Ownership, Control and Success of Large Companies*, Sweet & Maxwell (1961)

7 W. L. Guttsman, *British Political Elites*, MacGibbon (1963)
8 Counter Information Services, *The Recurrent Crisis of London:* Ante-report on the property developers C.I.S. (1973), p. 66
9 *ibid.*, p. 2
10 *New Society*, 'How the poorest live', *New Society* (1973), p. 16
11 B. Abel-Smith and P. Townsend, *The Poor and the Poorest*, Occasional Papers on Social Administration No. 17, Bell (1965)
12 E. Durkheim, *Suicide*, Routledge & Kegan Paul (1970)
13 C. W. Mills, *The Sociological Imagination*, Pelican (1971)
14 K. Coates and R. Silburn, *Poverty: the Forgotten Englishmen*, Penguin (1970)
15 *see* J. H. Goldthorpe, 'Social inequality and social integration: Britain', *Advancement of Science* (1969), 190–202
16 B. Abel-Smith and P. Townsend, *op. cit.* p. 66
17 M. Harrington, *The Other America*, Macmillan (New York, 1962)
18 R. Titmuss, *Essays on the Welfare State*, Allen & Unwin (1963)
19 Counter Information Services, *op. cit.* (1973), p. 3
20 *ibid.*, p. 36
21 *ibid.*, p. 33
22 G. Godwin, *Towns, Swamps and Social Bridges* (London, 1859)
23 F. Engels, *The Housing Question* (1872)
24 Counter Information Services, *op. cit.* (1973), p. 26
25 *ibid.*, p. 26
26 J. B. Cullingworth, *English Housing Trends*, Occasional Papers on Social Administration, no. 13, Bell (1965), pp. 32 and 33
27 Counter Information Services, *op. cit.* (1973), p. 30
28 *ibid.*
29 *Guardian*, 16.6.1972
30 *Guardian*, 24.5.1972
31 J. M. Simmie, *The Sociology of Internal Migration*, University Working Paper No. 15, Centre for Environmental Studies (1972)
32 D. Marquand and I. Clegg, *op. cit.*, p. 31
33 L. A. Coser and B. Rosenberg (eds.), *Sociological Theory: a book of readings*, Collier Macmillan (1957)
34 D. Lockwood, 'Social Mobility', in A. T. Welford, *et. al.* (eds.) *Society*, Routledge & Kegan Paul (1962)
35 B. Bernstein and D. Henderson, 'Social class differences in the relevance of language to socialisation', *Sociology*, **3** (1969)
36 B. Jackson, *Streaming: an education system in miniature*, Routledge & Kegan Paul (1964)
37 *New Society*, *op. cit.* (1973), p. 3
38 *ibid.*, p. 6

39 D. V. Glass (ed.), *Social Mobility in Britain*, Routledge & Kegan Paul (1954)
40 *ibid.*
41 *Times Higher Education Supplement*, 13.4.73
42 D. V. Donnison, *The Government of Housing*, Pelican (1967)
43 S. D. Chapman (ed.), *The History of Working Class Housing: a symposium*, David & Charles (1971)
44 F. Engels, *op. cit.* (1872)

5. Power, planning and distributional equity

Professionals and the public interest

The rapid multiplication of groups seeking professional status in post-industrial Britain has presented social scientists with, as yet, unresolved problems of analysis. On the one hand economists have consistently questioned the benefits of professionalism, pointing instead to the harmful monopolistic practices of professional associations,[1] and others have emphasised the threat posed by professionalisation to freedom. On the other hand it has been argued that the professions 'promise both a structural basis for a free and independent citizenry in a world threatened by bureaucratic tyranny'[2] and a form of rational control leading to the development of a meritocracy. Thus, in the 1950s Lewis and Maude[3] joined with Carr-Saunders and Wilson[4] in arguing that industrial and governmental bureaucracies were the major threat to the 'proper functioning of the professions in Britain'. For Parsons, this was axiomatically undesirable for he believed that the professions in industrial societies were the embodiment of what he called the 'primacy of cognitive rationality'.[5] It may be seen, therefore, that there is some considerable disagreement concerning the legitimate role of the professions in society and also over the effects that their activities produce.

There is, however, one strand of argument which appears repeatedly in the debates concerning the relationships of the professions to the power structure of their particular societies and to their own use of power. This is that the professions are altruistic bodies 'standing against the excesses of both laissez-faire individualism and state collectivism'.[6] In their dealings with the power structure and in their own use of power, the professions are therefore seen by many writers as being distinguished from other occupations primarily by their altruism, particularly when it is expressed in their orientation towards the service of the community as a whole. Parsons argued that the main distinguishing feature of the professions as opposed to other occupations was their collectivity-orientation rather than self-orientation.[7]

The main concept employed by town planners, which indicates their claim to serve altruistically the community as a whole, is that of the public interest. They tend to argue that in their allocation of land uses they take rational, altruistic decisions in the public interest. This is to say that the public as opposed to private interests are served in conditions of political neutrality and by employing rational, technical expertise. Writers on both sides of the Atlantic have emphasised the importance attached to seeking the public interest by town planners. Glass, for example, claims that the main raison d'être of British town planning is 'the rational and just pursuit of the public interest'.[8] Friedmann maintains that 'the public interest ... emerges as a key issue in planning theory and practice'.[9] Altshuler argues that 'the comprehensive planners [need to] understand the overall public interest, at least in connection with the subject matter ... of their plans; and that they [also] possess causal knowledge which enables them to gauge the approximate net effect of proposed actions on the public interest'.[10] And Davies, among others, has remarked on the commonly held belief among British town planners that they are 'responsible for defining and implementing the public interest'.[11]

In Britain, this doctrine of the public interest has been set against the competitive doctrine of laissez-faire and developed as an apparently neutral political concept. This apparent neutrality is attested by its espousal, at different times, by Liberal, Conservative and Labour Governments and their nominal extensions of state control over private enterprise in the use of land. This extension of government activity against the doctrine and effects of laissez-faire was fostered by the presentation of town planning in the public interest as a device for, in the words of Ruth Glass, 'making the best of all worlds: individualism and socialism; town and country; past and future; preservation and change. In other words, the planner promised the people that they could have their cake and eat it.'[12] This attractive prospect was designed to promote general political support for town planning. This was hard to resist for in such a version of the public interest it is not clear whose, if anybody's, interests would not be furthered.

In such a climate of consensus centred around the single concept of the public interest, it was but a short step from the identification of planning with political neutrality to the proposition that its logic rises above the erstwhile conflicts of political debate to something approaching the level of a scientific politics of the kind sought by social philosophers of the genre from Plato to Mannheim. This claim to scientific politics, resting on the pursuit of a generally accepted normative goal, the public interest – by the means of a rapidly developing technology including such weapons as cost-benefit analysis, location theory, systems theory, to name but a few – is designed to insinuate planners into final sovereignty over the state. Elected representatives in both central and local government are thus advised by bureaucrats (among them are town planners) to follow certain specified policies which are said to be in the public interest – a normative concept which overrides criticism on sectional political grounds – and which are supported by an apparently rational battery of techniques over which only the planners have professional mastery. Such a science of politics could only be resisted by men of bad faith seeking to advance the old, vested and sectional interests promoted by the doctrine of laissez-faire. The first dent in such a scientific politics is made by examining the different definitions of 'the public interest'.

Different conceptions of the public interest

A cursory glance at the literature on the public interest immediately reveals a wide variety of definitions and, particularly in American studies, agreement amongst the dissension that it does not provide an unambiguous goal for town planners to seek. Among the critics of the public interest as a concept are Meyerson and Banfield. The latter, who appended a 'Note on conceptual scheme' to their seminal work, *Politics, Planning and the Public Interest*,[13] argue that it is generally assumed by town planners that 'a decision [serves] special interests if it furthers the ends of some part of the public at the expense of the ends of the larger public. It is in the public interest if it serves the ends of the whole public rather than those of some sector of the public.'[14] But, in their study of public-housing policy-making in Chicago, Banfield argues that the public interest was defined differently by different groups to the extent that it was virtually impossible to make such a distinction.

On the one hand there were unitary conceptions of the public interest in which 'the whole may be conceived as a single set of ends which pertain equally to all members of the public',[15] while on the other there were 'individualistic' conceptions according to which,

> the ends of the plurality do not comprise a single system, either one which pertains to the plurality as an entity or one which is common to individuals. The relevant ends are those of individuals, whether shared or unshared. The ends of the plurality as a whole are simply the aggregate of ends entertained by individuals, and that decision is in the public interest which is consistent with as large a part of the whole as possible.[16]

That, however, was not the end of the confusion, for within these two major views of the public interest were to be found different versions of what it amounted to in practice. Among those holding a unitary view, two versions could be distinguished. An 'organismic' view held that the ends of the body politic were more than simply the summation of individual ends while a 'communalist' view argued that the ends of the plurality are common and that those which are not generally shared are not valued and should therefore not be sought. In contrast, among those holding 'individualistic' views of the public interest, three types could be distinguished. A 'utilitarian' view held that the ends of individuals should be sought and that if some were common, this gave them no special value. A 'quasi-utilitarian' view held that a greater value should be attached to some men's values then others. And finally, a 'qualified individualistic' conception held that the ends of the plurality are the aggregate of those selected by individuals but that only those ends selected from a group deemed appropriate are to count as being relevant in the making of policies.

Even without attempting to analyse the relative merits and demerits of these differing conceptions of the public interest, it is quite clear that the notion does not provide a clear and unambiguous goal for town planners. In fact, the reverse is the case, for as Banfield points out,

> It will be seen that since either the same or different decision-makers may employ opposed conceptions of the public interest, the question of which conception is to be regarded as the public interest, either in a specific situation or in general, may itself become a matter of controversy. Moreover, given agreement on any one conception of the formal nature of the

public interest, there may be controversy as to its concrete content. Indeed, the agreed upon conception may imply equally any one of a wide range of outcomes.[17]

It follows that there can be no such thing as the best or correct definition of the public interest without a previously agreed proposition concerning the legitimate role of government. Following the distinction between 'unitary' and 'individualistic' versions of the public interest – for example, before deciding which was relevant – a town planner would have to decide, as an agent of government, whether his legitimate role was to promote the interests of the polity as a supra-individual body or the aggregated interests of its members. In each case a different set of ends and means is suggested. This, in turn, would depend upon what discretion has been allocated to the town planner in such a choice by the sovereign body of the polity and consequently on the predominant choice mechanism of the society in which he found himself. In other words, the public interest represents not a rational goal for the town planner to achieve but a reflection of the ways in which the society in which he lives makes its choices about the distribution of its power and resources.

One of the major factors determining what a town planner seeks to do, and what he is able to do, is the discretion allocated to him by the governmental power structure and society. Normally, the former employs him and the latter contains his clients. The professional discretion allocated to town planners is a critical factor in defining both their ability to determine goals and their powers of implementation. Much attention has therefore focussed on the relationships between discretion, the definition of the public interest, the related structures of government and the results in terms of what town planners actually do in practice.

Johnson has discussed these issues in the context of professional relationships to the power structure and Schubert[18] has considered the same theme in his definitions of different concepts of the public interest and the resulting government structures. Johnson, for example, argues that 'there is an irreducible but variable minimum of uncertainty in any consumer-producer relationship and, depending on the degree of this indeterminancy and the social structural content, various institutions will arise to reduce the uncertainty. Power relationships will determine whether the uncertainty is reduced at the expense of producer or consumer.'[19] One of the main functions of a profession like town planning is to intervene in those power relations which exist between producers and consumers. The main characteristics of this intervention are said to be altruism, rationality and political neutrality as marked by the pursuit of the public interest.

Johnson and Schubert define three broad categories of intervention in the name of the public interest and, although the categories were arrived at quite independently, there is a surprising degree of similarity between them. Thus, for Schubert, one kind of public interest rests on the technical discretion given to or adopted by professional bureaucrats which includes the freedom to prescribe the means but not the ends of action. This leads, in Schubert's view, to what he calls a 'rationalist' view of the public interest. Rationalists envisage a political system in which the norms are all given, as far as, for example, the town planner is concerned, and his function is therefore to translate these given norms into planning policies. This definition corresponds in some respects with Johnson's identification of situations of patronage in producer/consumer relationships. In these circumstances 'the consumer defines his own needs and the manner in which they are to be met'.[20] This represents the case in which industrial, commercial and governmental institutions employ, or patronise, professions such as accountancy or town planning to supply the services required by their customers.

A second form of intervention on behalf of the public interest is that which allows the town planner to prescribe the means and also to clarify any ends which form only vague criteria in public policy. This Schubert terms the 'idealist' notion of the public interest and it results, in practice, in the exercise of authority in order to engage in social planning of the kind which has resulted, for example, in the new towns. This corresponds to Johnson's collegiate intervention in the power structure which is exemplified by the producer defining the 'needs of the consumer and the manner in which these needs are catered for'.[21] This is normally the case for the older professions such as medicine where doctors diagnose both the ills of the patient and prescribe the relevant treatment. In such cases the professions are themselves producers and tend to form autonomous occupational associations for the control and furtherance of the services they provide.

It is the third category which is most appropriate for an analysis of the relationships between town planners, the power structure, and society. In this instance discretion is allocated to town planners in prescribing means where the ends and criteria of action are ambiguous because they are in dispute. In this case the planner is allowed to use his ingenuity in political mediation. Schubert calls this the 'realist' version of the public interest in which the function of town planners is to engage in the political mediation of disputes between different goals, because these goals, and those who espouse them, are in conflict. This corresponds almost exactly with Johnson's category of mediation which is the most appropriate to an analysis of the intervention of town planners in the power relations existing between producers and consumers.

In the case of mediation, a third party (for example, town planners) 'mediates in the relationship between producers and consumers, defining both the needs and the manner in which the needs are met'.[22] Such mediation is intended to define the needs of consumers and to rationalise and regulate the ways in which these needs are satisfied. Mediation involves the intervention of the State and its agencies, such as town planning, in order to 'remove from the producer or the consumer the authority to determine the content and subjects of practice'.[23] It is therefore intended to invoke the altruistic and neutral mediation between conflicting claims for the appropriation and use of some resources and power. In the case of town planning, this involves mediation between different groups seeking to use land and to acquire those resources which town planners are also responsible for allocating to specific land uses. Such mediation takes place in two related areas. Town planners mediate in the market and in politics.

In situations of social conflict over the aims and aspirations of different groups to acquire scarce resources and power, the public interest turns out to be an inadequate goal for town planners to seek. In the first place there is no such thing as THE public interest. Rather there are a number of different and competing interests. For example, in the market, as Rodwin points out, 'there is a basic and often unavowed assumption of contemporary planning. It is that key errors, distortions, and imperfections of the market mechanisms can and will be corrected by the planners.'[24] Their main efforts in this direction as Hall says have been 'the implicit focus . . . on improvements in economic allocation. Planning was supposed to make for more efficient, that is more economical, use of resources and so [aid] the achievement of a high rate of economic growth.'[25] Dennis argues that one of the main reasons for such mediation and intervention in the market was 'to make life more pleasant for the people who are otherwise at a disadvantage'.[26]

Mediation in the market by town planners is therefore directed towards multiple ends. It is concerned with the rational regulation of market forces to achieve a more efficient use of resources in order to promote economic growth. At the same time it is also directed towards the altruistic and neutral allocation of existing and future resources, particularly to those groups in society who are disadvantaged, in the face of the conflicting claims to those resources by groups already enjoying a sufficiency of them. These ends themselves may be actually or supposedly in conflict. Thus, for example, the exigencies of economic growth may be argued to be incompatible with regulation of the market, particularly when such intervention also involves the redistribution of resources in favour of the disadvantaged. Conflict may also arise over whether resources should be concentrated on groups which exist in the present, or on future consumers. For, as Davies argues, 'It is the consumers of to-day who must pay for the commodities of the future.'[27] In such circumstances town planners may find themselves intervening in the market to determine the expenditure patterns of future consumers at the expense of contemporary and more pressing claims. Thus town planning mediation in the market can be between both manifest and latent, present and future groups.

The same is also true of mediation in politics. In this instance town planners are mediating between different interest groups possessing different degrees of political power, some of whom are organised and clearly manifest and some of whom are disorganised and latent quasi-groups. In this mediation, town planners are engaged in influencing one of the major decision making mechanisms of society. To have any significant effect on decisions taken in this field, planners themselves have to engage in political activities. According to Foley, 'Since town and regional planning is a governmental function, its doctrine needs to provide a broad and attractive rationale for winning over and maintaining the allegiance of political leaders, appointed officials, and citizens.'[28] In order to mediate successfully, town planning must appeal in some measure to many of the value stances and aspirations of different segments of all or most of these groups. One of the major problems in combining altruism with such activity is that the political system itself tends to emphasise individual self-interests as opposed to those of the community at large or its disadvantaged groups. Thus, in their attempts to mediate between different groups in politics, town planners are faced with the problem of maintaining a truly altruistic and neutral stance in the face of a system which naturally favours the furtherance of short-range and partial interests and to which they must appeal.

Town planning is fundamentally a political activity. It is much less an altruistic and rational policy making and implementing exercise. It is political in three senses. First, it was set up by government presumably to execute political wills on the subject of land use and regulation. Second, as an executive branch of government it is directly linked to the political power structure and indirectly to the rest of society both as voters and as clients. Third, the way town planning decisions are taken is political in the sense that they are usually the result of mediation and bargaining between different departments, levels of government, and political and interest groups. The political nature of town planning is illustrated by the case studies which have been made of how such decisions are arrived at.

The politics of planning

Among the few empirical studies of the political aspects of decision making in local government, those by Lee[29] and Bulpitt[30] are significant, the former because it has a section dealing specifically with the politics of controlled development in Cheshire and the latter because it provides a comparison of a number of local authorities in the north-west. Both show that the issues which generated dispute in the narrow party-political sense varied according to the historical, social and political characteristics of the particular local authority concerned. Lee found, for example, that in Cheshire, education and town planning were the issues most likely to raise party political conflict while Bulpitt found that, in the north-west, political conflict was more often generated in the field of housing policy. In this region town planning and the other functions did not usually generate political dispute.

Despite the manifest existence of political differences about the objectives and the means for achieving them and the highly individual nature of local politics in both studies, the planners, and many of the councillors, adopted a 'rationalist' posture in the definition of the public interest. In the north-west, both planners and councillors emphasised the need for 'good' government and administration with decisions based on common agreement and played down the part played by politics in decision making.

In Cheshire, many of the councillors, despite being elected on a party political ticket, preferred to be thought non-political and maintained that the introduction of party politics into local government by the rise of the Labour Party was a retrograde step.

In Cheshire, the town planners' definition of their position in the quest for the public interest was most explicitly rationalist. Their declared main function was the presentation of 'facts'. These took the form of showing what had happened in the past and 'therefore' what was possible in the future. These 'facts' were placed before the councillors by the county planning officers for their judgement on what was politically acceptable. Thus policy decisions were formally the responsibility of councillors weighing both the 'facts' submitted by the town planners and the arguments, not so much about their normative value as their political feasibility. The Skeffington Report[31] on participation in town planning, recommended an extension of this 'rationalistic' concept of the public interest and suggested that planning authorities should act openly and place the 'facts' not only before councillors but also before all the members of the public as well. This, together with the encouragement of members of the public to participate in town planning by collecting their own 'facts', was intended to ensure the logical pursuit of the public interest by the rational perusal of all the relevant 'facts' by those with final responsibility for town planning decisions.

In practice, however, this formal model of the rational pursuit of the public interest does not correspond closely to the informal procedures which are actually followed in deciding planning policy by town planners and others. In the first place, planning policy is the result of political conflict, defined in the widest sense of the term political, rather than in the narrow party political understanding of politics. Lee showed that in Cheshire – although the County Council was formally responsible for the public interest – actual control of town planning was in the hands of some of its elected representatives, its chief officer, divisional officers of the district councils, and senior civil servants. Town planning decisions were therefore the result of the interplay between these individuals and the different levels of government from whence they came. This interplay between them was of a political nature, especially when they did not agree among themselves. Even without overt disagreement, the public interest still emerged partly as a result of mediation between their different points of view, and hence corresponded more closely to the 'realist' than the 'rationalist' version of how it is formally supposed to be developed. Indeed, one of the main activities of the town planner was simply persuading the Ministry and their own committees to accept their proposals.

A further injection of political conflict into the development of planning policy resulted from the fact that the representatives of the three tiers of government, in addition to their own internal political environment, were subject to political pressure from other sources. In Cheshire this entailed accommodating the wishes and aspirations of private interests, other public bodies and ad hoc groups.

Landowners were among the private interests lobbying government officials and representatives. They engaged the professional advice of estate agents in order to increase the capital value of their land either by seeking housing permissions, or by seeking permission to develop land in which the local authority was interested, thereby increasing any possible compensation should the local authority decide to purchase. Also, foremost among the local pressure groups seeking to influence government officials and representatives in Cheshire, were the Council for the Preservation of Rural England and the National Farmers Union. The former, composed mainly of retired army officers and peers and the latter also representing a narrow sectional interest, exercised an influence, as they do nationally, out of all proportion to the numerical strength of their membership. This they often achieve by acquiring the support of their local Member of Parliament, who, naturally, is likely to rely on their political support in the business of getting re-elected at some point in the future.

Among the public bodies seeking to influence town planning decisions in Cheshire were either other departments of the same local authority such as hospital planners or the nationalised industries. Disputes between them again led to political conflict and again ensured that the public interest emerged, not so much as a result of 'rationalist' but rather as a result of 'realist' procedures.

The same was also true of the accommodation of pressures from ad hoc bodies. Generally, these groups were not able to effect much change in planning policy and the County Council was happy to let them expend their energies at the district level.

It may be seen, therefore, from the limited number of studies available and particularly from those of Lee and Bulpitt, that, as far as town planning is concerned, while the public interest is formally said to be politically neutral and identified by 'rationalist' procedures, in practice, it is a political goal whose details often emerge as the result of political mediation along the lines suggested by the 'realists'. In these circumstances, there is no reason to suppose that the public interest sought by town planners is different from or more than the aggregated interests of the articulate participants, or more narrowly, the aggregated interests of the most powerful coalition of participants in any given issue.

Bulpitt, for example, found that disputes in north-western council chambers did not mirror the kind of differences to be found among the general public. In particular, they did not reflect the basic division between ratepayers and the rest. Instead, it was the clashes between the personalities of individual members and differences of opinion over the implementation of schemes, irrespective of their 'objective' merits, which created most debate. The resulting policies represented an accommodation of these relatively irrational factors by the processes of political mediation. Lee also found that planned development in Cheshire was often the result of the resolution of conflicts between the different individuals, levels of government, private interests, other public bodies and ad hoc groups who participated in the planning process. He also found that even after these interests had been accommodated and planning policy decided, there were still those who did not accept the outcomes and concentrated their subsequent efforts on avoiding the town planning regulations.

Even in parts of the local government structure itself, efforts were directed to avoiding or ignoring the planning regulations. This was increasingly the case in successively lower echelons of local government and those at the district council level were most likely to ignore the regulations. A Fabian research pamphlet[32] also notes this tendency for the majority to become increasingly parochial and selfish, the lower their position in the hierarchy of authorities.

This limited evidence suggests, therefore, that the 'public interest' sought by town planners in Britain is often 'individualistic', composed of the aggregated interests of the most powerful coalition of groups of individuals who participate in the planning process, and is sought by 'realist' procedures which represent little more than the mediation of any conflicts between these groups and the accommodation of the resulting compromises that they are prepared to make. Even where 'idealist' procedures are used to develop the 'public interest', the eventual process of compromise is not much different from that found in the 'realist' case. The main difference is that, as in the case of Newcastle, so amusingly portrayed by Davies,[33] a different kind of power coalition arises. In Newcastle it was composed of a coincidence of purpose between Dan Smith, the Labour political leader, and Wilf Burns, the chief planner, and the political circumstance that the Labour Party had a majority in the local council. Even so, they were (in the terms of what they actually achieved) able to blame their lack of sufficient power for the comparative failure of the Rye Hill scheme. In other words, although holding a 'unitary' view of the public interest and seeking to achieve it by 'idealist' means, they in fact had to participate in the struggle for power to implement it. In this case, therefore, the town planners concerned, while eschewing the 'rationalistic' or 'realist' roles in the articulation of the public interest in favour of an 'idealist' position, and forming a power coalition with a local political leader, in practice found their ability to implement their schemes checked by other coalitions and the eventual overturn of the Labour majority by the local Conservative Party.

Hidden mechanisms of redistribution

In practice, therefore, British town planning has largely failed to define clearly its role as an important mediating agency in the allocation of power and resources. This failure to define its positions in the market and politics will have been crucial if these decision-making areas normally contain hidden mechanisms of redistribution. For, if town planning is to claim that it represents an altruistic, neutral and rational agency mediating on behalf of the public interest, it is necessary to be both explicit and accurate about which groups benefit and which groups lose by virtue of its activities. If it could be shown, for example, that failure to make these relationships clear has led to a regressive redistribution of power and resources as a result of town planning, then at best the planners must be chided for not exposing this situation and at worst they could be condemned for serving those groups who already possess a sufficiency of these scarce and desired commodities. It would also undermine their claims to provide an altruistic and neutral service to the public interest and call into question their claims to professional status in British society. Rather, they would be seen as merely the agents of the ruling classes.

Despite the fact that the 1947 Town and Country Planning Act conferred wide ranging powers on town planners to mediate in the allocation and distribution of land uses, employment, housing and the value of property, they tended to define their role in a narrower, physical sense. As McLoughlin says,

> Their primary interest was in land-use and their job, as they understood it, was to produce a development plan which was seen as a clear and simple policy instrument and a device for implementation. Their aim was to achieve, by these means, an attractive and efficient environment which displayed a consistent, balanced and orderly arrangement of land uses, which provided the physical basis for a healthy and civilised life.[34]

It was soon realised, however, that such an activity could not continue without regard at least to other government agencies which were making decisions about the use of land. Thus, in 1950, the Schuster Report argued that,

> The function [of town planning] is to create a well-balanced synthesis of what might otherwise be a mere collection of separate policies and claims, to combine them into one consistent policy for the use and development of land within the area in question, to devise the means of translating this policy in the physical conditions of that area into a plan that is practical, economic and aesthetically pleasing, and to organise the carrying through to realisation of the development for which the plan has made provision.[35]

The Schuster Report heralds the first intimations of the uncertainty surrounding the role of the planner which is now expressed as the difference between structure and corporate plans. It illustrates the distinction which is now made between the physical and the co-ordinating functions of the activity. In the 1950s, however, the latter role was seen primarily as one of co-ordinating the different demands for the use of land. As Hall says, 'the problems planning had to solve were defined in physical terms'.[36] This is echoed by Foley in relation to the Greater London Plan where planners 'viewed the metropolitan community as having a spatial, physical form that could be grasped and reduced to maplike graphic presentation'.[37] In 1965, however, planners were enjoined by the Planning Advisory Group (PAG) to take a broader view of their role and to take more account of people's expressed and felt needs and aspirations. This suggestion was supported in 1970 in the then Ministry of Housing and Local Government's Development Plans Manual. There, as McLoughlin says, it was 'suggested that the area of concern of planners should be broadened, and that the goals of planners should be the social and economic aspirations of the community'.[39]

The apparent realisation of the importance of social and economic aspirations and constraints by town planners in the 1970s is in reality somewhat illusory. As McLoughlin points out, 'the Development Plans Manual of 1970 still maintains that social and economic goals should be satisfied through physical solutions'.[39] In practice this has meant that often only lip service has been paid to the necessity to consider in depth the social, economic and political implications of town planning. Goodman has written with some justification that, 'For urban doctors there are supposedly no political questions, such as who gets what and through what process.'[40] Hall has pointed out that town planners often assume 'almost as an article of faith, that the problems [are] self-evident to all men of intelligence and goodwill, and that the remedies [are] generally . . . to the benefit of the entire community; conflicts of interest between individuals and groups (can) not arise'.[41] From this attitude derives the kind of approach to town planning found by Dennis in Sunderland, where the planners seemed to believe that, 'The ends are given, only the appropriate means remain to be chosen.'[42]

It may therefore be argued that even in the 1970s British town planning is characterised by a myopic view of implications of physical growth, decline, decay and change in the environment and an extremely superficial recognition of the importance of the social, economic and political forces at play in society. Nevertheless, whether town planners are clear about it or not it is now realised, as

Hall says, 'that many public policies, individually but also in their cumulative effect, act as hidden mechanisms of redistribution'.[43] Pahl has also drawn attention to the role of town planning which 'together with other instruments of social policy plays a crucial role in a mixed economy in redistributing spatial resources'.[44] While this part of their role is not clearly and accurately recognised by town planners, it would seem highly probable that if the hidden mechanisms of redistribution are fundamentally regressive then, other things being equal, the activities of town planners are also likely to be regressive in their effects on the distribution of power and resources. If town planners are not explicit about their role in the allocation of these commodities, then they are likely to be subject to forces of redistribution without their knowledge and without adopting a relevant position about whom they intend to benefit and who is going to shoulder the real burdens of the cost.

It is therefore necessary to examine the main mechanisms of distribution and to assess, other things being equal, who gains and who loses. The two most relevant of these mechanisms for town planners are those in which they wittingly or unwittingly mediate, namely politics and the market. These are also the two most important distributing mechanisms for society in general and it is this fact which makes the town planner's role in allocating power and resources so important.

Politics and redistribution

With respect to city politics in Britain, the first characteristic which a number of observers have commented on is its unitary style. Foley, for example, argues that 'two characteristics marked the London plans: their focus on containment and their unitary approach'.[45] This unitary approach is marked by attempts to build 'around a single comprehensive design for the entire urban community'.[46] But, as Hall recounts, such 'a unitary approach is typical of a paternalist system of government where an established ruling class is sure of its own values, so sure that it can impose them without question on the rest of the community'.[47] It must be suspected, however, that the imposition of a particular style of government is likely to bring most gains to those who impose it. Hence Hall correctly argues that,

As the rich will use their money to buy more private goods in the market place, so they will tend to use their knowledge and influence to unite more effectively in the pursuit of impure public goods. Since these goods tend to loom larger and larger in the total pattern of consumption in advanced societies, it can be expected that the richer and better advantaged sections of the population will tend to transfer their energies progressively from the market place to the political forum. In doing so they will naturally tend to argue in unitary political terms, i.e., that the defence of their interests is in the interests of society as a whole.[48]

On the face of it, therefore, unitary styles of city politics are likely to contain hidden redistribution effects which are normally regressive.

Nevertheless, British town planners tend to support this kind of government for two reasons. In the first place, as Dennis points out, 'the end of consensus also ends the pre-eminence of the technical expert'.[49] And in the second place, as Harvey says, 'if it becomes explicit as to who will lose and who will benefit, and by how much from a given allocation decision, then we must anticipate far greater difficulty in implementing the decision'.[50] Thus town planners have a vested interest in maintaining a unitary style of government in order to secure their position as 'technical experts' and also to facilitate the implementation of their plans. If such a style of government leads to regressive redistribution then town planning itself is likely to contribute to this kind of allocation by supporting it.

Maintaining the appearance of a unitary style of city politics does not, however, alter the realities of power. So, as Harvey again insists, 'Any attempt to understand the mechanisms generating inequalities in income must . . . involve an understanding of the political processes which operate in a city.'[51] In reality, these processes, far from being of uniform benefit to the community, are in fact 'a matter of jostling for and bargaining over the use and control of the hidden mechanisms for redistribution'.[52] This bargaining takes the form of attempts to organise the distribution of externality effects to gain some income advantage. It is local political activity which may be regarded 'as the basic mechanism for allocating the spatial externality fields in such a way as to reap indirect income advantages'.[53] Behind the unitary façade of city politics so often supported by town planners, Buchanon has identified the real nature of planning as 'a very ruthless bargaining process'.[54] Politics and planning are therefore arenas in which the struggle and conflict over scarce power and resources are fought out, often behind a misleading façade of unitary government purporting to serve the interests of the whole community rather than those of special groups.

There are a number of reasons for expecting that the outcomes of bargaining over the acquisition of those resources which town planners are responsible for allocating will be regressive. In the first place, groups will be bargaining in the political arena with votes, money, influence and information. Among these resources only votes are equally distributed to start with and these may be the least important in determining the outcome of decisions. In contrast, money, influence and information are distributed unequally between groups and therefore, other things being equal, those groups possessing most of them before bargaining commences are likely to be able to use them to ensure that they get more out of the political process than other groups. Thus, as Harvey argues,

It is theoretically possible to harness, by political activity and bargaining, the hidden mechanisms of income redistribution so as to achieve a balanced allocation of all impure goods and services over a spatially distributed population. But we can also conclude that this will only happen if the political process is so organized that it facilitates equality in bargaining between different but internally homogeneous interest groups.[55]

In such an inegalitarian society as Britain this is simply not the case.

Groups in Britain may be homogeneous but they are clearly not equal. Therefore it might be expected that, in the conflicts over political power, those groups with most information, education and finance in British society will dominate locational decisions. Unless town planners adopt a firmly progressive policy in the allocation of land uses, then it is to be expected that the rich will benefit most and the poor will gain least from their activities. This process is reinforced by the unrepresentative characteristics of the groups who voluntarily and effectively join in the new planning game of participation heralded by the Skeffington Report in 1969.

Participation and the acquisition of scarce resources

Given that British town planning is concerned with the pursuit of the public interest in the allocation of the factors of production in land, capital equipment and people; and given that the public interest is, in reality, defined by political processes (using political in the broadest sense of the term); then in practice, those who participate in the political determination of the concrete objectives of town planning, and are also able to form adequate coalitions of power, are likely to acquire a disproportionate share of those factors of production allocated by town planners. The rewards are high. A Fabian research pamphlet[56] pointed out that central government and its agencies, taken together, are responsible for more than half the national investment and actually spent about 40 per cent of the Gross National Product. By 1973 this figure had risen to 51 per cent of the GNP. Town planners play a significant part in deciding the priorities for some of this expenditure.

Those who participate in town planning, and consequently influence the distribution of those resources for which it is responsible, do not form a representative cross-section of society. For example, in a study by the author of the Parish Council of Wheatley,[57] conducted during the preparation of a plan for the village by the author and others, nearly half the population never discovered, despite extensive publicity, that the plan was in preparation. Of those who actually participated in its preparation, the leaders were normally drawn from the higher social classes while those who followed them were drawn disproportionately from the lower social classes. Of those who followed the preparation of the plan and who would therefore at least monitor their interests, again a disproportionate number were professional and intermediate workers with only a relatively small number of unskilled manual workers. In contrast, it is becoming generally accepted that nationally the poor, the sick, the old, the inadequate, the immobile and the under-housed characteristically do not compete in the struggle for power and resources. Because they do not compete, their interests and aspirations have not featured significantly in, for example, town planners' definitions of the public interest. Because their views are not significantly accommodated in the mediation between conflicting interests, which generates the material objectives of town planning, their relative share of resources has been dwindling since the 1950s.

Such individuals often find themselves trapped in the kind of cycle outlined by Harrington. He says,

> The poor get sick more than anyone else in society. That is because they live in slums, jammed together in unhygienic conditions; they have inadequate diets, and cannot get decent medical care. When they become

sick, they are sick longer than any other group in society. Because they are sick more often and longer than anyone else, they lose wages and work, and find it difficult to hold a steady job. And because of this they cannot pay for good housing, for a nutritious diet . . .[58]

The Skeffington Committee proposed that the town planners' answer to this dilemma should be to encourage not only active minorities but also passive majorities to participate in the planning process. Incidentally, it seemed, this increased participation in town planning might help to legitimise the activity in the eyes of more groups. In order to assist town planners to accommodate the interests and aspirations of those who do not characteristically participate, community development officers were to be appointed to encourage them and act as information gatherers.

Participation, however, can be interpreted by different groups in different ways. The town planning version is that participation increases the flow of information between planners and their clients, and thus improves town planning because decisions are more rationally arrived at on the basis of more data. It improves the planners' image because clients are able to discover why the rational decisions of town planners have been taken in a particular way. In reality, however, participation without power is a charade. In circumstances where the public interest is defined according to 'realist' principles by accommodating the requirements of different groups, it is clear that those without power do not carry much weight in the final mediation. This is why it is possible for county and county borough councils to let many ad hoc groups expend their participatory energies fruitlessly at lower tiers in the government structure. On the other hand, powerfully organised vested interests which stand to lose or gain most by planning decisions will shout longest and loudest and will insist on accommodation of their views.

Despite this, the call for increased participation in planning received widespread acceptance because not only did town planners and vested interests interpret it in a way which seemed favourable to their interests, but also other groups were able to do the same. As Whitaker[59] has argued, its popularity for some lay in the idea that it was a mechanism for transferring power from government to the people. As far as the poor and deprived are concerned, this has not been the case. The causes of deprivation and poverty are numerous and so, even ignoring the lack of appropriate middleclass skills necessary in a capitalist society, they do not have sufficient unity to form a power-coalition that can insist on its interests being served by town planners.

A second reason why such a coalition does not emerge is the paternalistic treatment of deprivation by most of the agencies of the Welfare State, including town planning. Instead of assisting individuals and families to help themselves, the Welfare State may render them less capable either by increasingly making them the passive recipients of services thought appropriate, by the absorption of their leaders into government agencies, or by allowing them to expend their participatory energies in ineffective action.

In order to overcome these problems, town planners would have to adopt more sophisticated techniques of market research to discover the requirements of different groups in the community and set these findings against the demands of predominantly middle-class interest groups such as the Council for the Protection of Rural England and the National Farmers Union. Without some clearly defined normative propositions, even this might prove ineffective. For, as Davies argues, 'the veto on redevelopment schemes . . . lies where it has always lain: with the possessors of large amounts of wealth, power and influence'.[60] Such groups can therefore prevent progressive redistribution taking place by their power of veto and can encourage regressive redistribution either by bringing superior power to bear in the political arena or by loading the 'rules of the game' in their own favour.

This second hidden mechanism of regressive redistribution has been noted by Pahl. As he says, 'The built environment is the result of conflicts, in the past and present, between those with different degrees of power in society – landowners, planners, developers, estate agents, local authorities, pressure groups of all kinds, insurance companies . . .'[61] These groups he calls the 'social gatekeepers' for they control the actual distribution of urban resources and also set the bureaucratic rules and procedures of allocation. It seems likely that they are either themselves members of or share the values and ideologies of the most powerful groups in society. They might be so similar as to constitute a ruling class in terms of the spatial structure. Certainly, they are often in a position to impose their ideologies and rules on those who lack power in the spatial structure. Conversely it seems likely that these ideologies and rules will be of benefit to themselves and to the power holders of society. Hence Davies may be correct to argue that, for example, the planning system 'complements and reflects the class structure, giving most to those who already have a lot and giving least to those who need it most'.[62] Hall also notes this tendency even under Labour Party control for, 'The Labour Party is mainly run, at the local level, by the lower middle and upper working-class members who tend to forget it. They have good reason to do so, because they are the beneficiaries.'[63]

One of the ways in which the setting of ideological and cultural norms is likely to benefit those who set the rules is that it may prevent groups with different beliefs from even taking up a valid bargaining position. Prior disputes about what is negotiable and what procedures are to be followed, or blank incomprehension by disadvantaged groups of what town planners consider to be relevant for their neighbourhoods, often prevents such groups from even negotiating effectively with the rulers of the urban system.

A further contributory factor to the naturally regressive nature of city politics in Britain is the institutional framework within which political activity is conducted. Thus, the structure of government, like planning itself, being determined by the holders of power, is not likely to contain an overabundance of checks on the use of that power. It is interesting to note, however, that many of the debates about town planning contain direct references to the effects of the structure of government on the efficacy of its policies. Thus Rodwin lays some of the blame for the failures of London's new towns at the door of 'errors of organization and administration'.[64] And Hall also notes the importance of the embarkation by the Labour Government of 1964–70 on a fundamental reform of local government in order to shift the balance of power from rural conservation to urban development.[65]

One of the more important mechanisms of redistribution is the institutional framework which exists for reaching collective decisions and arbitrating between different groups in society. Harvey notes that such institutions,

> [1.] partly reflect existing group activities and they are . . . far more able to take account of small-group pressures (special lobbies and special interests) than they are able to react to the needs and wishes of large groups.

[2.] An institutional structure, once it is created, may well become closed or partially closed.[66]

Low-income groups often find great difficulty in penetrating institutional structures and commencing effective negotiations. It could well be that the system of local government being constructed in Britain at this time will perpetuate exactly these problems. Thus, the large units are too small to overcome the parochial interests of privileged local groups and the small units are too large to provide a platform which could be effectively used by local, low-income groups to mount a campaign for significant reallocation of resources.

Redistribution in the market place

Politics, however, is not the only institution containing hidden mechanisms of redistribution. The market place is also a decision-making area in which planners consciously or unconsciously mediate. Pahl has succinctly summarised the importance of the market. As he says,

> There will always be scarce and desirable resources in any society. At present these resources are power, wealth and prestige, since with these, other resources can be obtained. The job market is one of the chief means of allocating these scarce resources: men who are highly paid gain security and power. Their position in the economic system determines their ability to benefit within the urban system.[67]

Thus the socio-economic system and its allocating mechanism, the market, comes to be the underlying basis of the structural part of the super-structure of society, along with politics and ideologies, all resting on the economic forces at play in society.

Like politics, the market is not a neutral mechanism. It also contains basic regressive tendencies. This is particularly the case in the spatial structure where conditions are neither those of perfect competition nor those of Pareto optimality. Most of the conditions of the former are broken in the spatial structure. As the collective purchasing of impure public goods supplants individual family decisions and as the importance of externalities grows, so conditions favouring monopoly, duopoly and oligopoly are developed. In such situations, the profit maximising solutions for producers are not likely to be the same as maximum benefit solutions for consumers.

Where consumers are poor and do not therefore bring many resources to the market, their losses in conditions of imperfect competition may be substantial. For example, while transfer payments mean more to the poor than to the rich, the former are more likely to sustain heavy external costs for small transfer increments just because they have so little to start with. They may therefore choose immediate advantages such as new airports because the poor are more desperate for employment than they are to object to the noise and inconvenience which are the external costs imposed by such a choice. Conversely, the employment generated by, for example, airports is of little or no consequence for the rich while they place a high, and often effective, value against the externalities.

Similarly, the market does not create conditions for Pareto optimality in the spatial structure. As Harvey says, 'a free market cannot give rise to prices conducive to Pareto optimum and . . . the housing market, for reasons of its own spatial internal logic, must contain group action if it is to function coherently'.[68] Other things being equal, therefore, one man's gain must be other men's losses in housing. A number of factors are responsible for this condition. In the first place, self-interested individuals are unlikely to form groups solely for the benefit of other groups in society nor are they likely to give up resources to make other groups better off. Those who have adequate housing are unlikely either to relinquish any of their property rights or cease to participate in the financial gains to be had from property ownership. The only way of distributing accommodation equally throughout society is therefore to generate more of it but, as the history of housing in Britain shows, the poor have never been able to generate adequate demand in either the private or public housing sectors. It seems unlikely that the market will ever, by itself, generate a situation where the rich stand still while the poor get better housing.

Another element in the market causing regressive redistribution in the spatial structure is the dynamics of economic growth. Town planners in their commitment to the efficient use of resources in the spatial structure have often sought to facilitate economic growth. The main argument in favour of growth, so far as the poor are concerned, is that as the Gross National Product gets larger, so increases in its size can be diverted to them without the need to introduce progressive redistribution. A Pareto optimum is sought in which the rich are not made worse off and at the same time the poor become better supplied with the necessities of life.

The main fallacy in this argument is that since the market has already produced an inegalitarian society by its hidden regressive mechanisms of redistribution, there is no reason to suppose that these mechanisms will not operate on the extra produce of economic growth. If the top 10 per cent of the population own 50 per cent of personal wealth and the bottom 90 per cent own the other 50 per cent, this is no *a priori* reason for expecting that the fruits of growth will be distributed differently. A 4 per cent economic growth rate might be distributed in the proportions of 2 per cent to the top 10 per cent of the population and 2 per cent to the remaining 90 per cent. Ignoring the problems of inflation, this represents a very small gain to those at the bottom of the market.

A final factor contributing to theoretically regressive redistribution via the market is the dynamics of urban growth, decline and change. Much urban modelling assumes that there exists some kind of natural equilibrium in the urban system. The system is therefore believed to be in a constant state of approach to this equilibrium. In fact, there is just as much reason to suppose that quite the opposite is the case and that no such equilibrium exists either in theory or in practice. Even if it is only allowed that different parts of the spatial structure change at different times and at different rates, then equilibrium analysis breaks down. Harvey points out that, 'Certain groups, particularly those with financial resources and education, are able to adapt far more rapidly to a change in the urban system and these differential abilities to respond to change are a major source in generating inequalities.'[69]

A crucial factor in the distribution of externalities and the value of property rights is location. Accessibility and proximity to such amenities as parks, for example, are important not only for their contribution to the value of property but also for the external benefits they confer. As the spatial structure changes so new opportunities open up and others decline for the use of such resources. Those groups in the population who are able to recognise and take advantage of these changes are first to benefit disproportionately from urban resources. Such groups are usually those who already possess greater amounts of education, wealth and resources than those who do not react quickly to such changes. Migrants are characteristically members of the more vigorous, educated and affluent sections of the social structure. As Harvey argues. 'The higher income and better educated groups tend to make an active use of space whereas lower income groups tend to be trapped by it.'[70]

Two reasons why lower income groups tend to be trapped by the spatial structure are firstly the rules governing their residential mobility and secondly the cultural deprivation which develops as a result of their territorial segregation. Many low-income groups are dependent on the rules governing housing allocation in particular local authorities. These rules tend to trap the poor in an area, both while waiting for local authority accommodation and once in it. Many local authorities, particularly in areas of housing stress, require lengthy periods of residence before families can qualify for accommodation. Even after qualification it is difficult for families to move either within or between local authority areas. They certainly do not have the choices or the resources to benefit from changes in spatial structure that the owners of private property have. It is these latter groups who benefit most from the changing patterns of externalities and property values.

Similarly, lower income groups may suffer cultural deprivation which deepens with increased length of residence in territorially deprived areas. The surest way to ensure that groups never begin to value parks, libraries, theatres and the countryside is to deprive them of all contact with these amenities which are so highly prized by members of the middle social classes. Such deprivation can be quite severe to the extent that some children in the east end of London, for example, are not clear how a basic commodity like milk is produced. If, as a child, one cannot cope with such simple problems, how is one to do well in an essentially middle-class school system? If one is not too successful in the school system then how does one get a good job, house, or move in the spatial or social structure?

It may therefore be argued that both politics and the market contain hidden mechanisms of regressive redistribution which favour the rich and disadvantage the poor. As they start from conditions of considerable inequality, it is therefore necessary for town planners to adopt explicit, specific and accurate policies for progressive redistribution in the spatial structure just to ensure that current inequalities are not increased. In order to actually reverse these trends they would need to generate a battery of related policies designed to promote an 'overkill' of the problems associated with deprivation. Above all, town planners should remember that they must run just to stand still over the matter of distributional equity in the spatial structure. In the past they have not done so.

The effects of town planning on distribution

Town planning affects the distribution of resources in the spatial structure in three ways. It can bring about changes in

1. The location of jobs and housing.
2. The value of property rights.
3. The price of resources to the consumer.

As Harvey says, 'These changes are themselves affected by the allocations of external costs and benefits to different regions in the urban system and by changes in accessibility and proximity.'[71]

If one turns first to the effects that town planning has had on the accessibility and proximity of jobs and housing, one may see that both the new towns and planned suburbanisation have been marginally regressive in their distribution of resources. Thomas has shown, for example, that all of London's new towns 'have a higher proportion of other non-manual workers than the country as a whole . . . [and] all of the new towns, without qualification, have a lower proportion of residents (in the low-income group other workers) . . . than both London and the country as a whole.'[72] At the same time, 'The growth industries attracted to the new towns tend to have a high proportion of professional and skilled workers, and most of the new town development corporations have not encouraged low-income families.'[73] Thus the new town policy followed around London has been actively regressive in its effects on the distribution of resources. Pahl is therefore correct when he argues that

> much of the physical planning on a regional scale has simply served to draw apart the more skilled workers, who have been able to consolidate and establish their new position in the new and expanding industries, from those with low or no skills who have put up with low pay as well as poor housing and access to other facilities back in the centre of London.[74]

Much planned and unplanned suburbanisation has had the same effect. The suburb has been dubbed by Mead as 'the most atrocious ekistical invention made in the history of the human race' and where 'people are segregated by age, by income, by ethnic group, by religion, and by a series of other wearisome temperamental characteristics'.[75] In Britain's large towns and conurbations most of the growth in new employment has been in or near the outer suburban rings. This relocation has favoured the affluent suburbanite at the expense of low-income inner-city dwellers, for the latter have lost sources of service employment while not themselves either being able to move out to the suburbs or to afford the increased journey-to-work costs involved in commuting to the suburbs. At the same time, those affluent members of the community who have moved to the suburbs or beyond, and have continued to work in central areas, have been served by expensive public transit systems in the form of road and rail links to the centre. In so far as these links are financed by public money, even the actual funding of them may be regressive.

Urban motorway programmes are a case in point. They penalise low-income groups in several ways. In the first place they tend to destroy more poor homes than rich ones while at the same time employing funds which, among other things, means the foregoing of other opportunities such as the building of more local authority housing. After they are built, they do not serve the poor unless they possess private transport. Such is not often the case among the unemployed, the low paid, the chronically sick, the old and children. Expenditure from public funds on urban motorways is therefore progressive in the benefits it generates and regressive in the incidence of costs.

Thus, it may be that both the structure of cities and the transit systems encouraged by British town planners are regressive. While, for example, redistribution is taking place in the London region as a result of the forces of suburbanisation, Foley has pointed out that 'a circular form of urban and metropolitan development seems to have maintained so strong a hold on British town and regional planners that they never seriously explored noncircular patterns'.[76] Consequently, just as inequality is a result of the characteristics of the social structure and the spatial structure is a reflection of the social structure, so it may be necessary to change both in order to bring about greater equity in the distribution of resources. British planners must therefore seriously consider alternative forms of spatial structure from the mono-nucleated, circular forms based on radial transit routes which they have favoured in the past if they are to be progressive in the allocation of urban resources.

The second way in which British town planners have encouraged regressive redistribution is in the contributions to the value of property rights. There seems to be a tendency for regulation to favour those who are making private or corporate investment decisions for it removes an element of uncertainty about the future which makes the calculation of gain that much easier. As Pahl says,

> Cynics might argue that, in the case of Britain, the various housing acts were simply a defence by the rich against the disease and possibly violence of the poor. Certainly for nearly a century the reforming zeal of the middle class created housing standards which found rents to be higher than the poor could afford so that collective responsibility to subsidize them was necessary. Similarly the reforming zeal of a more recent generation for Green Belts has forced a tax on those obliged to cross them between home and work.[77]

The most obvious example of regressive redistribution in the value of property rights is the financing of housing which is supported by town planners. The regressive nature of this distribution is reflected in the 1969/70 figures showing that the average government contribution to new permanent local authority dwellings was £26 per dwelling, plus £18 from local authority rate funds, making a total average of contribution of £44 per dwelling. The average benefit to house mortgagors in the form of tax relief on mortgages was, however, £45 per dwelling.[78]

The generally haphazard and regressive effect of housing policies on the poor has been documented by Glass in Camden. At the time of her study, only about 30 per cent of all households of semi-skilled or unskilled workers were in council accommodation. In contrast, among those in unfurnished privately rented dwellings, 45 per cent had less than £16 per week income, and among those in furnished privately rented accommodation, 54 per cent had less than £16 per week. Among those who had less than £12 per week, 45 per cent of the unfurnished and 78 per cent of the furnished tenants were paying one third or more of their income on housing. Glass comments that 'the poor are paying more, because many are paying no less than three supplementary housing taxes: on central area accommodation, on furnished accommodation and on accommodation for newcomers'.[79]

In contrast, as Hall points out,

> The more prosperous . . . have not done at all badly. The skilled worker enjoys his subsidized council or new town dwelling, and may use some of the surplus income to buy a car which gives him additional mobility, in seeking jobs for instance. He is in a similar position to the middle class white collar house buyer whose mortgage payments, though they have risen due to steepening interest rates, have been cushioned by the regressive tax relief arrangements. The fact here is that now, the white collar worker and the skilled blue collar worker find themselves on the same side of the real dividing line in British society.[80]

This is not entirely true as the main differences between them in the acquisition of wealth is their ownership of property and pension rights. The white collar home-owner with his greater participation in occupational pension schemes is accumulating wealth which his blue collar, property-renting counterpart is not. It nevertheless remains true that the poor have virtually none of the advantages of either.

Finally, let us examine the effects that British town planners have had on the price of resources and in particular the incidence of externalities. One of the main planks of British planning policy which has benefited the rich, and from which a whole sequence of regressive policies has flowed, is central business district imperialism. While trade and business interests concentrate resources in city centres and hence raise land values leading to increased housing costs for those who must also live there, Marriott has shown that, 'Certain insurance groups and private individuals have made fortunes out of stamping provincial England with the standard High Street of supermarket society.'[81]

While some groups make fortunes out of the spatial resource system, others derive very little. The pecking order which develops leaves those at the bottom with inadequate or non-existent supplies of public goods like schools, transport, housing and open space. At the same time, some of the costs of the attempts by town planners to alleviate these discrepancies have fallen most heavily on those they were meant to benefit. Redevelopment schemes often incur this characteristic and, as Dennis says, 'There can be little sense in a policy which is justified by reference to its beneficial effects, if the beneficiaries experience the results as hardship.'[82]

One of the problems in measuring the actual distributional effects in cases like redevelopment is that the value of a good is often set by the user in terms of some mental, social, emotional or cultural response to its use. Value measured in terms of one cultural system may not be the same as that imparted by a different system. Middle-class town planners can therefore inflict heavy real costs on the poor just because they do not share the same cultural values. The value, for example, attached to slum clearance, Parker Morris standards and open space by middle-class planners may be totally different from their importance to the poor.

However, the net results of town planning, in so far as they can be measured, seem to be that, as Hall says, 'After twenty-five years of effective town and country planning, nearly half of them under Labour, we find that the main distributive effect was to keep the poor, or a high proportion of them, poor.'[83]

Town planning and the legitimate use of power

There is thus a paradox in the professional stance adopted by town planners and in their legitimate use of power. On the one hand they seek to legitimate their role in society by reference to an altruistic, rational, politically neutral service of the public interest, while on the other they make few explicit statements concerning their views on the equity of the social and spatial structure but at the same time often contribute to making the latter less equitable. The questions that arise from this situation concern whose ends are served by town planning, how they are served and what normative propositions are advanced by planners to service these ends.

The answers to these questions which are advanced here are that:

1. British town planners are not altruistic because they serve (a) their own ends and (b) those of the existing power structure.

2. In such circumstances it is not possible to legitimate their use of power as being politically neutral and for the equal benefit of all members of the public.

3. Neither is it possible to argue that their use of power is both rational and legal, for while it may be the latter it is seldom the former, often because of a serious lack of relevant information.

4. Finally, town planners have no coherent and explicit set of normative propositions which either justify the effects of their use of power or provide debating points against which the validity of the ends they serve, and the criteria for the evaluation of their performance, may be assessed.

Turning first to the argument that town planners do not exercise professional altruism because they serve their own ends, Bakunin predicted that,

A scientific body entrusted with the government of society would soon end by devoting itself not to science but to quite another interest. And that, as is the case with all established powers, would consist in its endeavour to perpetuate itself in power and consolidating its position by rendering the society placed in its care even more stupid and consequently even more in need of being directed by such a body.[84]

Often this process starts by the seemingly innocuous conflicts which arise between the demands for service and administrative needs. In this process, as Johnson remarks, 'The attempt to guarantee services gives rise to an administrative framework, the efficient operation of which creates demands which are in conflict with the provision of those services for which they were created.'[85] It soon develops, however, into the sort of procedures, such as the standards which formed the basis of early town planning, which were basically convenient administrative formulae rather than solutions closely related to real problems.

Society is then apparently rendered more stupid by the promotion of mystification and an increasingly esoteric jargon having little or no meaning. It is also baffling to the public and probably some of the practitioners as well. This is also a peculiarly effective way of preventing uninitiated members of the public from participating in the planning process. In an area of Sunderland, for example, Dennis has documented the extreme difficulty that working-class households had in understanding the policy of 'lifing'.[86] Without understanding that, they could not follow the decisions made by the local authority and building societies on improvement grants and mortgages. What was even more perplexing was the fact that the original lives allocated to houses by the town planners often changed and in many cases by significant numbers of years. Thus one day a householder might find himself with a house he could mortgage and the next day not.

One day he might not qualify for a discretionary improvement grant and the next day he would. In such circumstances, as Davies recalls in a different location, 'the exercise of power has taken the place of the exercise of reason'.[87]

A second way in which town planners have served their own interests is in the use of the doctrine of professionalisation in their own struggle for status and income. They are in this sense the most direct and immediate beneficiaries of the planning system. Even *The Times* has been constrained to argue that 'a number of the restrictive practices carried on by professional groups and justified on the basis of community welfare [look] in fact rather like arrangements for making life easier for practitioners at the expense ... of their clients'.[88] The restrictive practices adopted by town planners in, for example, recruitment to the profession look too much like the attempts of a ruling group, who did not have to pass through those restrictions themselves, to limit the supply of apparently competent 'professionals' in order to benefit themselves from the effects of that policy on the price of their labour. In the bureaucratic organisational setting in which most town planners find themselves, this leads, as Morrison says, to policies which 'develop a most peculiar irrationality as questions of personal and institutional prestige come to take pre-eminence over the more important question of public accountability and the public interest'.[89]

While British town planners have been serving their own interests, they have also been facilitating those of the current power holders in society. The importance of this contribution is difficult to measure but should not be underestimated because, in common with many other professions, town planning has the inherent characteristic of bringing knowledge to the service of power. Young has even gone so far as to argue that 'the fusion of knowledge and power has created a new kind of professional technocrat who is in the process of replacing existing ruling groups'.[90] While this overstates the position of town planners, it is still the case that knowledge brings power and that therefore the current power holders can strengthen their positions by the use of the skills of those professional groups who are prepared to serve them. It is this possibility which lead both Veblen[91] and Merton[92] to reject the view that professionalisation inexorably leads to an increasingly participatory democratic society.

Certainly, the professionals' personal interest in the established order is unlikely to make him the servant of those groups seeking change. Rueschmeyer is probably correct in contending, therefore, that 'the profession's vested interest in a given legal order renders its service irrelevant to those groups in the society who seek radical change in the social order'.[93] The meagre evidence available seems to indicate that not only do town planners not serve radical change but also they benefit most those who already hold most of the power. In this context Davies argues that,

> The impact of planning on this society is rather like that of the educational system on that same society. It is least onerous and most advantageous to those who are already well-off or powerful, and it is most onerous and least advantageous to those who are relatively powerless or relatively poor. Planning is, in its effect on the socio-economic structure, a highly regressive form of indirect taxation.[94]

He is not contradicted by the evidence.

One of the main caveats which must be stressed in making such a statement, however, is the lack of significant evidence generated by town planners on such issues. Their claims to exercise rational legal authority must be questioned simply because many decisions are taken in a virtual data vacuum. From the early 1960s onwards, many external observers of British town planning have pointed to its inadequate data base, research and education. Nevertheless, as Davies says, 'The diagnoses and policies advanced by a genuine profession are capable of being falsified or verified by reference to a given body of fact.'[95] This is just not the case with British town planning. What is even more serious are the distortions in the collection by town planners of 'facts' which seem to creep into the work and prescribe what they find. As Goodman says, they 'operate from an ideological or value position and their so-called unbiased technical answers reflect this. Even the choice of what's to be studied, what trends they decide to project, involves considering one set of concerns that seems important and rejecting others that are supposedly not important.'[96]

One of the major factors contributing to the apparently regressive nature of planning is therefore the lack of explicit and relevant information on such topics as who gets what and why. One of the main manifestations of the failure to generate adequate data is the town planner's reliance on graphic representation of problems and proposals for their solution. This often leaves the impression that baffling social, economic and political problems can be reduced to a few lines and colours on a map and that whole communities and cultures can be swept aside by the bulldozers which so frequently follow these arbitrarily drawn lines. Few people who have witnessed urban motorways driven ruthlessly through poor housing areas, and clearance schemes which replace the human-scale slums of Victorian Britain with the ascetic concrete wildernesses of the twentieth century, can fail to wonder what problems these are the solutions to.

Finally, it cannot be stressed too forcefully that if planners are to make their relationships to the power structure clear and if they are to decide what data are worth collecting and what the data mean when they get them, they must develop an explicit normative social philosophy. Conversely, they must make explicit that which is unavoidably implicit in what they do anyway. Town planners tend to dodge this issue because it involves a set of social, political and ethical judgements upon which it is very difficult to obtain general agreement. But, as Harvey says, 'The trouble with merely dodging the issue is that judgements are inevitably implied by a decision, whether we like it or not.'[97]

For the structural-functionalists at least, one of the main functions of any profession is the application of knowledge to problems which are closely associated with the central values of society. Town planners, for example, are not separate from these values whether explicit or not. As important allocators of land uses and resources, town planners are making implicit normative evaluations of who should get what and, therefore, on the equity of this distribution. It is important, however, to make these judgements explicit. The problem then becomes that in order to expound their solutions to planning issues a clear social, moral and political philosophy becomes a prerequisite to any planning action. This should confront town planners with the major issue involved with their activities up to now, which is that their knowledge and actions are not of equal value to all groups in society. Indeed, the notions of social justice held by the power holders in society are unlikely to be the same as those of the powerless. If town planners are to mediate between different conceptions of justice and equity, they must be clear what they mean by these terms themselves. It is not enough to claim to be an altruistic profession. The constituents of altruistic mediation must be defined.

Conclusions

The relationship between town planners and the power structure are complex and intangible. They are nonetheless important for that. The implications of these relationships may be seen in the distributional equity of the social, political and economic structures in which planners operate and in the effects they have on the allocation of resources, and therefore power, to different groups in these structures.

The paradox that emerges in such an analysis is that while town planners strive to acquire professional status and income in society on the grounds that they provide an altruistic service to the public, in practice the benefits of this service have a tendency to accrue to those who are not most in need. This is the natural state of affairs in the market and in politics. These are both decision-making areas in which town planners mediate and therefore it might be expected that the effects of this mediation, if it were truly altruistic, would be to alter the natural outcomes of the market and politics in some significant way, and also not to benefit the better off groups more than the ones who have greater need. The converse seems to be the case.

Town planning alters the detailed practical effects of the market and politics in so far as decisions are taken and implementation follows. As a result, buildings come to look different and get put in different places. Many of these changes may be irrelevant permutations of how town planners think things should look and be located. Their effects on the distribution of resources and power may be marginal and regressive. In the most significant aspects of allocation, town planners achieve little in the way of really altering what would have happened without their mediation. Even the most obvious examples of town planning, the new towns, while involving large changes in what can be seen on the ground, have had little effect in providing more and better housing, employment, services and amenities to the poor. The main beneficiaries have been skilled manual workers. They would surely be among the main beneficiaries of any system.

Different countries, and in the case of the United States of America different parts of the same country, have markedly different planning policies and regulations. Two questions arise in this connection regarding town planning in Britain. The first is: Should the country publicly finance such an activity? The second is: If it should, what should be its broad, philosophical aims?

It may be argued that there is a real need for the administrative service provided by British town planning. Therefore the public or some other agency should, and would in any case, finance the activity. If this situation exists, but the outcomes are not markedly different according to whether the activity is publicly or privately financed, then it might be more economic, in terms of public expenditure, to allow the market and politics to make such planning decisions as are really necessary. This is almost what already happens in some parts of the United States of America. When these areas are compared with those where planning is publicly financed the similarities overwhelm the differences. This has led Banham, Barker, Hall and Price to ask of Britain:

> What would happen if there were no plan? What would people prefer to do, if their choice were untrammelled? Would matters be any better, or any worse, or much the same? (Might planning turn out to be rather like Eysenck's view of psychoanalysis: an activity which, insofar as it gets credit, gets it for benefits that would happen anyway – minds can cure themselves, maybe people can plan themselves?)[98]

The only argument that can be effectively advanced against such a proposition is that publicly financed town planning is necessary to the extent that it produces decisions and actions which are different from and 'better' than those produced by the market and politics under conditions of private planning. While it is difficult to assess how different public is from private planning, because few relevant contemporary comparisons can be made, it does not appear that British town planning produces decisions and actions which are markedly different from those of the market and politics. Thus, the effects of much town planning seem to be an improvement on the market and politics to the extent that decisions taken there are likely to be more regressive in their allocation of resources and power to different sectors of the social and spatial structures.

On the other hand, assessors of the efficacy of town planning must be able to define what they mean by 'better' in the context of planning decisions. For this, a social philosophy is necessary which contains substantially rational normative statements about what the desirable distributions of power and resources ought to be. Until statements of this nature can be argued through, it is impossible to decide what mixture of public and private planning would produce the results desired by society.

At the present time, however, it is impossible to argue, without too much fear of contradiction, that in view of the inegalitarian nature of British society it is only the rich whose interests would be served by expending public money to make it more inegalitarian. As the rich already have more than a sufficiency of power and resources, there is not much justification in giving them more. Therefore, publicly financed town planning should not be regressive. If British town planning is to be justified at all then it must at worst be neutral and at best progressive in its effect on the distribution of power and resources to the different social classes found in Britain today. At the present time, it does not appear to satisfy this criterion.

References

1 T. J. Johnson, *Professions and Power*, Macmillan (1972), p. 15
2 *ibid.*, p. 17
3 R. Lewis and A. Maude, *Professional People* (London, 1952)
4 A. M. Carr-Saunders and P. A. Wilson, *The Professions* (London, 1933)
5 T. Parsons, 'Professions', in *The International Encyclopaedia of the Social Sciences* (New York, 1968), 536–46
6 T. J. Johnson, *op. cit.* (1972), p. 12
7 T. Parsons, 'The professions and social structure', in *Essays in Sociological Theory*, rev. edn, Glencoe (1954), 34–49
8 R. Glass, 'The evaluation of planning: some sociological considerations', *International Social Science Journal*, **11** (3) (1959), 393–409
9 J. Friedmann, 'Planning as a vocation', *Plan*, **6** (3) (1966), 99–124
10 A. A. Altshuler, *Community Control*, Pegasus (New York, 1970)
11 J. G. Davies, *The Evangelistic Bureaucrat: a Study of a Planning Exercise in Newcastle-upon-Tyne*, Tavistock (1972), p. 96
12 R. Glass, *op. cit.*
13 M. Meyerson and E. C. Banfield, *Politics, Planning and the Public Interest*, Collier-Macmillan (1969)
14 *ibid.*, p. 322
15 *ibid.*, p. 324
16 *ibid.*, p. 325
17 *ibid.*, p. 326
18 G. Schubert, *The Public Interest*, The Free Press (Illinois, 1960)

19 T. J. Johnson, *op. cit.* (1972), p. 41
20 *ibid.*, p. 45
21 *ibid.*
22 *ibid.*
23 *ibid.*, p. 77
24 L. Rodwin, *The British New Town Policy*, Harvard University Press (1956), p. 201
25 P. Hall, 'Planning and the environment', in P. Townsend and N. Bosanquet (eds.), *Labour and Inequality*, Fabian Society (1972), p. 269
26 N. Dennis, *People and Planning*, Faber & Faber (1970), p. 360
27 J. G. Davies, *op. cit.* (1972), p. 105
28 D. L. Foley, *Controlling London's Growth: Planning the Great Wen 1940–1960,* California Press, (Berkeley, 1963), p. 53
29 J. M. Lee, *Social Leaders and Public Persons: a Study of Country Government in Cheshire since 1888,* Clarendon Press (1963)
30 J. G. Bulpitt, *Party Politics in English Local Government*, Longman (1967)
31 Ministry of Housing and Local Government, *People and Planning*, (Skeffington Report), HMSO (1969)
32 Fabian Society, *People, Participation and Government*, Fabian Research Series 293 (1972)
33 J. G. Davies, *op. cit.* (1972)
34 J. B. McLoughlin and J. Thornley, *Some Problems in Structure Planning: a Literature Review*, Centre for Environmental Studies, (London, 1972)
35 Committee on the Qualifications of Planners, Report to the Minister of Town and Country Planning of the *Committee on the Qualifications of Planners* (Chairman Sir George Schuster), HMSO (1950), Cmnd 8059
36 P. Hall, *op. cit.* (1972), p. 20
37 D. L. Foley, *op. cit.* (1963), p. 56
38 J. B. McLoughlin and J. Thornley, *op. cit.* (1972), p. 12
39 *ibid.*
40 R. Goodman, *After the Planners*, Penguin (1972), p. 207
41 P. Hall, *op. cit.* (1972), p. 268
42 N. Dennis, *op. cit.* (1970), p. 361
43 P. Hall, *op. cit.* (1972), p. 269
44 R. E. Pahl, *Whose City? And Other Essays on Sociology and Planning*, Longman (1970), p. 188
45 D. L. Foley, *op. cit.* (1963), p. 53
46 *ibid.*, p. 56
47 P. Hall, *op. cit.* (1972), p. 268
48 *ibid.*, p. 270

49 N. Dennis, *op. cit.* (1970), p. 361
50 D. Harvey, 'Social processes, spatial form and the redistribution of real income in an urban system', in M. Chisholm, A. E. Frey and P. Haggatt (eds.), *Regional Forecasting*, Proceedings of the Twenty-second Symposium of the Colston Research Society held in the University of Bristol, April 6th to 10th, 1970, Butterworth (1970), p. 268
51 *ibid.*, p. 283
52 *ibid.*
53 *ibid.*, p. 274
54 C. Buchanon, 'Presentation of the Gold Medal of the T.P.I.', *Journal of the Royal Town Planning Institute*, **54** (2), (1968) 49–55
55 D. Harvey, *op. cit.* (1970), p. 284
56 Fabian Society, *op. cit.* (1972)
57 J. M. Simmie, 'Public participation: a case study from Oxfordshire', *Journal of the Royal Town Planning Institute*, **57** (4), (1971), 161–2
58 M. Harrington, 'The betrayal of the poor', *Atlantic*, **225** (1), (January, 1970), 71–4
59 B. Whitaker, *Participation and Poverty*, Fabian Research Series 272 (1968)
60 J. G. Davies, *op. cit.* (1972), p. 228
61 R. E. Pahl, *op. cit.* (1970), p. 191
62 J. G. Davies, *op. cit.* (1972), p. 229
63 P. Hall, *op. cit.* (1972), p. 267
64 L. Rodwin, *op. cit.* (1956), p. 166
65 P. Hall, *op. cit.* (1972), p. 265
66 D. Harvey, *op. cit.* (1970), p. 286
67 R. E. Pahl, *op. cit.* (1970), p. 187
68 D. Harvey, *op. cit.* (1970), p. 279
69 *ibid.*, p. 270
70 *ibid.*, p. 290
71 *ibid.*, p. 292
72 R. Thomas, *London's New Towns: a Study of Self-contained and Balanced Communities*, Political and Economic Planning Broadsheet 510 (April, 1969), p. 419
73 *ibid.*
74 R. E. Pahl, *op. cit.* (1970), p. 239
75 M. Mead, 'Megalopolis: is it inevitable?', *Transactions of the Bartlett Society*, **3** (1964–5)
76 D. L. Foley, *op. cit.* (1963), p. 187
77 R. E. Pahl, *op. cit.* (1970), p. 187
78 Central Statistical Office, *Social Trends*, HMSO (1971), p. 131
79 R. Glass, 'Housing in Camden', *Town Planning Review*, **41** (1970)

80 P. Hall, *op. cit.* (1972), p. 267
81 O. Marriott, *The Property Boom*, Hamilton (1967)
82 N. Dennis, *op. cit.* (1970), p. 360
83 P. Hall, *op. cit.* (1972), p. 267
84 M. Bakunin, in G. E. Maximoff, *The Political Philosophy of Bakunin*, Collier-Macmillan (New York, 1953), p. 77
85 T. J. Johnson, *op. cit.* (1972), p. 85
86 N. Dennis, *Public Participation and Planners' Blight*, Faber & Faber (1972)
87 J. G. Davies, *op. cit.* (1972), p. 226
88 *The Times*, 29.2.70
89 A. Morrison, *see* J. G. Davies, *op. cit.* (1972), p. 126
90 M. Young, *The Rise of the Meritocracy*, Pelican (1958)
91 T. Veblen, *Engineers and the Price System*, (New York, 1921), p. 33
92 R. K. Merton, 'The machine, the worker and the engineer', *Science* CV (January, 1947), 79–81
93 D. Rueschmeyer, 'Doctors and lawyers: a comment on the theory of the professions', *Canadian Review of Sociology and Anthropology*, (February, 1964), 17–30
94 J. F. Davies, *op. cit.* (1972), p. 2
95 *ibid.*, p. 222
96 R. Goodman, *op. cit.* (1972), p. 199
97 D. Harvey, *op. cit.* (1970), p. 267
98 R. Banham, P. Barker, P. Hall and C. Price, 'Non-Plan: an experiment in freedom', *New Society*, 20 March (1969), 435–43

6. Social action and ideological conflict

Rationality versus ideology

The word 'ideology' was first coined by the French philosopher Destutt de Tracy at the end of the eighteenth century. He was seeking a way to arrive at a 'true' understanding of society other than by the traditional methods of faith and authority so insistently recommended by the Church and State, respectively. Later, the idea that such 'truth' could then be translated into social action was added by Hegel, Feuerbach and Marx. The latter agreed, however, that far from being 'objective' and 'true' views of society, ideologies were in fact reflections of the needs of specific groups. Thus 'truth' could only be discovered by uncovering the special interests served by ideologies and exposing how they served the particular interests of their authors.

In contrast to the Marxist prescription for the discovery of 'truth', British town planners have relied on the doctrine of rationality as their guide to objective, value-free reality and for the prescription of relevant policies. Indeed, the raison d'être of town planning, as Glass puts it, is assumed to be 'the rational and just pursuit of the public interest'.[1] Its decisions are said to differ from those arrived at through the ideologically coloured free-play of market forces or politics in that they pursue objectives like justice and the public interest in an 'objectively' rational way that entrepreneurs and politicians alike do not.

Friedmann notes that 'what renders planning so attractive in this view is its conception as a field for practical social reform, for widening the scope of rationality and order in society and for sharing in the exercise of power'.[2] The doctrine of rationality appeals to both utopians and reformers in planning as the criterion of the means by which their ends may be achieved. This general appeal as the means for achieving other doctrinal objectives helps to explain the widespread contemporary belief among planners that planning is virtually synonymous with rationality. For example, Morris and Binstock[3] assert that 'planning is now the generic term for rational problem solving'; Dahl and Lindblom[4] define planning as 'an attempt at rationally calculated action to achieve a goal'; and Simon *et al.*[5] define the activity as 'rational adaptive thought applied to the future'. Friedmann also notes that a 'major proposition of planning ideology is that planning is a specific form of social rationality'.[6] Planners are therefore arguing that their social action is based on 'value-free truth' which is discovered and pursued by the application of rational surveys, analyses and plans. There is no place for ideology in such social action.

It is argued here, however, that far from being a value-free and rational exercise, British town planning both reflects the current ideological conflicts in society and is not rational even within the terms of reference framed by the proponents of the concept.

Rational action

With regard to the notion that town planning is rational, the origins of this doctrine may be traced to the enlightenment and the utilitarian formulation of classical liberalism. 'Such views hold that problems may be solved given sufficient basic research, universal education and its application through institutions and communication.'[7] This reflects the contemporary elevation of reason and rationality over the emotional, subjective and irrational. This leads to the generally held assumption that decisions and actions ought to be rational and that the recipients of them will accept them more readily if they are argued to be so. In practical town planning this assumption often underpins the notion that the locational arrangement of work, residence, amenities and people should somehow be rational.

The rationalistic model of town planning also appeals because it harmonises with the two intellectual traditions of Dewy's rational economic man and Weber's theories of rational social action, both of which have represented a respectable intellectual tradition. They also account for the two categories, which have been identified by Dyckman, into which the study of decision-making falls. 'The first is normative, dealing with the quality of the decision as an act; the second is behavioural, dealing with the action context and the location of the action in the system of action.'[8] The former has been largely the concern of economics while the latter has been developed in the literature of organisation theory written mainly by sociologists. Again, as Dyckman has noted, 'economics and modern statistics, employing economic norms, focus on the tasks of rational action – that is to say, choosing and ranking ends or objectives, evaluating alternative courses of action, and sharpening the criteria for choice – the behavioural sciences focus on the spheres of competence for decision.'[9]

The traditional concern of economists for the normative element in rational planning is the result of the utilitarian foundations of modern economics, with its contention that 'rationality consists in always doing what would maximise interests . . . this assumes there is an optimum solution, which administrative man seeks if he is rational; it is an essentially Benthamite notion.'[10] Nevertheless, it is rational economic man whom the economists describe in their treatises on rationality. This being the case, it is immediately of concern that town planning should have adopted the doctrine of rationality so uncritically for, as Dyckman says, 'the main gaps in rationality which centralized planning has been asked to fill are the presumed deficiencies of other decision mechanisms in dealing with the future and the extensive repercussions of limited goals.'[11] In other words, while town planning was instituted to improve on the decisions taken in the market or politics in the development of towns and the quality of life in general, it is not immediately obvious that this may be achieved by adopting a similar doctrine of rationality to that found in those arenas.

Against this view, however, it may be argued that planning rationality improves on that of the market or politics in so far as it is more comprehensive and based on more information. Its comprehensive nature may lead to a more community-oriented balancing of interests, and its possession of more information than separate individuals may lead to decisions being taken nearer the conditions of perfect as opposed to imperfect competition. 'Such a model of rational optimum decisions can have its uses in situations where there is a finite number of variables, where alternatives are known and limited, and where there can be preference ranking among them.'[12] But, these conditions are hardly ever fulfilled in town planning where informational needs are almost infinite and the holistic or comprehensive view of the system imposes a huge burden of co-ordination in addition to the other problems of large scale public authority planning.

The classical rational-deductive ideal was first conceived in Western philosophy by Plato. It requires, as given, a generally agreed set of values expressed as general principles. Given these general principles or objectives it then requires that all of the alternatives open for achieving them, within the prevailing conditions, be examined. It also requires that all the consequences that would follow from the adoption of each alternative be examined. There are three types of theory, concerning these consequences, which may assist the town planner to estimate them. The first of these are certainty theories which assume that the town planner has complete and accurate knowledge of the consequences that will follow on each alternative. These theories correspond well with the assumptions of comprehensiveness and complete information. Second, however, there are risk theories which assume accurate knowledge only of a probability distribution of the consequences of each alternative. In such circumstances the town planner cannot be definite about either the validity of his information or the comprehensiveness of his plans. Finally, there are uncertainty theories which assume that the consequences of each alternative belong to some subset of all possible consequences, but that the town planner cannot assign definite probabilities to the occurrence of particular consequences. Neither in the case of risk nor uncertainty can the town planner claim to have fulfilled all the conditions of classical rationality, so that his claim to possess superior information and to be comprehensive and therefore superior in rationality to the market and politics is unjustified in these circumstances. In the case of certainty, however, he may go on to complete the last two steps in the production of a plan which is rational in the classical sense by (fourth) deriving a set of priorities from the given values or objectives which will serve as criteria against which the consequences of the different alternatives may be evaluated. And (fifth) selecting an alternative which will lead to the preferred or optimum set of consequences. It is clear, however, that in so far as the case of certainty rarely occurs in the problems that confront town planners in estimating the consequences of their actions, and in so far as they lack information and are unable to plan and actually implement comprehensive, co-ordinated strategies, it does not appear, at first sight, that it is practical for them to follow the doctrine of classical rationality and, at the same time, fulfil all its stringent conditions.

This would seem to be confirmed by Schoeffler, who has defined what he considers to be all the factors that need to be considered in the production of rational action in the 'real' world. These factors may be listed as:

1. The time dimension of action and of its consequences.
2. The multitudinous side-effects of action.
3. The inevitable uncertainty of the action in connection with the alternatives of action open to him and the consequences of each of these.
4. The costs of information gathering.
5. The costs of performing logical operations.
6. The variety of the value criteria of different actions.
7. The changes in the value criteria of any given action over time.
8. The tastes of the actor in relation to time-preference, risk-taking, logical processes, and the facing of uncertainty.[13]

This formidable list would appear to confirm the practical impossibility for the town planner to follow the doctrine of classical rationality.

In addition to the purely practical difficulties involved in following the rational ideal, serious doubt has been cast since the 1940s on the theoretical possibility of planning according to the requirements of classical rationality. In the first place, it does not make a clear distinction between the type of rational logic which leads to the establishment of general principles, goals or values and the criteria for evaluating them, and the type of rational logic which is the process adopted by town planners to decide and implement the course or courses of action which will best achieve their goals. Indeed, classical theory takes principles, values and goals as 'given'. The distinction between these two types of rational logic was first made by Mannheim. He defined the type of rationality that is concerned with the establishment of 'objective' goals as 'substantial rationality', and the type of rationality which reduces policies from these general principles as 'functional rationality'. Substantial rationality involves 'an act of thought which reveals intelligent insight into the inter-relations of events in a given situation'. Functional rationality involves the development of 'a series of actions organized in such a way that it leads to a previously defined goal, every element in the series receiving a functional position and role'.[14]

Functional rationality

Town planners, following the inherited traditions of utilitarian economics in the doctrine of classical rationality, have been generally pre-occupied with the efficient allocation of resources in market situations in which the rules of the game and the terms of the play are essentially fixed and the goals of the players obvious. Hence most town plans have been attempts to develop functionally rational programmes to achieve goals which have either been taken for granted or which have been specified in the market or politics.

The ability to be functionally rational in this way was first questioned by Neumann and Morgenstern in 1944. As Dyckman says, they 'established the end of innocence about the uniqueness of rational solutions and the straightforwardness of maximising and the purity of strategies'.[15] It became clear, therefore, that the classical synoptic ideal even when limited to the quest for functional rationality fails to account adequately for such difficulties as:

1. Man's limited problem solving capacities.
2. The inadequacy of information.
3. The costliness of analysis.
4. Failures in constructing a satisfactory evaluative method.
5. The closeness of observed relationships between fact and value in town planning.
6. The openness of systems variables with which it contends.
7. The analyst's need for strategic sequences of analytical moves.
8. The diverse forms in which town planning problems actually arise.

Accordingly, Neumann and Morgenstern proposed that superior functional rationality would arise if simple maximising was replaced by the criterion of 'minimax'. In this situation, the town planner, as an individual, abandons, for example, the old criterion that maximum welfare is achieved when it is impossible to make one person better off without making some other person worse off (the Pareto principle) in favour of minimising maximum risks.

This principle of minimising maximum risks overcomes some of the objections to the synoptic ideal in functionally rational town planning. Thus, it is no longer necessary for the planner to know all of the alternatives open to him at any given time nor all of the consequences attendant upon them. He may extend his operations from situations of certainty into those of risk. At the same time, his ability to define the range of probable consequences following from specified alternative proposals increases his significance as a professional expert and, at the same time, reduces the ability of the ordinary individual to counter-evaluate his plans. Consequently, social knowledge and the power of making decisions become more concentrated for purely practical reasons in a limited number of hands, among them those of the town planners. This increases the significance of the influence of the forces that create the power positions on the 'objectivity' of functionally rational plans. These forces, which have created the need for town planners and at the same time have created situations of complexity which force them into areas of risk as opposed to certainty, are generally those of industrialisation. The forces of industrialisation are also important for their influence in shaping the values of members of society, including town planners, and hence the nature of the alternative plans that are adopted. Suffice it, at this stage of the argument, to note that the forces of industrialisation are not noted for their promotion of substantial rationality.

Apart from these caveats concerning the limitations of functional rationality, three technical problems have to be faced by the town planners before they can claim to be functionally rational. The first is the problem of end reduction from multiple ends; the second, the evaluation of ends; and the third is the resistance of individuals and organisations to change.

Concerning end reduction from multiple ends, Meyerson and Banfield note that 'if only one end were relevant in the making of a plan, it would be a simple matter for the planner to choose a course of action. But almost always there are numerous ends to be served and no one course of action will maximise the attainment of all of them.'[16] First, this is a particularly acute problem for public planning agencies, because end reduction is more complicated than for private agencies following, for example, only the goal of profit. Second, the ramification of consequences for public agencies is likely to be much greater than for private ones. Third, the courses of action which will achieve even the principal ends of public agencies decreases rapidly with the number of secondary objectives which must be considered. Also, the hazard of unanticipated consequences which may be of radical importance is high for agencies seeking to follow several ends without certain knowledge of all their consequences.

Concerning the evaluation of ends, two points should be made. The first is that even where the ends are given to planners in a situation of functional rationality, some evaluation will necessarily have to be made in order to decide their priority ranking. This calls for an element of substantial rationality not theoretically present in the situation. Second, the ends themselves may generate the values inherent in the judgements that planners must make in choosing between alternative policies – so that here again it is not possible to avoid the necessity for an element of substantial rationality.

Finally, concerning the resistance by individuals and organisations to change, functional rationality tends to apply more to static than to dynamic situations. Generally speaking, town planners prefer policy alternatives that represent the continuation of present programmes as opposed to those entailing change. This is partly because alternatives to current actions are not sought unless those actions are in some sense unsatisfactory. This realisation, however, calls for an admission that past policies have been at least partially wrong, or reference to new normative standards which are not generated under conditions of functional rationality.

Town planning in practice

Despite these difficulties, town planning decisions do follow the doctrine of functional rationality. In practice, however, this doctrine is much modified even from the minimax criterion proposed by Neumann and Morgenstern. This modification is primarily the work of Simon who 'doubted the prevalence of such clever and foresighted action, and posited a more intuitive [and perhaps more myopic] decision maker.'[17] He replaced Neumann's minimaxing planner with satisficing planning within the limits of bounded rationality. His theory of rational choice, incorporates two fundamental characteristics:

1. Choice is always exercised with respect to a limited, approximate, simplified model of the real situation . . .

2. The elements of the definition of the situation are not given . . . but are themselves the outcome of psychological and sociological processes, including the chooser's own activities and the activities of others in his environment.[18]

The boundaries of rationality consist primarily of the properties of human beings as organisms capable of evoking and executing relatively well-defined programmes but able to handle programmes only of limited complexity.

Actual policy making therefore tends to focus on problem solving based on simplified models of the real world and executed within a bounded area of functional rationality. Bruner, Goodnow and Austin have experimentally identified four possible strategies for problem solving in this context. They are simultaneous scanning in which all possible hypotheses are investigated at the same time. Successive scanning in which hypotheses are investigated sequentially, conservative focussing in which one positive response leads to alteration in the search procedures, and other parts of the policy are sought to fit in with that evoking a positive response. And, finally, focus gambling in which one or more alternatives are picked at random and policies built around those positive responses.[19] Braybrook and Lindblom point out that 'under the conditions of this experiment, it is not true that the best way to solve a problem is to be comprehensive . . . when time is short – it may be best to trust to a degree of luck.'[20] This procedure is likely to happen quite often in practice because, in the search for possible courses of action, alternatives will be tested sequentially. As soon as a few possible solutions to the problems at hand are found, then these will be evaluated. If one of them proves to be relatively satisfactory, it is likely to be adopted and the search for optimum plans replaced by ones which satisfy.

Simon argues that in most human decision making, whether individual or organisational, the search is for satisfactory alternatives. Only in very exceptional circumstances is it concerned with optimum solutions. The main technical reason for this is that to optimise requires processes several orders of magnitude more complex than those required to satisfy.

In many ways the criterion of minimax risk is one method of satisficing when it entails selecting the least worst combination of the worst consequences that could possibly flow from alternative plans. In 1963, however, Braybrooke and Lindblom proposed an even more potentially conservative strategy of decision. They argued that, in practice, most planning is disjointed and incremental. It is disjointed, according to the authors, because the planner:

[1.] Chooses as relevant objectives only those worth considering in view of the means at hand or likely to become available.[21]

[2.] He automatically incorporates consideration of the costliness of achieving the objective into his marginal comparison, for an examination of incremental differences in value consequences of various means tells him at what price in terms of one value he is obtaining an increment of another.[22]

[3.] While he contemplates means, he continues at the same time to contemplate objectives, unlike the synoptic analyst who ideally must at some point finally stabilise his objectives and then select the proper means.[23]

Over time, this kind of town planning leads to the adjustment of aspirations to the level of achievement and also discourages innovation. This, combined with increasing job security and cynicism among town planners as their careers progress, materially contributes to the conservative nature of British town planning in practice. This has led to the argument that, in the light of the limits on human planning capacity in centralised positive planning, town planning should be decentralised. The ultimate in decentralisation is a return to the market, a proposition recently advocated by Banham, Barker, Hall and Price.[24]

Substantial rationality

If the ability of town planners is as limited as Neumann, Morgenstern, Simon, Braybrooke and Lindblom argue in the field of functional rationality, then the main argument for the doctrine of rationality in British town planning must be that it introduces an element of substantial rationality not found in a sufficiently predominant position in either economics or politics.

Substantial rationality requires the application of rational analysis to the statement and elaboration of goals. The process leading to the formulation and clarification of these goals may be termed normative planning. The differences between the normative goals of town planning and those of economics and politics are that while economic analysis defines the object of the exercise as the maximisation of profit and politics is primarily concerned with the struggle for power, it may be contended that the goals of town planning are the comprehensive maximisation of welfare in the public interest.

There is some doubt, however, as to whether individual goals can be aggregated to form comprehensive normative statements of welfare. The seminal work on the aggregation of individual values into a social value scale was published by Arrow in 1951.[25] Dyckman notes that his problem was familiar,

> given preference rankings of m alternatives ... by n individuals ..., define fair methods for aggregating these into a single ranking (social welfare function). In a startling demonstration, Arrow showed that five innocuously appearing requirements of fairness are inconsistent (no welfare function exists which satisfies them all).[26]

These conditions are:

1. Universal domain, that is, which resolves all possible preference patterns.
2. Positive association of individual values.
3. Independence of irrelevant alternatives.
4. Citizen sovereignty.
5. Non-dictatorship.

'Arrow proceeded to show that if a function satisfied the first three conditions, it was either imposed or dictatorial.'[27] The possible answers to the dilemma posed by Arrow's Impossibility Theorem have been summarised by Luce and Raiffa. According to them,

> Social choice problems still arise and must be resolved, and so the impasse must be sidestepped. As we see it, there are two distinct possibilities:
>
> 1. to keep Arrow's formulation of the problem and to reject one of his conditions as being too restrictive: or
> 2. to alter the formulation of the problem itself by changing the given and/or the demands on society's final product.[28]

Dyckman comments perceptively on this proposition that 'the game approach of Luce and Raiffa, equally with Simon's assault on the optimizing criterion, strikes at the planning problem by re-defining it in ways which eliminate the traditional role of the planner'.[29] It may clearly be argued that the solutions to the impasses of functional and substantial rationality, proposed by Simon, and Luce and Raiffa, respectively, in fact mean that town planners are neither functionally nor substantially rational in the production of plans and that therefore the doctrine of rationality is of as little value as those of reform and utopianism.

Social action and ideology

From a phenomenological point of view all social action is based upon an ideological interpretation and definition of the 'facts'. The social action prescribed by normative planning and executed by a series of 'logical' steps springs from the ideological frames of reference to town planners themselves. These frames of reference are the result of the influence of the contemporary ideologies in society on town planners via their social, educational and institutional environments. While town planners continue to present society with programmes of action which are said to be 'objectively' developed from 'generally agreed' goals by the use of rational argument and techniques, the sceptic must seek to discover the ideological basis of these propositions and whose interests and aims they serve. One may agree with Goldthorpe's analogous criticism of

> those who interpret the making of social policy as a pragmatic and necessary response to social crisis. These explanations, he argues, are essentially functionalist and neglect certain key issues. Any attempt at explaining the development of social policy in Britain must analyse the situation in terms of the ends involved and the groups in conflict with each other, rather than in terms of the needs of society, considered as a whole.[30]

One question which arises from this kind of analysis is whether Marx was correct to argue not only that ideas should not be taken at their face value – rather that one should search for the interests they serve – but also that the test of the 'truth' of these ideas is to see what class interests they serve. If, for example, there is some identity between the ideologies of those groups who reap the greatest benefits from the spatial structure and those of town planners, then it could be argued that the doubtful rationality of the latter's plans is more sinister than a simple failure of technique. Thus, while Horton's proposition[31] that any attempt to explain social problems 'invariably involve(s) normative theory, values, ideologies, or whatever one may care to call the subjective categories of our thinking about society' may be generally accepted, it is a much more serious indictment of a government agency to add to this the proposition that, in practice, these ideologies are used to legitimate social action which serves the interests of, for example, a ruling class.

In order to assess whether this latter is the case with British town planners it is first necessary to illustrate the ideological conflicts and the ensuing policies which influence their social, educational and institutional environments.

In 1960, Bell argued that the events of 1930–50 had led to the exhaustion of political ideas in the fifties, and consequently to the end of ideology. This was exemplified by modifications in capitalism and the rise of the Welfare State. Thus, 'In the Western World . . . there is to-day a rough consensus among intellectuals on political issues: the acceptance of a Welfare State; the desirability of decentralized power, a system of mixed economy and of political pluralism.'[32] He went on to say that 'economic development has become a new ideology that washes away the memory of old disillusionments'.[33] This description fits quite well with the conventional political wisdom of the early fifties in Britain.

The idea grew, nourished by the Conservative Government of the time, that the establishment of the Welfare State after the Second World War had led to the modification of the hard face of capitalism seen during the depression and to the amelioration of life in general. Power was increasingly thought to be shared, particularly because of the mixture of public and private ownership of capital. These beliefs led Johnson,[34] for example, to pose the problem of what to do as the Welfare State worked its way out of existence and sociology as the critical discipline of society became redundant with the approach of the millennium. Elections could be won on the basis of Macmillan's immortal phrase 'You've never had it so good.'

In reality, far from heralding the end of ideology, this 'happy' state of affairs marked a period of the ascendancy of liberal ideology, and a pause in the ideological conflict with socialist ideology, while the proponents of the latter awaited the revelations of, for example, Abel-Smith and Townsend in *The Poor and the Poorest*. Thus the

1950s, in Britain, were characterised by more general acceptance of liberal than socialist ideology and the consequent legitimation of sound action and policies based on that view of the 'facts'.

The main propositions of liberal ideology are characterised by Gallie as:

[1.] Justice is essentially a commutative conception, grounded on the familiar claim that rewards or returns should be proportional to merit.

[2.] Commutative justice is best assured when each individual is left free to decide in what ways he will use his own capacities and property, subject to the proviso that his way shall not prevent others from using their capacities and property in their ways.

[3.] Evidently the system of free contract is an admirable device for ensuring this result whenever men choose to divide and 'mix' their labour.

[4.] The main functions of good government [which follow from this ideological position], are negative and preventive, e.g. defence of country and protection of life and property. The positive function of government is to safeguard the greatest possible freedom of choice for every citizen; and probably the best way of doing this is to facilitate and simplify the making of free contracts and to enforce these once they are made.[35]

The kind of policies and priorities followed by government and its agencies based on this ideological definition of reality have been sketched by Donnison. He argues that,

the standpoint of the tough-minded, economically oriented Right, goes something like this:

1. When policies are to be decided, top priority should normally be given to economic growth.

2. Economic growth means growth in the goods and services produced by private enterprise.

3. The fruits of growth should reach people in the form of money because it is healthier, both for the individual and for the country, if people buy what they want rather than getting things free through the social services.

4. To succour the casualties growth leaves in its wake there must be some redistribution of incomes. This is brought about through the social services which confer most of their benefits on poorer people, at the cost of taxes levied mainly on richer people.

5. So far as the poor are concerned, our aim must be to raise their living standards to an adequate minimum from which they should be encouraged to make further advances by their own efforts.

6. The growth of the social services must wait on the growth of the

private sector of the economy for it is only from the surplus generated in this sector that the resources for the expansion can be found.

7. Greater equality of incomes may be morally desirable, but it tends to be economically self-defeating because it is inflationary (the poor having low marginal propensities to save) and because it penalises the most productive, rewards the idle and thus frustrates growth itself.

8. The success or failure of individuals is largely due to their psychological inheritance, cultivated by will and character. It is thus impossible to create a much more equal society than the one we now have.[36]

It is clear, therefore, that the end of ideology was not reached in Britain during the 1950s. On the contrary, the stress given to economic growth, the residual nature of the Welfare State, and the idea that the combination of economic growth and residual social policies were giving those with ability the good life and those without the opportunity to 'have it', was the liberal ideology of laissez-faire in its twentieth century guise. Furthermore, as Wedderburn was to argue later, the residue of the universalist British welfare state that was left by the 1960s was neither particularly socialist nor radical and amounted to little more than a tempering of the prevailing winds of competition.[37]

The question therefore arises as to who seems to benefit most from such social action and policies legitimated by liberal ideology. This depends on the nature of the distribution of economic resources and political power in the first instance. If society is characterised by inequality in these distributions, then it is likely that economic growth will increase rather than decrease this inequality. So if 1 per cent of the population get 99 per cent of dividends and profits then, in so far as these are the fruits of economic growth, this minority will benefit first and most from growth. This situation is reinforced if economic growth is defined primarily as growth in the goods and services produced by private enterprise. Similarly, if some of the fruits of growth are distributed in the form of money to labour, the secondary effect of this form of distribution will be to increase the rewards to capital either in the form of increased consumption or inflation. Indeed, capital has a vested interest in continued inflation because of its powers of substitution and ability to outstrip the price of labour. Through inflation, originally expensive fixed assets became cheaper or, in the case of property, either increase in value faster than average rates of inflation or can be substituted for more or different property without the expenditure of any effort whatsoever on the part of the owners.

Conversely, to succour the casualties of such a system by using selective welfare services is the least expensive way to provide acceptable levels of social benefits. The cost to the rich is also minimised by providing a limit to such benefits beyond which individuals are expected to compete once again in the market. Furthermore, if growth of the social services must wait on growth in the private sector this again limits their cost but at the same time ensures that levels of benefits are always just inadequate. They will always lag behind the gains to the private sector and never overcome the erosion of their real value as a result of the inflation attendant upon economic growth.

The arguments against greater equality of income also benefit the rich most, for they legitimise their possession of wealth on the grounds that wealth demonstrates worth. Such arguments seek to institutionalise an inegalitarian distribution of economic resources to the obvious advantage of those who have rather than those who have not. The suggestion that this might change in time is also proscribed by the argument that success or failure depends on the psychological characteristics of individuals rather than the structure of society.

The main beneficiaries of societies, social action and government policies based on liberal ideologies are those who start with most economic resources and political power. Those who gain least are those who start with least.

Socialist ideology

In conflict with this ideology of the free market and politics is that of the socialists. It is a protest against the kind of society which results from social action based on liberal ideology. As Gallie points out:

> [1.] It complains that the liberal account of justice is defective or misleading since: it suggests that the capacities and property of different individuals are either things given by nature or else in some way meritoriously owned whereas, in fact, property – and hence to some extent capacity – are usually the result of inheritance.
>
> [2.] The system of free contract does not in fact always or even usually result in the greatest possible fairness in rewards.

[3.] The liberal account of good government rests on the factual (but false) assumption that no important improvements in governmental machinery can ever be devised and hence that all government or collective action must remain basically of a restrictive and repressive kind.[38]

Instead, socialist ideology seeks to gain the acceptance of distributive justice, the contributing individual, freedom as essentially freedom to be, not to get, and collective action in economic affairs as the goals of social action. The reasons for adopting such goals are essentially moral ones. It is argued, therefore, that society has a moral duty to provide an adequate material basis of life for all its members and also to secure the kind of freedoms which are associated with the highest states of human existence.

The free market economy does not achieve this felicitous state so it is therefore necessary to socialise the economy. This may increase its efficiency by removing the wastefulness of competition and also ensure that the production of basic essentials is not left to the whims of individual enterprise. It also may have moral benefits in that any decline in competition and acquisitiveness is likely to lead to a more co-operative society based on the kind of desirable human values found in non-competitive societies and institutions. Socialist ideology relies heavily on moral arguments for its prescriptive force.

The kind of policies that follow from these arguments have again been outlined by Donnison. He says that,

The standpoint of the tender-minded, socially oriented left goes somewhat as follows:

1. When policies are to be decided, top priority should normally be given to the equalisation of incomes and living standards. That should be achieved by raising the standards of the poorest.

2. Equality is valued for essentially moral reasons: the more equal we become, the more civilised and compassionate will be our relationships with our fellow citizens.

3. Poverty does not mean a failure to attain a fixed minimum, but exclusion from the continually rising standards of the country's middle income groups. Thus the problem of poverty can only be resolved by movement towards greater equality of rewards and living conditions.

4. The main instruments for redistribution are the social services . . .

5. Economic growth, which is valuable if it enables the country to move towards greater equality, consists partly of the growth of the social services.

6. It is healthier, both for the individual and for the country, to distribute many of the basic essentials of life, according to need and preferably without payment, rather than through the market.
7. The success or failure of individuals is largely due to environmental influences, many of which society is capable of modifying.[39]

Again the question arises as to who benefits most from these sorts of policy.

This is not too difficult to define, at least in intention. Whether social policies actually achieve these objectives is another matter. The aim of socialist ideology is clearly to benefit the disadvantaged members of society at the expense of the privileged. This is to be achieved by removing the obstacles to participation by the poor in the continually rising standards of the average family. An improvement in the quality of social interaction in society at large is supposed to result.

The main agencies of this social action are those of the social services. Paradoxically this means that the most immediate beneficiaries of such policies are not the poor but the employees of new and expanding agencies of welfare. Not too many of these employees of the welfare industry will be underprivileged.

Thus, socialist ideology contains some serious deficiencies as an effective counter to liberal laissez-faire. In the first place there is no obvious reason why the rich in a market economy should agree to having some of their income and wealth transferred to other groups. Both Runciman[40] and Rawls[41] argue that both the distribution of economic resources and political power must be justified to the losers. The onus is placed on the rich man to argue why his income should not immediately be transferred to the poorest old age pensioner. It is argued that in the hypothetical situation where men did not know in advance whether they would be rich or poor, powerful or powerless, a rational man would choose to insure himself against the exigencies of being poor and powerless. To do this, he would have to agree in advance to a social structure which did not contain extremes radically different from the median. Unfortunately, there is little prescriptive force in this argument in a society stressing competition and acquisitiveness unless one is predisposed to such an ideological position in the first place.

To convince the rich and powerful who do not accept the socialist premises of such an argument that they should insure themselves against the possibility of becoming less rich and less powerful, such a situation would have to be an objective possibility. This is precisely not the case in a market economy. There, the best insurances against poverty and powerlessness are wealth and power. They are also the best means to acquire the impure public goods supplied or subsidised by government agencies. Even in the universal services of health and education great advantages are gained by those who can buy either, while at the same time what they buy is also being subsidised by the community at large. A further difficulty with socialist ideology is that, as Runciman has shown, it plays 'little part in the feelings even of those whose unformulated claims it would vindicate'; instead he suggests that 'most people's lives are governed more by the resentment of narrow inequalities, the cultivation of modest ambitions and the preservation of small differentials than by attitudes to public policy or the structure of society as such'.[42] In so far as this is true, then the best way for the rich and powerful to maintain their position is to ensure that the differentials between themselves and the rest of society are maintained at a level which is beyond the comprehension of most of the majority; to maintain a system where the best form of insurance against the vagaries of life is wealth and power; and to seek to legitimate such a situation on the basis of liberal ideology.

The creation of such a society in market economies produces a situation where inequalities are not generally perceived and where liberal ideology is more readily accepted than its socialist rival. The acceptance of this situation by some members of society whose needs are not served by the resulting distributions of power and resources has led to elaborations of the concept of 'false consciousness'. This concept is used to argue that 'the citizens of advanced industrial society are so repressed that they are incapable of recognizing the extent of their own deprivation'.[43] During the nineteenth century, Marx, the originator of the concept, was able to point to very large 'objective' differences between the rich and the poor in the newly emerged capitalist countries following their respective industrial revolutions. The inability of the poor to recognise the extent of these differences or to construct relevant general pictures of their society, combined with some acceptance of the liberal ideology of the day, all gave rise to a clear case of false consciousness. Clear, that is, when looked at with the benefit of hindsight against the background of twentieth-century conditions. It was not clear nor generally accepted at the time. Indeed, for several decades, Marx was regarded in much the same light as Marcuse is in contemporary society.

For Marcuse, the problem is not only that it is not clear to everybody in advanced capitalist societies who benefits most from their arrangement, but also that the Welfare State is used to 'decrease the likelihood of this recognition'. Marcuse argues that the 'Welfare State is a part of a universe of administration in which depressions are controlled and conflict stabilized by the beneficial effects of growing productivity'.[44] At the same time, the benefits of welfare policies must await economic growth and only be distributed in sufficient quantity to prevent large-scale disaffection with the 'system' rather than to remove all its inequalities.

Unfortunately, again like the prescriptions for distributive justice advanced by Rawls and Runciman, the explanation, in terms of false consciousness, of why more people do not see and define the problem of inequality lies in its lack of force for those who are not ideologically predisposed towards such a view. Thus few people are willing to accept that their view of 'truth' is incorrect. The problem of convincing the beneficiaries of a market economy that social justice consists in redistributing some of their gains to other groups, and of convincing numbers of the population that they are in fact suffering from false consciousness in their understanding of society, is a problem of the same magnitude that would be involved in convincing the Protestants of Northern Ireland that they should become Catholics!

This being the case for socialist ideology, the same may also be said for liberal ideology. Thus, the latter has little prescriptive force for those who are not predisposed to accept it. At the same time it has serious moral problems in seeking to justify a system of gains which accrue to a minority of society, particularly when that minority is also largely responsible for the attempts to gain general acceptance of the same ideology. Furthermore, it does look suspiciously like a rationalisation of self-interest when the debate centres on the contention that wealth and worth are closely related. Any examination of the ways that individuals have accumulated and held wealth provides many examples of where wealth seems inversely related to worth. It could well be, therefore, that a more telling attack on liberal ideology could be mounted on the basis of an extensive analysis of the rich.

Instead of concentrating on the poor, inequality and explaining the failure of the individuals to appreciate the concept in terms of false consciousness, those seeking a more egalitarian society might do well to turn their attention to the rich. It would be most enlightening to develop an analysis of the paradoxes between liberal ideology and the behaviour of the rich. These paradoxes could well be illuminated by devoting more attention to how and in what forms wealth is acquired; what effects it has on the ownership of resources and the control of political power; what the connections between wealth holders are; how they transmit their wealth to successive generations; and what avenues these generations pass through to institutionalise their position. Such an analysis would show the degree to which self-interest is served by liberal ideology and also the degree to which the pursuit of gain through competition leads the rich to distort even the Machiavellian morality of the market place.

The ideologies of town planning

The ideologies of British town planners reflect those currently existent in the wider economic, political and social context of society. Thus, while there is not a one-to-one relationship between men and ideas, the definitions of town planning which form the basis of the normative stances of its practitioners clearly reflect the main ideological divisions in British society. On the one hand there are those of the tough-minded, economically oriented Right who argue that town planning is a specific form of social rationality designed to promote an efficient and economic allocation of physical land uses. On the other hand there are those of the tender-minded, socially oriented Left who argue that town planning is a more general social activity concerned with politics, philosophy and government.

Either way, town planning is a primarily ideological activity. As Friedmann points out, 'Planning is done by individuals whose fundamental motivations derive in part from an ideological interpretation of the function of planning in society. This influences the choice of problems, method of work and proposed solutions. It introduces an important normative element in planning.'[45] The result is that those subscribing to physical definitions of town planning choose different problems, methods of work and propose different solutions from those who subscribe to social science definitions of planning. Ideologies are therefore important, as Foley says, in providing 'a basic operating rationale'.[46] They constitute the rudimentary theories of practice which lead to the different types of professional action. Nearly all town planning starts from and contains ideological propositions. These often contain the substantial or normative rationality of the activity. But, in so far as little substantially rational argument is forthcoming to support these ideological stances, and in so far as ideological implications are anathema to functional rationality, so the 'objective' and 'value neutral' stance of town planning must be viewed with scepticism.

Furthermore, in so far as town planning is ideological in the Marxist sense of the term, then it is to be expected that its practitioners will serve particular rather than general interests. Nevertheless, the 'official' position as described by Kantorowich is that 'Town Planning . . . has emerged fully in response to a social need as a distinct professional process'.[47] And, according to Ling, 'the Royal Town Planning Institute exists only because of society's need for planning'.[48] Non-planners are therefore asked to believe that town planning serves their own best interests in the same way as, for example, the civil engineer when he bridges a previously impassable obstacle. But this is by no means always the case, as groups arise seeking professional status and exclusiveness.

The main interests served by the professionalisation of town planning have been those of its practitioners. The debate about the definition of planning has been conspicuously marked by what Cockburn describes as 'an endeavour on the part of the profession to remain in control of job opportunities'.[49] This is reflected in the continuous demarcation disputes, particularly those that occur between architects and planners. But, while the tough-minded, economically oriented Right maintain that 'planning is the job of the Chartered Planner, assisted by contributors to the planning process',[50] it does seem as though other kinds of people are also planning with little or no effect on the quality of the outcomes. This is clearly reflected in the multiple membership of members of the Royal Town Planning Institute. In 1968, Ling noted that '75% of our present members also belong to another profession or discipline (60% are also architects, engineers and surveyors)'.[51] Now if the sick could equally well be treated by doctors, vets, chemists or faith healers, society would be entitled to ask why the faith healers, for example, should claim to be the only body competent to cure the sick. If the main advantage of this claim was that faith healers got more jobs and pay, then the ideological nature of such a claim would be exposed.

Often society is fully able to make such distinctions, and so, as Chetwynd notes, 'an occupation only becomes a profession when society in general recognizes it as such'.[52] This society has conspicuously failed to do for the town planner. Clapham amusingly notes that a planner as seen by the public

> is a close relative of the Income Tax Inspector. He has no personal relatives since his parentage is doubtful . . . Most planners are employed by local authorities solely to create problems in order that they might justify their existence . . . A planner's dearest wish is to send everything back first time round to see whether the applicant means it . . . Only he could really appreciate the logic in refusing your own modest extension to your outside bog as being detrimental to the blood boiling factory and multi-storey chip shop next door . . . The planner's written word is sheer poetry – or something. His vocabulary and his language are unique and completely unintelligible.[53]

Many members of the public find this description all too true to be amusing.

The general public does not accord the town planner professional status. Hence, although the planner may claim to serve the needs of the community in general, many people suspect that such assertions do not sit well with demarcation disputes and closed-shop tactics. At the same time, the fact that the ability to become a town planner does not preclude the time and ability to become any one of a number of other quasi-professions – combined with the impossible range of planning education – must cause many people to ponder on the significance of what lies behind these professional façades.

In the case of town planning, the quasi-professional façade is composed largely of ideological definitions of what constitutes the activity. This is particularly so in the case of the tough-minded economically oriented Right who seek to provide exclusive definitions of town planning. While these definitions change over time, their substance remains much the same. Up to the late forties, this view held that to plan was 'to express in a drawing the form of existing or proposed land uses and buildings'.[54] This view did not change much during the fifties, so that by the end of the decade Keeble was still describing planning as being 'concerned with the arrangement of land uses and communication routes in the most satisfactory practicable form'.[55] Looking back on the period the American observer Foley summarised this ideological stance as the contention that, 'Town planning's central function is to provide a good (or better) physical environment; a physical environment of such good quality is essential for the promotion of a healthy and civilized life.'[56] He went on to say that this simplified view of planning could be given technical expression in terms of space standards and density control which in turn contributed to a professional style of behaviour. This again calls into question whether such behaviour serves the community or professional interests.

Nevertheless the view was again reiterated by Kantorowich when, in 1967, he claimed that town planning 'is dedicated to the promotion of an efficient and life-enhancing relationship between man and his physical environment'. He went on to say that, 'In this often very complicated activity, persons from a number of disciplines are usually involved, each playing a significant part.' But his professional self-interest emerged clearly when he concluded that, nevertheless, 'the town planner is called upon to carry the central and crucial professional responsibility because his special skill is a command of the planning process as a whole'.[57] A claim which many dispute.

As a result of the grip that the Royal Town Planning Institute has maintained on education – the main form of secondary socialisation of members seeking its recognition – and Kantorowich's association with its educational policy, a new generation of planners has emerged subscribing to this same ideology. Thus, in 1971, two young products of the planning schools could still assert that, 'We are talking about physical planning, which we regard as a discipline and a professional activity in its own right, [as being] primarily responsible for the physical aspects of the total development process.'[58] There is little else for which they can argue. As the produce of the planning schools subscribing to this ideology, they would be practically unemployable if the nature of planning were to become different. The ideology of physical planning is maintained largely because of the spectre of technological unemployment which faces those who have been educated in its shadow.

The ideology of physical planning may have provided its adherents with a practice theory, but it has proved conspicuously unsuccessful in convincing the general public of the need for such planning and in demarcation disputes. The latter failure is particularly serious from the point of view of the town planner. The existence of physical planning as a separate and distinct activity has always been in doubt partly because of its antecedents among architects, surveyors and engineers. This situation was exacerbated in 1965 when the Institute both failed to broaden its membership policy and at the same time fell back on physical definitions of its activities. The result has been an increased challenge, particularly by architects, to the planner's authority in matters of physical design. This is reflected in educational patterns where, as Cockburn notes, 'many educationalists are still concerned mainly with design and some among them are moving back towards urban design which they feel has particular application in action area planning'.[59] The concept of urban design can be and is extended by architects to cover most of the physical aspects of planning up to the scale of whole towns and country landscapes.

Town planning as co-ordination

To meet this ideological challenge for employment by architects and others, town planners have played down the design element of physical planning and emphasised its co-ordinating and synthesising role. Kantorowich argues that 'planning is one of the synthesizing specialisms' and quotes with approval from the Introduction to the New Syllabus for the Final Examination, which asserts that the planner is 'the professional whose special skill is his synoptic integrating view of systems of land-use and settlement and the factors affecting them'.[60] A whole new practice theory has been built on these ideological foundations.

The systems school in Britain, founded mainly on the work of its able exponent McLoughlin, seeks to formalise the synthesising and co-ordinating functions of physical planning. It 'attempts to consider the environment as a system, organic in nature, of complex interrelationship'.[61] So, according to McLoughlin, 'if we see the city as a dynamic system that evolves in response to many influences, it follows that plans for it must be cast in a similar form . . plans for the nature, rate, quantity and quality of urban change – for a process of development'.[62] To accomplish this feat, however, all planners would have to be 'direct descendants from Solomon and . . . closely related to Einstein, St John and Gordon Banks'.[63] Such men are a trifle rare in the corridors of planning offices.

The serious objections to systems theory are, however, that it rests on hidden ideological foundations, requires impossible feats of functional rationality, and is substantially irrational and does not deal with elements of cities which are readily identifiable or relevant. As to the first objection, the ideology of physical planning, stressing co-ordination and based on systems theory, is fundamentally conservative. It contains the idea that the natural or normal state of the system is some kind of integrated equilibrium to which the system itself is, or policies should be, directed. Thus it contains an implicit reification of the status quo. In ignoring the possibility that social systems are at all times more or less in states of dynamic tension as different interests struggle for resources and power, the systems ideology tends to support the interests of those who have most of these commodities at any given point in time. As Brooks and Stegman correctly suspect, 'planners have been interested primarily in securing for their programmes, the co-operation and approval of one rather specific subgroup, namely, the political and economic leadership of the community'.[64]

Such beliefs combine to make the relationships between the tough-minded, economically oriented Right and those planners who subscribe to the ideology of physical and co-ordinating planning, extremely close indeed. Social action coloured by these ideological beliefs is therefore fundamentally conservative.

Its conservative nature is also partly the result of its institutional setting. Although the claims of professional competence are founded on assertions of functional rationality, it is neither likely in theory nor borne out in practice that physical planning is a purely technical or logically 'correct' activity. It has already been argued that, in theory, in situations of risk and uncertainty it is unlikely that planning is functionally rational. At the same time its attempts to overcome these situations produce a somewhat diffident and timorous pattern of behaviour amounting to conservatism in the face of impossibly complex situations. In practice, such behaviour is compounded by the nature of the bureaucratic organisations for which most planners work.

The traditional doctrine of rationality in formal organisations is inherited largely from the work of the German sociologist Weber. It derives from his interest in the concept of authority and its relationships with legitimate systems of social control. He defines authority as 'the probability that certain specific commands (or all commands) from a given source will be obeyed by a given group of persons'.[65] The two criteria distinguishing authority from other forms of control and legitimating this kind of command are 'voluntary compliance with legitimate commands and the suspension of judgement in advance of command'.[66] The key characteristic of authority is the willingness of individuals to follow directives, not because they can be enforced by physical means, but rather because of the general social acceptance of their legitimacy and the role of the individual or organisation issuing the directives.

Weber identified three types of authority. The first is legitimated by the sanctity of tradition. In this case the ruling person or group is usually defined by heredity and directives are obeyed by other individuals because of their belief in the sanctity and relevance of this traditional order. The second type of authority is legitimated by the special qualities of an individual who gives directives. The charismatic leader relies upon his personal magnetism and its ready acceptance by his followers to legitimate his claims to authority. The third type of authority, the one most relevant to the study of rational decision making in formal organisations, is legitimated by a belief in the supremacy of law. Rational, legal authority relies for its acceptance on the general belief in the validity of the laws and the efficacy of the rule of law. According to Weber, the authority exercised by all modern bureaucracies is legitimated on the grounds that it is both rational and legal.

It is therefore to the study of bureaucracies that we must turn in order to investigate whether town planning decisions are taken within a rational organisational context and to determine how far such a context determines that the outcomes are fundamentally conservative.

Weber constructed an 'ideal' or 'pure' type of bureaucracy which, while only a mental construct, is said to show all the salient features of bureaucracy in sharp focus and may be thought of as a template against which bureaucratic structures may be compared and studied. The main features of the Weberian model are the following:

1. Hierarchy of office, each with its own area of competence and ordered by official rules.
2. A hierarchy of status among members corresponding to the hierarchy of office.
3. Calculability of the behaviour of members which is important both in the efficient running of the organisation and in its relationships with clients.
4. An allocation of roles, filled from above, the top posts sometimes being filled by election.
5. A high security of tenure and remuneration associated with posts.
6. Assistance in a career to be followed without reference to pressure from outside and ensuring the loyalty of the official to the bureaucracy.
7. Maintenance of impersonality in the social relationships between the members of the organisation and their clients.

Not surprisingly, no bureaucracy fits exactly this pure type model, since it was not intended to be a description of an existing bureaucracy.

Nevertheless, the reasons for adopting an organisational form similar to that outlined above are, according to Weber, that,

> experience tends universally to show that the purely bureaucratic type of administrative organization . . . is, from a purely technical point of view, capable of attaining the highest degree of efficiency and is in this sense formally the most rational known means of carrying out imperative control over human beings. It is superior to any other form in precision, in stability, in the stringency of its discipline, and in its reliability. It thus makes possible a particularly high degree of calculability of results for the heads of the organization and for those acting in relation to it. It is finally superior both in intensive efficiency and in the scope of its operations and is formally capable of application to all kinds of administrative tasks.[67]

He goes on to argue that 'bureaucratic administration is, other things being equal, always, from a formal technical point of view the most rational type'.[68] It owes its superiority to the 'role of technical knowledge which, through the development of modern technology and business methods in the production of goods, has become completely indispensable'.[69]

This remarkable analysis of the nature of bureaucratic organisations is the starting point for all subsequent studies of the context within which town planning and other types of decisions are taken. Doubts on whether bureaucracies actually functioned in the rational way outlined by Weber were first voiced by Merton. He distinguished between the formal and informal behaviour patterns in organisations. The latter were argued to introduce dysfunctions into the formal patterns which bureaucracies were said to follow by Weber.

Merton outlined one such set of dysfunctions that followed from the demand for control made on an organisation by its top hierarchy. This demand, he argued, takes the form of an increased emphasis on the reliability of behaviour within the organisation. This results in a reduction of the amount of personalised relations between members; an increase in the internalisation of the rules of the organisation by the participants; and an increase in the use of categorisation as a decision-making technique. The unintended consequences of this action are, however, to increase the rigidity of behaviour and the propensity of members of the organisation to defend their status, which in turn leads to an increase in the amount of difficulty experienced with clients. This leads to an increase in the perceived need for the defensibility of individual bureaucratic action and hence to further emphasis on the reliability of behaviour and its rigidity. Thus, although the original demands for reliability and defensibility of action may be satisfied, this comes at the expense of increased conflict with clients, something which most organisations wish to avoid. Nevertheless, emphasis on defensibility, reliability and the resulting rigidity, contribute materially to the conservative nature of organisational behaviour in general and town planning bureaucracies in particular.

A second critique of Weber's classic formulation of organisational behaviour was voiced by Selznick in 1949. March and Simon point out that 'where Merton emphasized rules and response to the demand for control, Selznick emphasizes the delegation of authority. Like Merton, however, Selznick wishes to show how the use of a control technique . . . brings about a series of unanticipated consequences.'[70] In the Selznick model, the demand for control by top hierarchy results in the increased delegation of authority. The intended consequence of this is an increase in the demand for training in specialised competences. This has the effect of decreasing the difference between organisational goals and achievements and consequently stimulates more delegation. The unintended consequences of this action are, however, an increase in departmentalisation resulting in what Selznick calls the 'bifurcation of interests' between the different departments. This leads to increased conflict among organisational subunits, and hence to the familiar situation that the content of decisions made within the organisation increasingly depends upon considerations of internal strategy – particularly if the internalisation of organisational goals by participants is limited.

The results of the unintended consequences of the delegation are an increase in the difference between organisational goals and achievement which, if not recognised, leads to further delegation of authority which exacerbates the problem even more. The conflict between parts of an organisation, leading to decisions being highly coloured by the strategies of individual departments as opposed to those of the total organisation, is familiar to anyone working in large bureaucratic structures.

The Royal Town Planning Institute itself is guilty of trying to foster just such a situation in its proposals for the changing shape of the planning process. There they recommend, for the organisation of the new primary local authorities, a bifurcated structure split into departments dealing with social and economic objectives, land and physical, and one dealing with money.[71] The net effect of such a deliberate bifurcation of interests is again to make the most likely form of bureaucratic behaviour a conservative one. The town planner who does not recommend new departures in policies is the least likely to come into conflict with other departments or tiers in the structure of government.

A third critique of the rationality of formal organisations was developed by Gouldner in 1954. 'Like Merton, Gouldner is concerned with the consequences of bureaucratic rules for the maintenance of organization structure. Like both Merton and Selznick, he attempts to show how a control technique is designed to maintain the equilibrium of a larger system, with a subsequential feedback on the subsystem.'[72] Gouldner argues that the use of general and impersonal rules regulating work procedures is one of the responses to the demand for control from the top hierarchy. One consequence of such rules is to decrease the visibility of power relations. Because the visibility of authority-differences within the work-group interacts with the extent to which equality norms are held, changes in their visibility influences the legitimacy of supervisory roles in the organisation. If the norm of equality is widely accepted, then a decrease in the visibility of power relations can lead to a reduction in interpersonal tension and an increase in the legitimacy of supervisory roles.

On the other hand, the use of general, impersonal rules, 'by defining unacceptable behaviour, . . . increase the knowledge about minimum acceptable behaviour'.[73] This, in combination with a low level of internationalisation of organisational goals, can lead to an increase in the difference between those goals and achievement. This is seen by top members of the organisation as failure. It also cancels out the internal stabilising effect of the rules by unbalancing the larger organisation as a whole. The response to this unbalance is an increase in the closeness of supervision which increases the visibility of power relations within the organization, raises the tension level in the work groups, and thereby upsets the equilibrium originally based on the institution of rules. It also means that, again, the best way for lower-level members of the hierarchy to avoid conflict and tension is to behave in a conservative way and follow the minimum acceptable behaviour prescribed by the rules.

Recent research has suggested 'that in many cases organizations with structures opposite to those prescribed by Weber exist and are conducive to a high degree of efficiency'.[74] Among the members of this flexible school of thought are Gouldner,[75] Stinchcombe,[76] Janowitz,[77] and Litwak.[78] Litwak, for example, concluded that jobs which stress uniform situations or traditional areas of knowledge tend to generate organisational structures similar to the Weberian model, but that those 'which require social skills tend to create organizations which stress primary relations and organizational goals'.[79]

He has produced a discretionary model of organisations that hypothesises the relationships between these and the authority structure, vertical communication, co-ordination or activities, normative supervisory control, the employee compliance structure, effectivity in interpersonal relations and productivity. The burden of his and other work among architects, for example, is that in decisions which require special social skills such as town planning, non-hierarchical, democratic and flexible organisations result in higher productivity than those structured along Weberian lines. This would seem to be in sharp contrast to most organisations specialising in the production and implementation of town planning decisions in Britain.

Nevertheless, a characteristic of the tough-minded, economical oriented Right, subscribing to the physical and co-ordinating ideology of town planning, is a belief in the efficacy of clearly defined procedures enshrined in carefully regulated bureaucracies. Such procedures eschew explicit substantial rationality as being either irrelevant or given, or the province of other groups such as politicians. Such practice, based on systems theory, may therefore be substantially irrational in two senses.

In the first sense, the procedures themselves generate no principles or criteria from which the relative success or failure of plans may be effectively evaluated. In lieu of such endogenous principles, the results of such exercises usually express the predilections of participants all too often in a quasi-mathematical form which renders their nonsense less susceptible to public or political control. Andreski gives a less controversial example of this process in another context. He relates how the Swiss mathematician Euler, while at the court of Catherine II of Russia, became bored with arguing against Voltaireans about the existence of God. Calling for a blackboard, he wrote on it: $(x-y)^2 = x^2-2xy+y^2$. Therefore God exists. The Voltaireans capitulated before this 'scientific' proof.[80] The Euler test should be applied to all 'mathematical' planning.

Finally, the ideology of physical, co-ordinating planning must be questioned as to how far it deals with identifiable or relevant aspects of cities. In its physical and systems form such planning deals mainly with the effects of societal decisions. Thus, buildings, communications, population change, economic growth and location are all examples of decisions that have been made by groups and individuals according to a wide variety of criteria. In designing, mapping or studying the interrelationships between such factors, planners are attempting to influence the symptoms rather than the causes of the forms of settlements. Systems analysis, for example, is rendered irrelevant by the cumulative effect of quite small societal decisions such as how many children families decide to have in any given year. Systems analogies can be shown to be defective simply by projecting them backwards. In such circumstances they soon require alterations in their basic assumptions to make them relevant.

A further difficulty with rational, physical and systematic planning is that because of information lags it is inevitably somewhat in arrears of current situations. Despite its ability to adapt over time, this means that planning into the future can only be seriously attempted over relatively short time horizons. Although much public investment will last several decades into the future, physical planning cannot seriously predict situations beyond about a decade.

The main reason for both these serious problems is that such planning deals mainly with the effects rather than the causes of societal decisions. An example of this is that until comparatively recently physical planners were not prepared to accept that even an intermediate causal factor such as poverty was of serious relevance to the problems of physically bad housing. Even in some planning schools perfectly adequate dissertations linking these two factors have been deemed marginal simply because they did not primarily treat the physical effects of poverty!

Such myopia may be partially explained in terms of the relationships which exist between liberal morality, the tough-minded and economically oriented Right, and the ideology of physical, systematic and co-ordinating planning. While these relationships are not one-to-one, are not exclusive, and are extremely complex, nevertheless there is a clear reflection of the proposition that the main aim of government policies with respect to the casualties of society is to place them, at least cost, in a situation where they can then compete in the usual way with the rest of society, and the view that planning is almost exclusively concerned with the creation of a good physical environment. This latter view, often loosely associated with physical determinism, results in a segmented view of life where the promise of good housing can be seen as an isolated pursuit valuable in its own right just because it puts a Parker Morris roof over people's heads. But often this roof is in the wrong location, too expensive or designed according to architectural fantasies of what those snared in the lower echelons of the socio-economic structure need. Simply providing a family with a 'good environment' can therefore be a way of avoiding substantially rational issues in favour of packaging them in neat, twentieth-century, ticky-tacky, functional surroundings. In this way, according to Davidoff, 'we cope with the problems of the alienated man with a recommendation for reducing the time of the journey to work'.[81]

Alternative planning

So far, it has been argued that traditional definitions of town planning are ideological and irrelevant to the main problems of contemporary life. They are ideological in two senses. First, they spring from an ideological view of the nature of society which, in British terms, is associated with those who extol the virtues of the market place. Second, they serve the particular interests of the better-off classes and town planners themselves rather than, for example, those of disadvantaged groups. They are irrelevant in so far as capitalist and mixed economies tend to serve those sorts of interest anyway and also because they focus on areas of social action which may either be successfully accomplished by other groups or which are the effects of more important causes, or because they attempt the impossible.

This has lead critics, influenced by the ideological understanding of society of the tender-minded, socially oriented Left, to argue, as Friedmann says, that,

> Planning in the sense of rational conduct is impossible because man is not omniscient and therefore unable to foretell the consequences of his actions. Others declare that the value man appears to place upon the future is illusory, since all of his activities may be reduced to a political contest for power, influence, and social position from which he seeks the immediate gratification of insatiable wants. A third view maintains that history, the sum total of human experience, has a driving force of its own which cannot be subdued by human will but sweeps mankind along its inevitable and senseless path: rational planning is an illusion. A fourth will claim that planning must of necessity lead to the enslavement of the individual by rendering him subservient to the arbitrary purposes of an arrogant elite.[82]

The ideological stance of physical planning as represented in the 'official' definitions of the activity, advanced successively over the years by adherents like Keeble, Kantorowich, the Association of Student Planners and the Royal Town Planning Institute, needs to answer these charges. This will not be an easy task. It has been argued here, for example, that in conditions of risk and uncertainty it is impossible for the physical planner to be functionally rational according to the criteria of classical rationality with respect to foretelling the consequences of his actions. It has also been argued that the dominant substantial rationality in a mixed economy tends to reflect the contests for resources, power and ideological supremacy between different groups in that society. It has further been argued that the effects of physical planning on the historical development of settlements, whether reformatory or utopian in interest, have not significantly altered the course of history in ways that are very different from what might have happened without such intervention. Finally, it has also been argued that the interests served by the ideology of physical planning seem to be primarily those of the political and economic elites in society in general and those of town planners in particular.

Some might be persuaded, therefore, that the narrow definition of town planning which confines the activity to physical problems does not promote a significant element of substantial rationality in British cities. Some might take the conditions prevailing in their inner areas and the ultimate conflict in Northern Ireland as conclusive evidence of the irrelevance of physical planning to the 'real' issues confronting those who live in contemporary cities. Often those who are convinced of this are also sympathetic to the ideological understanding of society based on socialist morality and resulting in the kind of policies recommended by the tender-minded, socially oriented Left.

The ideology of societal planning has a lengthy lineage even within the context of town planning. As long ago as 1947, Silkin called for 'a new approach to training to correspond to the vast changes taking place in our conception and our practice of planning'.[83] These changes were outlined in 1950 by the Schuster Report. There it was argued that 'planning is now primarily a social and economic activity limited but not determined by the technical possibilities of design'.[84] Later, in 1965, Burns argued that in contrast to traditional physical definitions of planning, the activity was, in reality, 'a highly complex operation where such things as primary road networks, modal splits, social satisfactions, politics, employment difficulties, housing standards and leisure problems, are all interwoven and all require specialist analysis to formulate properly a comprehensive plan'.[85] The ideology of societal planning received its latest definition in 1969, when Hall argued that there was a view 'opposed to the idea that there is something called planning and this is town and country planning and that this is the province of the Town Planning

Institute. Some of us feel that planning is a near universal condition of modern life and that town and country planning is only a particular aspect of it.'[86]

This view was substantially supported by Friend and Jessop in the same year with the publication of their work on Coventry which showed the interrelatedness of decisions made by the various committees of the City Council and the importance of general strategic planning above and beyond the work of the town planning department and committee.[87] Thus, the ideology of societal planning may be summarised as follows: 'It begins with societal goals, with considerations of economic and social opportunity and, necessarily, only comprises spatial planning as one of its elements.'[88]

The ideology of societal planning may therefore be outlined as follows. First, if one looks at society in general it may be observed that planning of one sort or another is an activity common to virtually all of its institutions and organisations. Second, planning is an activity of great variety but is always a phenomenon associated with truly human as opposed to instinctive life. Third, planning is always associated with political, economic or social values. It always implicitly or explicitly begins with *a priori* moral judgements based on these values. Fourth, therefore the main objectives of planning are the translation of political, economic or social values into functionally rational programmes of action in order to create situations which implement those values. Traditional physical planning is some way down the chain of programmes but is nonetheless influenced by the ascendant values of its environing society.

Within this general planning context common to firms and individuals alike, government agencies have a special, different and complicated role to play. This role is largely determined by the ascendant values of society. For example, planners in Cuba are allotted a different role from planners in Australia. In Britain, a country accustomed to the acceptance of authority and characterised by centralised forms of government and a mixed economy, the role of government agencies is complex and often paradoxical. It is complex because of the continuing debate over the legitimate roles of government and private enterprise in the economy and also because of the conflict over whose ends should be served by public agencies. It is paradoxical because although public agencies are held to be democratic and responsive to all groups in society, often centralised government agencies can be effectively swung into operation in the interests of some groups rather than others and without the possibility of effective checks and balances being operated, particularly by disadvantaged minorities. In many ways this is what has happened and continues to happen in the inner areas of Britain's major cities. There, considerable gains have accrued to property developers, commercial interests and migratory elites, while those with few skills – the old, the chronically sick, fatherless families, the unemployed, the poor and coloured immigrants – often find themselves net losers.

The main *a priori* moral judgement which underlies the ideology of societal planning and which provides the starting point for the normative debates of government agencies is that social values should be put before political and economic goals. Thus the main functions of public agencies of welfare are to evaluate what happens without their intervention in a mixed economy according to a set of substantially rational principles or values. Second, to intervene in the political arena and the market place when the results of those decision-making areas are not consistent with the application of substantially rational social principles. Third, to insure that such intervention takes place even on behalf of groups who are not dominant in politics or the market place. Fourth, to achieve this intervention in such a way that the minimum number of people are excluded from governing their own lives and the minimum number of people become entirely dependent on forces and agencies beyond their control for their very existence.

In practice, this means that one of the main general aims of societal planning in a mixed economy is to equalise the abilities of different groups to compete in the market and in politics. All groups must be equally able to demand and take the basic essentials of a truly human life. Everybody in an advanced, affluent industrial society like Britain should be able to get appropriate housing, work, food, fuel, clothing, medical services, education and care. Societal planning is concerned with the distributive justice of the allocation of these goods and services, equality of opportunity on the part of different groups to acquire them, and freedom from want allowing individuals to lead secure lives free from the worst exigencies of the market place and politics.

In the context of local area planning, the furtherance of justice, equality and freedom would require first an explicit debate about these issues so that the position of the supplying agencies is clarified. This debate and the conflicts that would arise at this stage of the planning process are the most important points at which different groups, particularly the disadvantaged, must be able to participate. The second stage of the planning process would be the collective assessment by all public local supplying agencies of how they could contribute to the general principles hammered out during the conflicts over the general normative aims of their local authority. Owing to the inevitable disagreements over some of the general principles, changes in the distribution of power and man's limited technical forecasting ability, most of these contributions would have to be incremental, achievable in less than a decade and susceptible to checks and balances.

Once these collective contributions had been worked out then the technical activity of physical planning would become relevant in the co-ordinated location of facilities; transport planning in developing linkages between them; and urban designers (last but not least) in translating the foregoing decisions into three-dimensional forms. In the context of societal planning, physical planning is neither teamwork nor management. It is the co-ordinated location of physical facilities in such a way that they best accomplish the co-ordinated objectives of all the agencies of local government according to the substantially rational normative goals of local people as expressed by themselves and channelled through their political representatives.

The primary weakness in this ideological position is the familiar one that distributive justice, equality of opportunity and freedom of the individual are all *a priori* moral judgements only having a convincing prescriptive force for those who are predisposed to accept them in the first place. If it was possible to justify these goals in substantially rational terms then the chimera of a scientific politics would become a reality and the continuing conflict between liberal and socialist morality would subside. Failing the arrival of this millenium, the most practical step adherents of the ideology of societal planning can take is to transfer maximum 'power to the people'. Their objective would be to help people to help themselves. The multitude of activities that would contribute to this objective would take exponents a long way from the cosy institutional setting of a bureaucracy whose entrants are all approved by the Royal Town Planning Institute. Both this movement and the explicit debate about normative goals are also likely to have the effect of making the latent conflicts in British society much more manifest and relevant to agencies of government.

The ideological objectives in stimulating such conflict would be concerned with promoting the interests of the poor rather than the rich, of the working rather than the ruling class, of the powerless rather than the powerful and of those with few rather than many resources. Thus the link with socialist morality and the tender-minded, socially oriented Left is clear.

It is also clear that the ideologists of physical planning have a different area of concern from those of societal planning. While the former are primarily concerned with the demarcation of an area of professional competence, the latter are trying to harness government in general to social purposes of which they approve. The outputs of the former are concerned with the physical structure of settlements, the latter with their social structure. While both may exist at the same time, they are bound to generate ideological conflict because societal planning necessarily must seek to control physical planners in order to define whose interests they serve and how that is to be accomplished. Physical planners, on the other hand, will resist this control because it will confine their activities to a technical level and prescribe their employment opportunities. In the last resort, the outcome of this conflict will depend on the degree to which different groups seek to control the agencies of government found in Britain.

Conclusions

Despite the reification of rationality in a scientific age and despite claims that ideology is dead, social action continues to be characterised by irrationality and ideological conflicts. In Britain the ideological stances of the Left and Right continue to differ and result in different interpretations of social reality and consequently different actions relevant to the perceived problems contained in that reality. This is reflected in the planning of settlements.

It can therefore be argued that British town planning is neither substantially nor functionally rational nor does it necessarily take place in a rational bureaucratic setting or environing society. Conversely it may be argued that the activity is essentially ideological in its normative intent. While it sprang from reforming and utopian origins, since the 1950s it has reflected liberal ideologies and followed policies somewhat along the lines advocated by the tough-minded, economically oriented Right. In so doing it has also served its own 'professional' interests.

In conflict with the physical interpretation of planning ideology, societal planning stresses the ideological goals of distributive justice, equality of opportunity and individual freedom as the guiding principles of government action in general and town planning in particular. Societal planning seeks to institute control over physical planning, particularly by those with relatively little power and resources in society. As yet there is no systematic institutional setting for societal planning. It therefore takes place on an ad hoc basis mainly in a political context. This means that at present it is largely concerned with the struggle for power and the harnessing of any gains to social purposes. Its social purposes are closely related to those of socialist morality and policies linked with those of the tender-minded socially oriented Left.

Both positions depend upon *a priori* moral judgements. As yet, there is no substantially rational way to resolve the conflicts between such judgements, so ascendancy depends upon which groups or interests in society can acquire the most power and resources.

References

1 R. Glass, 'The evaluation of planning: some sociological considerations', *International Social Science Journal*, **II** (3), (1959), 393–409
2 J. Friedmann, 'Planning as a vocation', *Plan*, **6** (3), (1966), 99–124
3 R. Morris and R. H. Binstock, *Feasible Planning for Social Change*, Columbia University Press (New York, 1966), p. VII
4 R. A. Dahl and C. E. Lindblom, *Politics, Economics and Welfare*, Harper Bros. (New York, 1953)
5 H. A. Simon, D. W. Smithberg and V. A. Thompson, *Public Administration*, Knopf, (New York, 1968), p. 423
6 J. Friedmann, *op. cit.* (1966)
7 *ibid.*
8 J. W. Dyckman, 'Planning and decision theory', *Journal of the American Institute of Planners*, **27** (1961), 335–45
9 *ibid.*
10 D. Emmet, *Rules, Roles and Relations*, Macmillan (1966), 186–87
11 J. W. Dyckman, *op. cit.* (1961)

12 D. Emmet, *op. cit.* (1966)
13 S. Schoeffler, 'Toward a general definition of rational action', *Kyklos*, VII (1954), 245–71
14 K. Mannheim, *Man and Society in an Age of Reconstruction*, Trans. by E. A. Shils, Routledge & Kegan Paul (1940), p. 30
15 J. W. Dyckman, *op. cit.* (1961)
16 M. Meyerson and E. C. Banfield, *Politics, Planning and the Public Interest*, Collier-Macmillan (1955), p. 316
17 *see* J. W. Dyckman, *op. cit.* (1961)
18 J. G. March and H. A. Simon, *Organisations*, Wiley (New York, 1958), p. 139
19 D. Braybrooke and C. E. Lindblom, *A Strategy of Decision*, Free Press (New York, 1963), p. 42
20 *ibid.*, p. 43
21 *ibid.*
22 *ibid.*, p. 74
23 *ibid.*, p. 94
24 R. Banham, P. Barker, P. Hall and C. Price, 'Non-plan: an experiment in freedom', *New Society* (1969)
25 K. J. Arrow, *Social Choice and Individual Values*, Wiley (New York, 1951)
26 J. W. Dyckman, *op. cit.* (1961)
27 *ibid.*
28 R. D. Luce and H. Raiffa, *Games and Decisions*, Wiley (New York, 1957)
29 J. W. Dyckman, *op. cit.* (1961)
30 J. Goldthorpe, 'The development of social policy in England, 1800–1914, notes on a sociological approach to a problem in historical explanation', *Transactions of the Fifth World Congress of Sociology* (Washington, D.C., 1962)
31 J. Horton, 'Order and conflict theories of social problems as competing ideologies', *American Journal of Sociology*, **LXXI** (6), (1966), p. 713
32 D. Bell, *The End of Ideology: on the Exhaustion of Political Ideas in the Fifties*, Free Press (New York, 1965), p. 402
33 *ibid.*, p. 403
34 T. J. Johnson, *Professional Power*, Macmillan (1972)
35 W. B. Gallie, 'Liberal morality and socialist morality', in P. Laslett (ed.), *Philosophy, Politics and Society*, Blackwell (1967), 123–25
36 D. V. Donnison, *The Government of Housing*, Penguin (1967)
37 D. Wedderburn, 'Facts and theories of the welfare state', in R. Miliband and J. Saville (eds.), *The Socialist Register*, Merlin Press (1965)
38 W. B. Gallie, *op. cit.* (1967), p. 125
39 D. V. Donnison, *op. cit.* (1967)

40 W. G. Runciman, *Relative Deprivation and Social Justice*, Routledge & Kegan Paul (1966)
41 J. Rawls, 'Justice as fairness', in P. Laslett and W. G. Runciman (eds.), *Philosophy, Politics and Society*, **II**, Blackwell (1962), 132–57
42 W. G. Runciman, *op. cit.* (1966), p. 285
43 R. Pinker, *Social Theory and Social Policy*, Heinemann (1971), p. 116
44 H. Marcuse, *One-Dimensional Man*, Beacon Press (Boston, 1966), p. 49
45 J. Friedmann, *op. cit.* (1966)
46 D. L. Foley, 'British town planning: one ideology or three?', *British Journal of Sociology* (1960), 211–31
47 R. H. Kantorowich, 'Education for planning', *Journal of the Royal Town Planning Institute*, May (1967), 175–81
48 A. Ling, 'Planning and the Institute', *Journal of the Royal Town Planning Institute*, November (1968), 419–25
49 C. Cockburn, 'Opinion and planning education', *Information Paper 21*, Centre for Environmental Planning (London, 1970), p. 61
50 *ibid.*, p. 55
51 A. Ling, *op. cit.* (1968)
52 A. Chetwynd, 'Professionalism and the public interest', *Town and Country Planning Summer School*, University of St Andrews (1972)
53 R. C. Clapham, 'A planner as seen by the public', *Journal of the Royal Town Planning Institute*, May (1970), p. 403
54 C. Cockburn, *op. cit.* (1970), p. 20
55 L. B. Keeble, 'Problems of planning education', *Town and Country Planning*, July (1953)
56 D. L. Foley, *op. cit.* (1960)
57 R. H. Kantorowich, *op. cit.* (1967)
58 T. Kitchen and J. Perry, 'Planning education and planning research', *Journal of the Royal Town Planning Institute*, December (1971), 455–7
59 C. Cockburn, *op. cit.* (1970), p. 41
60 R. H. Kantorowich, *op. cit.* (1967)
61 Association of Student Planners, *Planning Education* (1966), p. 35
62 J. B. McLoughlin, *Urban and Regional Planning: a Systems Approach*, Faber & Faber (1969)
63 R. C. Clapham, *op. cit.* (1970)
64 M. P. Brooks and A. Stegman, 'Urban social policy, race, and the education of planners', *Journal of the American Institute of Planners*, September (1968), 275–86
65 M. Weber, *The Theory of Social and Economic Organization*, trans. by A. M. Henderson and T. Parsons, Wing Press (1947), p. 324
66 P. M. Blau and R. W. Scott, *Formal Organizations: a Comparative Approach*, Routledge & Kegan Paul (1963), p. 28
67 M. Weber, 'The ideal bureaucracy', in G. D. Bell (ed.), *Organizations*

and Human Behaviour: a book of readings, Prentice Hall (New Jersey, 1967), p. 86
68 *ibid.*
69 *ibid.*
70 J. G. March and H. A. Simon, 'Dysfunctions in organizations', in G. D. Bell (ed.), (1967), *op. cit.*, p. 93
71 The Town Planning Institute, 'The changing shape of the planning process', Royal Town Planning Institute (1971)
72 J. G. March and H. A. Simon, in G. D. Bell (ed.), *op. cit.* (1967), p. 94
73 *ibid.*, p. 95
74 G. D. Bell (ed.), *op. cit.* (1967), p. 98
75 A. Gouldner, 'Organizational analysis', in *Sociology Today*, R. Merton, *et. al.* (eds.), Basic Books (New York, 1959)
76 A. Stinchcombe, 'Bureaucratic and craft administration of production: a comparative study', *Administrative Science Quarterly*, 4 September (1959)
77 M. Janowitz, 'Changing patterns of organizational authority: the military establishment', *Administrative Science Quarterly*, 3 March (1959), 473–93
78 E. Litwak, 'Models of bureaucracy which permit conflict', *American Journal of Sociology*, **67**, September (1961), 177–84
79 *ibid.*
80 S. Andreski, *Social Sciences as Sorcery*, Andre Deutsch (1972), p. 127
81 P. Davidoff, 'Advocacy and pluralism in planning', *Journal of the American Institute of Planners*, **XXXI**, November (1965)
82 J. Friedmann, *op. cit.* (1966)
83 L. Silkin, Address as Minister of Town and Country Planning to the Town and Country Planning Summer School at Reading University, *Town Planning Institute*: Proceedings of the Summer School, July (1947)
84 Ministry of Town and Country Planning, *Report of Committee on Qualifications of Planners*, Prepared by a committee under the chairmanship of Sir George Schuster (1950)
85 W. Burns, 'Contribution to a discussion following the Presidential Address', *Journal of the Royal Town Planning Institute*, November (1965)
86 P. Hall, 'Report of a conference on the theme: the new planning courses', *Regional Studies Association*, July (1969)
87 J. K. Friend and W. N. Jessop, *Local Government and Strategic Choice*, Tavistock (1969)
88 C. Cockburn, *op. cit.* (1970), p. 40

7. The planning of change

The price of criticism

It is generally agreed that the price of criticism is a sound alternative. This is a high price indeed, especially when radical changes are urgently required. The radical dilemma is of necessity posed by the perceived need to generate significant immediate change and the problem of devising feasible strategies to achieve that end in a mixed economy. In this context it is reasonable to assume that revolutionary alternatives will not solve immediate problems but at the same time the forces of reaction found in a mixed economy will resist far reaching radical but peaceful proposals for change.

This is illustrated by the misconceptions of the 'futurists' who are becoming the delphic oracles of the planning profession. The futurists tend to make two assumptions. First that rapid change is now the 'normal' state of society and second that the ramifications of all this change lead to increasing complexity which renders society less comprehensible to all but the futurists and planners. There is some truth in these assertions. For example, national growth rates of 3 per cent or 4 per cent per annum are confidently planned. Such continuous rates of growth are as high as anything experienced at the height of the industrial revolution in England. Comparatively speaking, therefore, this represents a rapid rate of change. Similarly, some people equate the current technological explosion with significant change. The gimmicks and gadgets of the second half of the twentieth century seem to mark the march of progress for many futurists. A great many long term plans seem to rely heavily on such technological gadgets as videophones, vacuum transmission tubes, travolators, powerful automatic computers, and the like. It is also frequently assumed that what the 'trendies' perceive now, the masses will avidly demand in the future as a result of their embourgeoisement and higher incomes.

It must be seriously questioned, however, whether this coming 'Disneyland Society' constitutes real change or merely the more extreme lengths that a society geared to consumption must go to in order to persuade its members to continue consuming. In Britain during the 1970s, for example, while it has become possible for almost anyone to purchase his own pocket computer, only the top 10 per cent of income earners can now purchase a house for the first time without having to provide large amounts of additional capital. The technological 'Disneyland Society' may create artificial growth and wants and yet fail to satisfy more 'real' and basic needs. The richest country in the world has not yet devised the means or the will to create freedom from want.

The first priority, therefore, in devising an alternative strategy for the planning of change is to get quite clear what is to count as significant change. The simplest answer to this problem is that the most important changes in a society are changes which take place in the social structure. In practice this means things such as demographic change, including alterations to birth and death rates; changes in the size, scope and pervasiveness of the family; the opening of the stratification system and shifts from ascribed to achieved status; the levelling of culture with mass communication and education; high levels of education; the secularisation and bureaucratisation of society. These may be summarised as changes in the structure, habits and equipment of society.

If one looks at twentieth century British society and expects to find rapid and continuous change in all these factors, the surprising thing is how little they have changed over two or even three generations. The social class structure, for example, has changed remarkably little during the twentieth century. Marsh has estimated, for example, that of the males and females with specified occupations, 4 per cent in 1901 and 6 per cent in 1951 provided professional services. The proportion of people making things in factories, workshops or on building sites was 36 per cent in 1901 and 29 per cent in 1951. While in 1901 the proportion of general dealers, labourers or undefined occupations was 5 per cent, it was 8 per cent in 1951. Marsh goes on to say that,

> The main conclusions to be drawn about the changing pattern of occupational distribution between 1881 and 1951 are that the proportion of the occupied population engaged in agriculture, fishing, mining, quarrying,

and personal service occupations declined; the proportion engaged in manufacturing, building, transport and communications remained relatively stable; that there was an appreciable increase in the proportion concerned with administration, defence, commerce and finance, and a slight increase in professional and technical occupations.[1]

Nevertheless, by 1966 the proportions of the economically active population found in different categories were remarkably like those of 1901. What is more, many of the differences are accounted for because the figures are not directly comparable either because of the rise of new occupations such as computer programmers or because of the reclassification of people such as welfare workers. Thus, in 1966, 2·9 per cent of the economically active population were professional workers; about 39 per cent were making things in factories, workshops or on building sites; and about 9 per cent were unskilled labourers or in inadequately described occupations.[2]

While the social class structure has not changed radically during the twentieth century, some people have believed that it is possible for individuals to move and change their position within it. Until recently, most of the evidence gleaned in Britain and other advanced, industrial western countries has shown this not to be the case. In 1954, Glass *et. al.* showed that there was virtually no significant mobility in Britain during the first half of the twentieth century.[3] Lipset and Bendix examined other industrial countries and found little mobility over some forty years.[4] Recently Blau and Duncan came to much the same conclusion about American society.[5] The only dissenting voice in this general picture of relatively little changes and mobility is Goldthorpe who, on the basis of work conducted at Nuffield College, argues that at least social mobility is on the increase rather than decrease.[6] There is a very long way to go, however, before it would be correct to describe the British social class structure as relatively stable but marked by its openness and social mobility.

One of the reasons why the British social class structure has remained remarkably stable, despite the prodigous efforts of a relatively comprehensive system of welfare to improve the lot of those at the bottom, is the emphasis placed on equality of opportunity rather than outcome. For example, it has often wrongly been assumed that the universal provision of free and compulsory education must lead to the emergence of a certified meritocracy. Equality of opportunity, however, is a sophisticated version of laissez-faire where all those who come to the market place or school can compete but not on equal terms. Those who arrive at school with most advantages take most of the certificates when they go. The Robbins Report showed that, of 18 year-olds from non-manual homes, 8·9 per cent entered university in 1928 to 1947 and 16·8 per cent in 1960; from manual homes, 1·4 per cent of the 18 year-olds entered in 1928 to 1947 and 2·6 per cent in 1960.[7] These figures should be compared with the fact that in 1961 the proportion of non-manual homes in Great Britain was about 17 per cent as compared with 83 per cent for non-manual ones.[8] Education in general and university education in particular are classic examples of the effects of welfare expenditure based on the principle of equality of opportunity. In general, those who have most to start with get most of the significant benefits.

Not surprisingly, therefore, the main basis of the social class structure, namely, income and wealth, has not changed a great deal over the twentieth century. The benefits of technological change and economic growth have been felt first and most at the top, and last and least at the bottom of the social class structure. Such change as does take place has to be measured in decades. Thus between 1961 and 1969 the Gini-coefficient of concentration of wealth did actually fall from 72 to 65 and the share of wealth of the top 10 per cent of owners fell from 62·5 per cent to 52·7 per cent.[9] Much of this fall can be accounted for by the spreading of individual wealth among trusts and members of the same family in order to avoid death duties. The changes taking place below the top 10 per cent have been much more marginal.

The distribution of post-tax incomes has changed even less. In 1949/50 the lower quartiles received 32 per cent less and the upper quartiles 39 per cent more than the median post-tax income. In 1969/70 the figures were virtually identical. The lower quartiles received 33 per cent less and the upper quartiles received 39 per cent more than the median.[10] Thus the poorer sections of the population were marginally and relatively worse off in 1969/70 than they had been in 1949/50, and there had been no relative equalisation of post-tax incomes.

Despite these figures, that indicate the lack of significant change in the bases of the social class structure, one is often invited to believe that even the poorest members of the community are relatively better off now than they have been in the past because average weekly earnings have risen faster than retail prices. In other words, the benefits of economic growth are greater than its costs.

Before such an assertion is accepted, it is vital to disaggregate different prices and different income and wealth categories. Such an analysis shows that the prices of basic essentials such as housing, fuel and light have risen faster since 1951 than average retail prices, and at times faster than the average weekly earnings of manual workers. As manual workers form a majority of the economically active population, this is reflected in total consumer expenditure. In 1951 consumers spent 8·7 per cent and in 1970, 12·5 per cent of their budgets on housing. During the same period they spent 3·9 per cent and 4·8 per cent respectively on fuel and light.[11] While it may be the case that some of these consumers were paying more for better housing, this is probably not the case with poor groups living in the inner areas of our cities. Indeed, due to the demise of the private rented sector of the housing market, many of them are paying more for worse accommodation.

It is, therefore, possible to argue that town planners in particular and welfare policy makers in general are not confronted in the 1970s by rapid and truly significant change in the social structure, habits and equipment of British society. Furthermore, the explosion in the technological gadgets of the 'Disneyland Society' should not be confused with significant change nor should it be thought to affect equally the total population.

Conflict and planning

The real, immediate issue facing town planners, and indeed all institutions of welfare at the present time, is the fair, equitable and just distribution of the current equipment, income and wealth of society. This will not take place if, for example, town planners continue to believe that the various parts of society are organically and functionally related, nor if they continue to believe that all the groups in society share a common set of values and interests. It is also false to assume that distributional injustice is minimised by economic growth. Both in the United States of America and in Europe 'the most intractable problems of relative poverty (occurred) and . . . (grow) at an enormous rate, not in the peripheral and poorer regions but in the most prosperous regions'.[12] Because the capitalist system based on laissez-faire, other things being equal, distributes most to those who already have most and least to those who have least, economic growth, expressed as increases in income and wealth, generally increases inequality.

Meade has demonstrated that there is a fundamental conflict between economic efficiency, as defined in capitalist terms, and distributional justice.[13] Societies dominated by the idea of efficiency normally become increasingly unequal societies. Thus Webber is absolutely correct to argue that,

> The industrial age was dominated by the idea of efficiency. The post-industrial age is likely to be dominated by conflicts over equity. The over-riding question for planners will be how should the social product of an increasingly affluent and increasingly capable society be distributed? . . . Who shall pay? Who shall profit? And who shall decide?[14]

The first lesson that town planners must learn from the application of conflict theory to town planning is that the old standards approach is now irrelevant. The production of a structure or a corporate or a local plan based on the assumption that a geographic area necessarily contains one community sharing common values, and therefore having standard requirements, is increasingly a recipe for conflict. In the first place such public action necessarily shifts the distribution of gains and losses among the population. It is therefore necessary, as Webber says, to 'make group-specific evaluations about the distribution of goods and services among the various communities'.[15] Even when this is possible, however, there is no reason to suppose that town planners will or can produce a more equitable distribution. This is because the kind of values to which town planners subscribe are often those of the upper social classes and the resulting standards they devise for administrative convenience seem too often to further the onset of the 'Disneyland Society'.

Other things being equal, it is therefore not unreasonable to expect increasing conflict over the distributions of resources and power, and ideological conflicts over 'relevant' values. Some of these conflicts will fall within the current province of town planners. Lest anyone should minimise the extent of these possible conflicts, two reminders may serve to illustrate the point. Northern Ireland is part of the

United Kingdom in 1974. The Protestant domination of distribution of resources such as housing and jobs and the Unionist Party's domination of political power clearly fuelled the start of violence. The ideological conflict between Protestants and Catholics also has the same effect. Second, the social class composition of the inner areas of our cities is creating a polarisation between rich and poor. While the poor are mostly the old, young children, and fatherless families, this may not lead to much physical conflict. When many of the poor are also young, unemployed, badly housed and racially distinct, then all the ingredients of extreme physical conflict arise.

The main problems to be confronted by town planners are the resolution of conflicts over the distribution of resources and power and over ideologies. While it is possible to pick out those parts of these issues which are currently the statutory responsibility of town planners, this is something of an artificial task. In the first place the problems do not confine themselves to different parts of the statute books and in the second place, even if town planners got their part 'right', these efforts could be easily undone by other parts of the total welfare system. Thus, although continuing efforts will be made to highlight those areas for which town planners are currently legally responsible, one of the main conclusions drawn from the analysis will be that interest-specific professions and departments are a hinderance rather than a help to the resolution of conflict.

Planning the distribution of resources

In planning the distribution of resources, it will be necessary to break away from conditions of Pareto optimality where policies are thought to be satisfactory if they make one person better off and nobody worse off. Even if only the fruits of future economic growth are to be redistributed, the rich must forgo opportunities in favour of the poor. Although a sustained growth rate of only 3 per cent per annum would raise British per capita income from £590 in 1966 to £1400 in the year 2000, there is no *a priori* reason to suppose that this would make any more relative difference to the social class structure in the last third of the century than it did in the first two thirds. Indeed, there is more reason to assume that, other things being equal, the fruits of this coming affluence will be unequally distributed and that in fact differences may increase. As Webber says: 'Those who have the social and cognitive skills that will permit entry into the affluent sectors of post-industrial society are likely to fare very well indeed during the next generations. Those who lack these skills may find the entry points are closed.'[16] In this country this means, for example, that the vast majority of children from manual-workers' homes who do not go to university are not likely to be impressed by the resource gains of their generation. Consequently, if the relative proportions of wealth and income do change over the next thirty years, it is more likely that they will change for the worse rather than the better as far as the poor are concerned.

Furthermore, reliance on such long time periods for the generation of wealth is both illusory and irrelevant. The problem of poverty, for example, exists now and must be solved immediately. Our ability to forecast situations and the effects of programmes beyond about a decade is almost negligible. The possibility of cake tomorrow is no substitute for the lack of bread today. Town planners should therefore confine themselves to relatively short time horizons in planning the distribution of resources.

The United Kingdom already has enough resources to go round. In 1970 the average per capita income was about £560. At an average of nearly three persons per household this means that if the nation's total incomes had been equally distributed every family could have had about £1680. Similarly, if the wealth of only the top 1 per cent of wealth owners had been confiscated in 1969 and distributed equally, every individual could have received a further £350 making a total average family income of £2730. Clearly there is no 'absolute' need to wait for a generation before average family incomes reach such levels.

Such notional figures however, only provide the context within which the most pressing practical problems in planning the distribution of resources must be solved and solved quickly. Paramount among these is the need to break the cycle of poverty which successive generations have experienced and are experiencing particularly in the inner areas of our cities. This will require significant interference with market forces – on the grounds that the market place, even with massive economic growth, is both incapable and unwilling to deal with poverty.

The basic ingredients of the poverty cycle are low income, poor living conditions, poor educational opportunities and unskilled work or unemployment. Clearly, town planning is concerned primarily with poor living conditions. When it comes to the practical implementation of policies that could well be the area in which the town planner would, under present statutory and departmental arrangements, be most active. But it makes no sense at all to produce Parker Morris living conditions in areas of high unemployment where the poor cannot pay for them or acquire the kind of education which would probably make them unwilling to live in those areas anyway. In other words, effective town planning depends just as much on employment, income and educational policies as these areas depend upon town planning. The Centre for Environmental Studies was constrained to say of the Greater London Development Plan: 'Clearly the aims of the Plan cannot be attained within the confines of the present locations of jobs, the present distribution of incomes, the present transport system, and the present policies for housing, social security, taxation and subsidies. Either these patterns must be changed or some of the generally agreed goals must be jettisoned.'[17] The greatest barrier to the achievement of adequate policies on all these issues designed to achieve desired total effects is the single interest profession or department. Whether town planners or the departments themselves like it or not, the Department of Health and Social Security, the Lord Chancellor's Department and their local representatives are all closely involved in the planning of our cities.

The main objectives of the total planning exercise, therefore, should be to devise mechanisms which would automatically redistribute income and wealth from the top of the social class structure to the bottom and thus increase the effective demand of the poor, and to supply this demand with relevant material resources. In this way, the different values of the poor could be expressed in the market place and the effectiveness of planning could be judged by client rather than producer satisfaction. One way of making planning more responsive to the different needs of different groups rather than to the production of standards is therefore to use quasi-market processes.

The first requirement of effective demand is money. The most pressing need is therefore for a battery of policies concerned with maintaining an adequate level of family income. Minimum wage legislation and a negative income tax or social dividend seem the most promising possibilities in this area. Minimum wage legislation could introduce a moving floor of, say, not less than half the average manual worker's pay in any given year. In 1970, this would have meant that everyone in employment would have been paid at least £14 per week. The floor would rise every time the average manual worker's pay went up. Such an arrangement would have the additional advantage of harnessing the energies of the strong trade unions to improving the pay of all workers. It might also have the advantage of encouraging employers to use labour more efficiently.

The minimum wage level would also provide the point either at which negative income tax would operate or at which a social dividend would be paid. In the case of negative income tax anyone who, for whatever reason, became unemployed would automatically have the minimum wage transferred to them from government funds. This would apply mainly to pensioners, the sick and fatherless families. This policy has the advantage that the machinery for its implementation already exists and it could therefore be instituted as fast as Parliament could agree to the necessary legislation. It also has the advantage that it would be able to distribute funds to those most in need and therefore make the best and most appropriate use of scarce resources.

The social dividend on the other hand would be distributed to every family in the land. This has the merit that, unlike selective policies where applicants must claim their rights and thus incur stigma, one would be reasonably sure that everyone who needed and was entitled to support actually received it. Subsequently, either the dividend could be clawed back from those who did not need it or higher rates of income tax would be levied on all additional incomes. If the income tax machinery is to be employed anyway, it would seem that the advantages in rapid implementation and non-stigmatising selection make the negative income tax on balance a better proposition than the social dividend.

The principle that should be employed in deciding who is to pay for the benefits of a negative income tax should be that of redistribution. Thus the cost of a negative income tax should be met by the introduction of a progressive annual wealth tax. This might involve for example, charging all those families whose net wealth amounts to more than £25 000 an annual and progressive levy on their assets at whatever level was necessary to finance at least most of the payments made under a negative income tax scheme. Such payments would have the additional merit of moving towards a situation of equality of outcome rather than equality of opportunity.

Once a minimum basic income level for all has been secured, adequate basic living conditions within the means of this income level should be provided. Under present statutory and departmental arrangements, this is where regional, corporate, structure and local planners come into the picture. Their overriding problem is to provide appropriate housing located in the right places, that is, where different groups want to live, where employment is to be found, where their cultural and social lives can be fulfilled, and where the basic infrastructure of life can be provided most economically at a price within the means of those on the minimum income level. One of the difficulties in pursuing these objectives is that the relative importance of the individual elements changes in different circumstances. The lack of sufficient employment looms larger in areas of economic decline, and the shortage of land and housing is more pressing in areas of economic growth. Nevertheless, while these different conditions change the relative difficulty of achieving the basic objectives in different areas, they remain as a check-list of what needs to be done.

Unfortunately up to the present time the British town planners have singularly failed to achieve any of these objectives with respect to the lowest social class. Instead they have been systematically destroying our great cities by pursuing policies of planned decentralisation involving suburbanisation – new and expanded towns combined with a restrictive land use policy based on the simplistic concept of green belts. This has increasingly changed the inner areas of our cities into places where most people cannot afford adequate and acceptable living conditions. Consequently many have been forced to leave for the suburbs and beyond. This urban exodus has been translated into a self-fulfilling prophecy by subsidised commuter travel, urban motorways, urban redevelopment and new and expanded towns. All these have been developed not only at the expense of cities in general but also at the expense of the lowest social class in particular.

These policies cannot and should not continue indefinitely. They cannot continue, for example, because a glance at the location of new and expanded towns shows that most of them simply follow the main axes of existing population and employment. There is a limit to the number of such developments that can be located between London and Liverpool, Glasgow and Edinburgh, and around the Tyne and the Tees, without simply creating what amount to low-density, poly-nucleated conurbations. This is precisely the feature that the policies were originally designed to prevent. Also, they should not continue because they represent a wasteful and inefficient use of resources such as administration and infrastructure. At the same time a disproportionate amount of these wasted resources is distributed to those who are not most in need.

The major objective of town planning should therefore be to develop existing cities in such a way that families both want and can afford to live in them. The advantages of existing large cities is that they generally have a varied and viable economic base and an existing infrastructure. The major problem then becomes one of locating appropriate housing at reasonable cost in the right places and in relation to the various kinds of available employment. Increasingly, the two barriers to achieving this objective are the price and scarcity of building land, and the radial structure of most cities. The two are linked. The only way to solve the land problem without nationalisation which, with market compensation, has now become too expensive to contemplate, is to appropriate land, which the community already owns, at zero cost; to insist that all employers make a given percentage of their floor space available as accommodation; to alter the basic structure of our cities; and to compulsorily purchase at agricultural values more than enough land to supply the cities' needs for any following decade.

Owing to the nationalisation of the railways, gas and electricity, the national community already owns large tracts of either derelict or used land in and around cities. At present, when this land is redeveloped or brought into multi-use, the national community is asked to pay market rates a second time for this privilege. This should not be the case. Land belonging to the nationalised industries should immediately be made available at zero cost to local authorities for development, for housing, or for multi-use. The redevelopment of railway stations as housing and employment centres and the decking over of railway tracks would also provide additional land space for these purposes.

An important additional factor arising from this kind of policy would be that cities could be restructured around a public transport system rather than roads and the private motor car. This change in policy could result in a redistribution of resources. Thus expenditure on roads, particularly urban motorways, is regressive in its incidence on different groups. In the case of Westway in London, the benefits accrued to the users of private transport while some of the heaviest costs were incurred by the poor who lived in or near its path. Cities structured around public transport can greatly improve the housing opportunities of the lowest social class by such policies as special working men's fares, free transport before, say, eight in the morning, or free transport paid for by progressive local taxes. A cheap public transport policy combined with the location of housing and employment on transportation nodes reduces the restrictions placed upon the poor by their need to live close to their work.

Such a policy could be reinforced by a requirement that all employers provide, say, 20 per cent of their floor space free of charge as accommodation. This could be placed in a metropolitan-wide pool giving first priority to anyone living on the minimum income level, either just to gain accommodation or to live above their work. Again, this would have the benefit of redistributing resources from the wealthy industrial and commercial institutions to the lowest social class.

In the location of future development based on public transport it would be necessary to break away from the old radial structure of cities. The two main reasons for this are that radial lines of communication do not produce efficient public transport networks. And, more important, the radial structure of cities is the spatial manifestation of market forces operating in the competition for the use of land. It has already been argued that such forces and their results are inherently inequitable. It is therefore to be expected that the modification of market forces will alter the 'natural' structure of cities anyway. This is illustrated by the effects of the location of public authority housing. Town planners dedicated to the purpose of equitable redistribution of resources and efficient public transport should therefore consider what spatial structures may best promote these purposes.

One of the greatest single mistakes in the planning of London, when viewed in this light, was the adoption of the Abercrombie rather than the MARS[18] plan after the devastation resulting from the

Second World War. The latter plan held out the opportunity of an efficient deployment of jobs, housing and transport which could have been used to promote greater equity. The former has made Inner London virtually uninhabitable at an adequate quality of life for all but the rich.

The main principle guiding the restructuring of cities on a more equitable basis is that its components should be linked by public transport and should be located in such a way that these links vary in inverse proportion to the quantitative volume of their use. This means simply that the best locational arrangement of components is that which keeps the linkage receiving maximum use to minimum length. One of the few structures which satisfies this criterion is the linear city. Poly-nucleated patterns can also be arranged to satisfy this requirement.

If town planners were to adopt, for example, a policy of developing linear cities, then the problem of land allocation again comes to the fore. Supposing Edinburgh and Glasgow, or Portsmouth and Southampton, were to be developed as linear cities, then the authorities concerned would need to purchase compulsorily all the land between them at agricultural prices if most of the gains of such a scheme were not to accrue to land speculators. It is already too late in the case of Portsmouth and Southampton, for as soon as the plans for a city on the Solent were mooted, land speculators moved in and bought up as much of the potential building land in the area as they could get. In the restructuring of cities it is, therefore, crucially important to municipalise the increase in land values which results from the public decision and to allocate more than enough land for the various components of cities, so that artificial scarcity does not drive up the price of other land. One way of avoiding such artificial scarcity is to abandon the green belt policy as we know it today. Cities should be allowed to expand in certain directions and in a controlled manner without necessarily setting limits to the extent of this growth.

Again, the question arises: Who is to pay? In the case of the extension of cities to increase the supply of building land and housing, a minority of land owners would have to forgo the opportunity to charge urban rates for their land. On the other hand they would acquire market compensation at agricultural values. This money would, of necessity, have to come from central government. Hopefully it could be collected by progressive forms of taxation so that those who have derived most benefit from the community bear most of the costs for improving its environment.

Finally, in the progressive improvement of the living and particularly the housing conditions of the lowest social class, attention must be directed to the current operation of the housing market. Many town planners do not regard this as one of their primary concerns. Nevertheless, it cannot be ignored particularly where inner boroughs like Camden can find themselves in a situation where the interest charges on their public housing loans are greater than their total housing revenue. No solution to the housing problems of the lowest social class will be forthcoming without altering the current operation of the housing market.

The first objective must be to make the operation of the housing market progressive and related to quality, rather than regressive. In this context, the tax relief on mortgage interest charges should be abolished and redirected to pay for the abolition of rate charges on houses which lack any of the five basic amenities. This would make a greater average subsidy available to the poorest quality housing than to local authority or owner-occupied houses.

The second objective should be to balance the increased supply of building land and housing, resulting from the release of land in public ownership, and the breaching of green belts by improving the effective demand, particularly of the lowest social class. This could be done as, for example, in Australia, by requiring all financial institutions to set aside a percentage of their funds to be lent to house purchasers. These funds could be used in Britain to provide interest-free loans to poor owner-occupiers or renters to improve and rehabilitate their properties. This might also be achieved by doubling or trebling the present discretionary grant levels, but only allocating them in proportion to income-tax ratings. A family on a minimum wage line might thus qualify for up to £3600 grant in some areas while others on higher incomes would get much less assistance.

The main problem in this exercise would be to create an effective demand for and at the same time produce low-cost housing. Without balancing both supply and demand, administrators risk generating demand-pull inflation and thereby leaving very few people in better housing than when the policy started. To do this, local authorities will have to rely much more heavily on a progressively managed policy of rehabilitation rather than redevelopment. All too often redevelopment has also meant the replacement of the very poor by the not too badly off.

If one turns from some of the issues to be faced in poor living conditions, one comes next to poor educational opportunities associated with the poverty cycle. The problem then is to define what would constitute relevant educational opportunities for the lowest social class. In general, current education is an almost exclusively upper-middle social class concern providing that group with certificates to set against the advantages of wealth and power in the struggle for access to scarce resources. Upper middle-class values predominate in schools and universities and provide a justification for self-esteem even in the face of economic adversity. Such a service is of little or no value to the children of the lowest social class even if it was provided in sufficient quantity and quality in the inner areas of cities.

The improvement of poor educational opportunities is a two-headed problem. On the one hand what is taught must be of some use to the lowest social class, so that more of what exists at the moment will not do. On the other hand if some kinds of curriculae could be devised that were relevant, then certainly more funds, schools and teachers would be required. Clearly the money for more education in deprived areas will have to come from the central government and be collected by means of progressive taxation in conjunction with possible cuts in such things as defence expenditure. The problem of what to teach is, if possible, more difficult. Part of the dilemma is to decide whether the children should be trained to fill the low-skilled jobs which may be available to them, or whether they should be educated to expect something which most of them, under present conditions, may not attain. If they are trained for the former, then this is likely to perpetuate rather than break the poverty cycle. If they are educated to expect the latter, then a potential for anomie and conflict is generated. Frequently, in deprived areas these already take the form of delinquency and crime. Education for the children of the lowest social class is therefore something of a knotty and unresolved problem. One cannot be too optimistic in these circumstances about the likely successes of educational priority areas. While they may provide more, they do not necessarily provide relevant educational opportunities.

The remaining element in the poverty cycle is unskilled work or unemployment. As to the latter, the right to work surely must be guaranteed by the state. If a man falls out of work and is unable to find employment in the private sector, then he should automatically be employed by the public sector of the economy. It should be the ultimate responsibility of local authorities and nationalised industries to employ people who are willing to work but unable to gain employment. Again, it should be the wealthy financial, commercial and industrial institutions who should pay for this employment.

If such a policy of guaranteed work was pursued in conjunction with massive local efforts to train unskilled workers, then much of the problem created by unskilled work or unemployment could be eradicated. For the remainder, who cannot get or hold skilled jobs, the local authorities could well provide many more sheltered workshops, particularly for the more marginal elements of the work force. This again would be a policy in which many departments ranging from health to prisons could co-operate.

It may be seen, therefore, that planning for changes in the distribution of resources with the object of breaking the poverty cycle has many ramifications. Many different efforts need to be brought to bear on different aspects of the problem and co-ordinated so as to produce the most effective results. It would seem unlikely that such a degree of co-ordination can be produced by single-interest professions like town planning or those with fragmented departmental responsibilities.

Planning the power structure

Parallel with planning the distribution of resources must go planning of the power structure. Without the simultaneous generation of political will and administrative machinery, resource planning is an empty exercise. This is particularly the case where it is being argued that the gains and losses of different groups with different resources, power and value systems must be assessed. As soon as these distributional questions are brought into the open, then the inherently political nature of planning is forced to the surface. This is because the technical equipment of planners provides no basis for determining how benefits should be distributed. As Baumol says, 'There is nothing in economic analysis which permits us to say that individual

A should optimally receive [a fixed amount of income or other benefit more than] B. The value judgements involved in recommending a distribution of income must somehow be grafted onto the economic information . . .'[19]

In exposing the importance of the distributional consequences of town planning, only the incidence of gains and losses may be measured technically. When it comes to deciding how they *ought to be distributed* between different groups, one enters the realms of social and political philosophy. When it comes to deciding *to distribute* differential gains and losses, then one is firmly in the realm of practical politics.

The power structure reflects the market place. This means that their main distributive characteristics are roughly similar. In both cases those who start with the most gain the greatest benefits and those who start with the least often gain the least and incur the most losses. The lowest social class lack both money and power. If an objective of planning is the redistribution of resources to this group, then one of the major problems is the current management of the power structure.

Politics and the power structure

Two of the main elements in the power structure are political and executive power. These will be dealt with separately. First, with respect to political power, as with economic resources, the problem is that it is highly concentrated in a few hands. In both central and local government, for example, a relatively small number of politicians control and direct affairs within the limits of public tolerance. Their main allegiances are to power itself and to those who finance and support them. Neither at central or local government level is there any pressing necessity for such politicians to consider the plight of the poor on other than social, philosophical or moral grounds. At present these reasons do not carry much weight in political deliberations.

A further difficulty for the lowest social class is that neither of the two main national power groupings, namely capital and labour, are primarily interested in their problems. Politicians seeking power, and therefore to capture a majority of the middle ground between capital and labour, are not forced to make concessions to the lowest social class in order to achieve their aim. While the extremely wealthy are fully able to look after themselves because of their economic resources, the poor have neither money, power nor politicians courting their favours. Consequently the poor are the only group who have virtually no bargaining power whatsoever in British society.

There is thus a fundamental conflict of interest between the way power is distributed and operated in Britain and, at the very least, the lowest social class. For distributional questions have no technical answers – only political ones. Political answers are arrived at by the interplay of different groups and therefore represent the situation where 'might is right'. This kind of answer, which is also that produced in the market place, is based on the implicit assumption that what is wanted is right and consequently those groups who get most of what is wanted are the most worthy groups. Thus for many powerful decision-making groups, people are thought to be poor because they deserve to be poor.

Such conflicts are coming into the open increasingly at small-scale local levels. Squatting, rent and rate strikes, demands for playgrounds, refusal to accept the dictates of town planners, are all examples of isolated conflicts arising from the effects of the unequal distribution of resources and power. Such conflicts are becoming more general and frequent to the extent that the SNAP report talks of the 'them and us syndrome which characterises the relationship between all deprived areas and authority'.[20]

Peaceful and co-operative attempts to overcome these problems have not succeeded in large enough measure in redressing the balance between rich and poor. Often neighbourhood organisations are neutralised by absorbing them or their leaders into the bureaucracy. Alternatively, groups without upper-middle class status, values and habits of speech and argument are ignored or pushed aside in negotiations. The time has come to take more directly political steps and to demand adequate incomes, living conditions, education and employment. Such action would have to be taken by organised labour on a national scale. The trade union movement should therefore be induced to mobilise its economic power in the interests of the lowest social class and its own members to demand, particularly in our large cities, the destruction of the poverty cycle.

The movement should therefore widen its field of interest to include policies, not just on income and employment, but also on living conditions and education. The pursuit of these policies should be demanded in areas such as London's dockland where, for example, town planning is actively in the process of creating an upper-middle class and speculator's paradise at the direct expense of the lower social classes. So far, even the trade unions directly concerned have done nothing to effectively prevent this process taking place. This, despite the fact that dockland provides a clear example of capital benefiting at the expense of labour.

The involvement of the trade union movement in town planning could also provide a co-ordinating framework for local militant action designed to end homelessness, provide adequate housing for all, relevant education and leisure activities for children, proper services for the elderly or sick, and so on. This isolated group action which can now so easily be rendered harmless by local authorities could be co-ordinated and establish the situation where all local branches of government must always ask themselves first: 'What does this policy do for the poor?' And if the answer should come back 'nothing' then it should not be possible to implement the policy until such time as the poverty cycle is eradicated.

Alongside the involvement of organised labour in town planning, it also will be necessary to make local government more sensitive and responsive to the needs of small groups, whether minorities or not, and also able to accommodate their collective needs. In this connection, the recent restructuring of local government has moved towards a greater ability to satisfy collective needs by reducing the numbers of primary authorities and enlarging them to cover more meaningful resource and political areas. It could be argued, however, that these areas are still not large enough to provide room and resources to solve their own problems.

The metropolitan counties, for example, are all too small to solve their own problems. This is shown clearly by the inability of Greater London to solve either its land or housing problems within its own boundaries. Londoners are therefore being euphemistically 'decanted' to almost any part of southern England that will have them. Problems of this magnitude can only be dealt with at a regional or at the very least sub-regional level in such a small country. Thus, if Northern Ireland, Scotland and even Wales can have regional parliaments, why not the other major regions of England? Meaningful resources and power could be devolved from Whitehall to these bodies so that they could generate both the will and the means to tackle their own specific problems.

Conversely, the new district councils are not small enough to generate any personal involvement or sensitivity to small group need at the local level. Some evidence of this has already been provided by the extremely small proportion of the electorate who have even bothered to vote for their members. In one recent election the poll was as low as 10 per cent of the electorate. So, although homogeneous minority groups are not usually conveniently segregated on a purely geographic basis, small local authority areas such as neighbourhood or street councils often prove at least a sensitive sounding board for local needs and conflicts.

In order to generate interest, participation and real sensitivity to local needs, micro-politics, as it has come to be known, should be developed. This might be done on a ward basis. Small councils or preferably assemblies should be instituted for each ward. Government by assembly has the advantage that anyone may participate and extensive selection and election procedures, often dominated by the major parties, are not required. Strangely enough, the kind of political rights and organisation enjoyed by full citizens of Athens during the fifth century B.C. might serve as a model for micro-councils.

The overriding principle which should guide involvement in regional and micro-councils, and in the formation of new coalitions of power, is that groups should be encouraged to do things for themselves. This might turn out to be the most relevant educational experience for the lowest social class. It is also the only way to keep a political momentum and ability going over a continuous period of time. The great weaknesses of advocacy planning, for example, are that it does not render the poor more capable of helping themselves; it often involves the definition of their needs by people from different social classes, and the results often collapse with the departure of the advocates. As the SNAP report says, 'Advocacy therefore tends to enoble planning schools and enliven professional journals rather than effect any shift of resources to those in real need.'[21]

Bureaucracy and the power structure

Marris and Rein argue that, 'Bureaucracy, as the instrument of power, can be taken to reflect the interests of the dominant social classes.'[22] The problem of planning the power structure is, however, not just one of shifting power from the dominant classes to the lowest social class but also of establishing efficient executive machinery for implementing the wishes and satisfying the needs of the poor. In seeking to achieve this end, no faith can be placed in large, hierarchically structured bureaucracies divided up into single interest departments. Much evidence now shows that the main beneficiaries of such a system are the administrators themselves.

Many of the social 'professions', including town planning, have been in the business of serving themselves rather than their clients. This has resulted in what the SNAP report described as a 'conclusive picture of welfare anarchy'.[23] This anarchy included interdepartmental conflict where departments guarded their functions so jealously as to prevent effective co-ordination of policies; unnecessarily complicated departmental procedures providing a smokescreen behind which the bureaucrats could hide; self-defeating policies because one department was undoing the work of another, and so on.

One of the common denominators of all this chaos was the fact that departments are oriented to measuring their success in terms of inputs and the acclaim of their peers. Some town planning departments, for example, measure their efficacy in terms of the size of their staff or budget, the number of planning applications processed, the length of roads planned or the number of houses built. The introduction of organisation and methods people into government has contributed materially to this state of affairs. The result is that for many town planners the object of the exercises is 'the sheer application of the available means'.[24] Such a situation where success is measured purely in terms of the slavish pursuit of the existing rules is a typical feature of hierarchically organised bureaucracies.

The first major change required from our welfare bureaucracies is therefore that their success should be measured entirely in terms of the demonstrated effectiveness of their outcomes. Success should be measured on the output and not the input side. Bureaucracies must therefore be subject to control by their clients. This should be enforced both at the political level and on the ground.

At the political level, assuming that relevant structures and power conditions are in operation, then further alterations are needed in the way bureaucracies are directed. As virtually none of their officials share the value systems of the lower social classes nor have any conception of what it is like to be poor, representatives of the lower social classes should be co-opted on to the corporate planning committee. This could be done via the local trade unions and micro-councils. More important, perhaps, even than this, is that at least the holders of chief executive offices should have to seek election from their constituents. If we must have chief town planning officers, then let them seek election by those they are supposed to serve. This could be the most effective way to gain consumer sensitivity from bureaucracies.

As far as the output from bureaucracies is concerned, it would seem that both at the policy planning level and at the local planning level, all the evidence from the work of management consultants and voluntary local bodies points to the need for multi-interest agencies and co-ordination. It would seem, therefore, that the needs of consumers can be satisfied better on a ward by ward basis, with only a corporate planning and budgeting function directing and co-ordinating their efforts, than it is at present by centralised and separated departments. It should be possible, therefore, for clients to go to one local office in their ward and find out from one man what it now takes a dozen different visits to as many different offices to unearth.

Such a system requires, as a pressing necessity, the demise of the single interest profession and department in favour of a more flexible and democratic form of organisation geared to the satisfaction of consumer needs. This will also require the substitution of quasi-market forces and politics for the kind of standards approach so frequently found in contemporary town planning. The technology for this is already emerging in the form of social indicators, market research, benefit-cost and cost-effectiveness analysis and programme budgeting.

A paradox emerges, therefore, that in order to improve the client sensitivity of our welfare bureaucracies, which arose because of deficiencies in the market and politics, it may be necessary to return to the modified versions of those very decision-making mechanisms. This is a step which would have to be taken with extreme caution. At best, however, it might arrest the unnecessary further growth of bureaucracies and make the remainder a more effective force for social equality.

Planning ideological change

There is no reason to suppose, however, that any ideological commitment to greater social equality will be forthcoming from the kind of people and training now embedded in current administrative systems. The education of town planners is a case in point.

At present, potential town planners are usually trained in institutions of higher education. This means that, other things being equal, they are likely to come from the same unrepresentative cross section of society that most of the other students in higher education come from. Thus they often have no experience, empathy or knowledge of other than middle-class life-styles, values and aspirations.

These predispositions are seldom, if ever, dispelled or altered much while students are in the planning schools. Rather they are socialised into accepting the importance of town planning as a separate and distinct activity and into playing the professional status-game by following their own personal career interests within this framework. There are a number of theses, for example, produced in planning schools on the subject of professionalisation which actually extol these very virtues.

The actual content of most town planning courses does nothing to increase the critical self-awareness of students on these issues. Very often the courses consist of practising a series of functionally rational techniques with no thought to the substantially rational framework into which they may or may not fit. In this way students are incorrectly brought to believe that they can actually make substantially rational decisions on the basis of mathematical techniques, location theory, or cost-benefit analysis which are, in fact, only functionally rational. In other words, potential town planners are actually taught at college to concentrate their efforts on the sheer application of the available means.

Part of the inadequacy of town planning education must rest with the Institute. For too long now it has handed down dictates to the schools based on the outmoded prejudices of its older members. Even this, however, is not quite as serious as the predilections of the staff at planning schools for consultancy rather than research. The use of positions in the schools as sinecures while large and profitable private practices are built up is nothing short of scandalous. It contributes, in most cases, nothing whatsoever to planning thought or education, and, in so far as it is possible to generalise on these matters, it makes some individuals considerable money for doing what their students would be happy to do just as well for nothing. Colleges should pose the choice to their staff, research or private practice, but not both.

If a revolution is needed anywhere it is certainly needed in British planning schools. At the moment they are simply over-producing an irrelevant body of generalists who will surely be unemployable within the next decade, either because there are not enough jobs for them or because their education has been too irrelevant for them to be desirable employees in changing circumstances. What is needed in these circumstances, running alongside the re-organisation of administration, is the development of a small number of schools of public administration concerned with all facets of government and administration. The curricula would contain social philosophy, politics, economics, sociology, social administration, government, urban design, and so on. They would be centres of research and teaching only.

Equal importance would be given not only to what was taught, but also who taught it and who it was taught to. Ideally, the institutions would be open for four quarters each year – not only to full-time students, but also to community action workers, bureaucrats, elected representatives, and indeed, almost anyone expressing an interest in their affairs. The roles within the schools should also be subject to regular change so that teachers, for example, might spend one quarter out of four in a local authority, or working with local groups. Students would have to work with local groups as part of their training. Nobody should be allowed to leave the institution without knowing what it is like to be poor and planned. Altogether, the institutions should be integrated with 'real life' as opposed to isolated havens for the maintenance of the career chances of the upper middle classes and the incomes of the professoriate.

Such proposals are, of course, a recipe for ideological conflict. Even if this conflict only resulted in town planners re-examining the purposes of their activities, this would be no mean achievement. Much more than this will be needed, however, if the exasperations of living in the inner areas of our cities are not to explode in more recognisable forms of conflict. The future is there to be guided and influenced. There is no reason to suppose that once the real basis of society has been exposed as conflict over the distribution of resources and power that the forces of history cannot be altered to make these distributions more equal. The problem is to find the will.

References

1 D. C. Marsh, *Changing Social Structure of England and Wales 1871–1961*, Routledge & Kegan Paul (1967), p. 148
2 Central Statistical Office, *Social Trends*, HMSO, (1971), p. 59
3 D. V. Glass (ed.), *Social Mobility in Britain*, Routledge & Kegan Paul (1954)
4 S. M. Lipset and R. Bendix, *Social Mobility in Industrial Society*, Heinemann (1959)
5 P. M. Blau and O. D. Duncan, *The American Occupational Structure*, Wiley (1967), p. 424
6 J. H. Goldthorpe, *Times Higher Educational Supplement*, 13.4.73, p. 6
7 HMSO, *Higher Education*, Appendix I (1963), p. 54
8 Central Statistical Office, *op. cit.* (1971), p. 59
9 *ibid.*, p. 81
10 *ibid.*, p. 74
11 *ibid.*, p. 82
12 SNAP 69/72, *Liverpool Shelter Neighbourhood Action Project*, Shelter (London, 1973), p. 176
13 J. E. Meade, *Efficiency, Equality and the Ownership of Property*, Allen & Unwin (1964)
14 M. M. Webber, 'Planning in an environment of change', in J. B. Cullingworth (ed.), *Problems of an Urban Society*, Volume III, *Planning for Change*, Allen & Unwin (1973)
15 *ibid.*, p. 54
16 *ibid.*, p. 38
17 D. V. Donnison, *et al.*, 'Observations on the Greater London Development Plan submitted to the Greater London Development Plan Inquiry by the Centre for Environmental Studies', in J. B. Cullingworth (ed.), *op. cit.* (1973), p. 81
18 A. Korn and F. J. Samuely, 'A Master Plan for London, Town Planning Committee of the MARS Group', *Architectural Review*, **XCI**, January–June (1942)
19 W. J. Baumol, *Economic Theory and Operations Analysis*, Prentice Hall (New York, 1965), p. 356
20 SNAP 69/72, *op. cit.*, p. 133
21 *ibid.*, p. 143
22 P. Marris and M. Rein, *Dilemmas of Social Reform*, Routledge & Kegan Paul (1967), p. 45
23 SNAP 69/72, *op. cit.*, p. 141
24 M. M. Webber, *op. cit.* (1973), p. 60

Subject Index

Subject Index

Administration (See Bureaucracy), 13, 155, 226; structure of government, 225
Alienation, 14, 37–41; organic analogy, 30–2
Anomie, 14, 37–41; organic analogy, 30
Association of student planners, 193
Australia, 195
Authority, 186

Barnsbury, 103
Behaviour and environmental determinism, 75
Bethnal Green, 70
Biological theories, 7
Bournville, 73
Bureaucracy, 186–9; ideology, 91; power structure, 223–5

Camden, 102, 147
Capitalism, 172
Central government, expenditure, 137; land, 214
Centre Point, 100
Change and planning, 203–27
Chartism, 73
Cheshire, 127, 128, 129, 130
Chicago School, 23, 30, 121
Children, 69
Cholera, 68
Club and Institute Union, 73
Committee on Housing in Greater London, 103
Community, 14, 31–2; plan, 6; studies, 30
Conflict, 14, 79; planning, 207–9; public interest, 125–7; social structure, 85–6; theory, 48–63
Congestion, 67, 75
Conservative Party, 131, 172
Corn Laws, 66
Corporate planning, 5, 47
Cost-benefit analysis, 121
Council for Protection of Rural England, 129, 139
Counter Information Services, 91, 99
Coventry, 195
Crime, 67, 75
Cuba, 195
Culture, deprivation and, 144; norms, 140

Darwinism, 49
Decision theory (*see* Bureaucracy), 161–2, 163, 165–9
Development Plans Manual, 4, 133
Distribution (*see* Economics), 50, 75, 88–99, 134, 139, 142, 143, 145, 153; externalities, 143; housing, 147; ideology, 179; of income and wealth, 206–7; justice, 177; land use controls, 76–8; planning, 209–19; politics, 134–40; power and, 131–4; power structure, 220; town planning, 74–7; transport, 216

Ecology, 26
Economics, distribution and, 141; growth, 126, 142–3, 174, 203, 209; rationality, 162; social class, 88–99
Edinburgh, 216, 217
Education, 112–13, 161, 205; poverty cycle, 218; of town planners, 183, 184, 226–7
Elites (*see* Social class), 51–3
Employment (*see* Economics), 211; poverty cycle, 219

England, 222
Equality, 63, 174–5, 180, 206; distribution of wealth, 143; social mobility, 110–12
Eton, 91
Europe, 207
Euston Centre, 91, 100

Family, 27; expenditure survey, 97
First World War, 78
Fraternity, 63
French Revolution, 8
Freshwater, 105
Future, 161, 162; futurists and, 203

Garden City planning, 22, 74
General Strike, 74
Gentrification, 103
Giffin paradox, 100
Glasgow, 216, 217
Goals, 15, 161, 164, 166–7, 169–70
Government, 13
Greater London Plan, 133
Greater London Council, 102
Greenwich, 5
Greenwood Slum Clearance Act 1930, 79
Gross National Product, 137, 142
Grosvenor Square, 92
Growth (*see* Economics), 126, 174, 203, 209

Hampstead, 69; Garden Suburb, 74
Health (*see* Welfare), 67, 75
History and social conflict, 64–80
Housing, 28, 78–9, 100–9, 142, 147, 213; Act 1919, 73; finance, 217; Finance Act 1972, 104, 105; location, 214; new towns, 75–6; social class, 103–9; squatting, 221; subsidies, 147
Hull, 5

Idealism, 8
Ideology, 15, 50, 53–4, 67, 69–70, 78, 139, 141, 152, 160; change, 226–7; conflict theory, 54–5; laissez-faire, 66; Liberal, 173; social action, 171; Socialist, 175–6
Ill health, 75
Industrial revolution, 8, 65
Inequality, 88

Justice, 63, 160, 173, 175–6, 177, 179; power and, 177–8

Labour administration, 6
Labour Party, 74, 131, 140; Representative Committee, 73
Laissez-faire, 53, 65, 66, 67, 71, 72, 121, 177
Letchworth, 4, 73, 76
Liberal Party, 78
Liberty, 63
Liverpool, 5, 70, 72, 216, 217
Lloyds Bank, 88
Local Government, 5; district councils, 223; participation, 137; and politics, 127–31; Regional government, 223
Local plans, 47
Location theory, 121
London, 69, 70, 72, 99, 102, 144, 216, 217; County Council, 100; Stock Exchange, 99

Manchester, 70, 100
Manifesto of the Communist Party, 51
MARS Plan, 215
Mortality, 67

National Farmers Union, 129, 139
National Insurance, 92
Nationwide Building Society, 101
Neighbourhood, 14, 27–33; unit, 28, 75
Newcastle, 131
New Earswick, 73
New Lanark, 67
New town, 31, 140; middle-class ideas and, 75
New York, 100
Northern Ireland, 194, 222
Nuffield College, 205

Organicism, 7, 8, 17, 20–21
Organisation (*see* Bureaucracy), 189
Overcrowding, 67

Pareto Optimality, 141, 142
Participation (*see* Politics), 137, 138, 223; distribution and, 136–41; standard of living and, 177
Philosophy of history, 7, 8
Planning Advisory Group, 133

Policy plans, 47
Political philosophy, 7
Political reform, 7, 8
Politics, 15, 126, 127, 135, 141; electoral reform, 66; nineteenth century change, 73–4; planning, 127–31; power structure, 220–3; rationality, 162
Poor Law Commission Report 1909, 72
Population, 65
Portsmouth, 216
Positivism, 7
Poverty, 56, 67, 75, 92–9, 142, 192, 207–8, 210; cycle, 210; institutional structures, 141; participation and, 137–40
Power (*see* Politics), 14, 50, 51, 58, 75, 123, 125, 137, 160; planning and, 219–20; professionalism and, 119–20
Profession, 119, 124, 151, 182; ideologies, 181–3; job opportunities, 181; neutrality, 150; power and, 123–7; public interest, 119–21; ruling groups, 151–2; status, 151
Public Health Act 1875, 71
Public interest (*see* Politics), 15, 120, 121, 122, 123, 124, 128, 131, 137, 149; definitions, 121–3, 124–5; power and, 123

Rationality, 15, 120, 149, 160–71; functional, 165; public interest, 160; rational deductive ideal and, 163; substantial rationality, 169–71
Redevelopment (*see* Development Plans Manual), 139, 148, 149
Reform (*see* Social planning), 67–74, 160
Residential mobility, 114–15
Royal Town Planning Institute, 3, 183, 193
Rye Hill, 131

Saltaire, 67
Scotland, 222
Second World War, 4, 27, 76, 112, 172, 216
Shoreditch, 69
Slums (*see* Housing), 115–16, 153
SNAP, 221, 223, 224
Socialism, 72; origins of the Labour Party and, 73–4; social policies, 176–7
Socialisation of town planners, 183
Social action, 10
Social balance, 28–9, 32, 75
Social change, 52
Social class, 23, 50, 61–2, 87–8, 204; false consciousness, 178; housing, 79, 213; power structure, 220–21, 224; residential mobility, 115; ruling class and, 65–6, 91, 99–100; spatial structure, 99–109
Social control, 31
Social ecology, 23–7; social interaction and, 106–9
Social facts, 9
Social interaction, 10, 14, 15, 17, 18, 55, 85
Social mobility (*see* Social class), 109–14, 205
Social planning, ideology, 171; Liberal ideology, 173–4; societal planning and, 194–8
Social reform, 7, 8
Social relationships, 9
Social structure (*see* Social class), 26, 85, 146; social change and, 204–6; social class and, 86–8
Social survey, 8
Society, 11; forms of social interaction, 10–12
Sociology, 7, 8; definitions, 9–10; origins, 7–9; in town planning, 14–16; of town planning, 12–13
Southampton, 26
Stock Conversion and Investment Trust, 91
Structural-functionalism, 17–22; professionalisation, 153; social mobility, 110
Structure planning, 17, 47
Systems theory, 33–37, 121, 184–5
Suburbs, 31
Sunderland, 27, 29, 133, 150
Surrey, 70
Southwark, 100

Theories of evolution, 8
Town and Country Planning Association, 22, 74

Town Planning; 1909 Act, 74, 76; 1947 Act, 2; 1968 Act, 3; Abercrombie Plan, 215; alternative planning, 193–8; as co-ordination, 185; corporate planning 5; definitions, 2–7; development plans, 4; distribution and, 145–9; functional rationality, 167–9; ideology, 180–5; Planning Advisory Group, 3; power and, 149–53; power structure, 153; strategic planning, 5; structural-functionalism, 20–2; structure plans, 3
Trade Union Congress, 73

Unions (*see* Politics), 221–2
Unionist Party, 209
United States, 207
Urbanisation, 14, 65; effects of Industrial Revolution, 67–74; urban structure, 146–7
Urbanism, 14; alienation, 40–1; anomie, 38–9
Utopia (*see* Social planning), 20

Values, 12, 14, 139, 161, 176, 207, 208
Voters (*see* Politics), 223

Wales, 222
Wealth, 88–92, 143
Welfare, 177; false consciousness, 179; measurement of success, 224–5; social welfare function, 170; Welfare State and, 51, 80, 93, 139, 172, 174, 179
Welwyn Garden City, 74
Westway, 215
Wheatley Housing Act 1974, 79
Wheatley Parish Council, 137

York, 73, 93

Author Index

Author Index

Abel-Smith, B., 93–6, 117n, 172–3
Abercrombie, 215
Altshuler, A. A., 120, 156n
Andreski, S., 191, 202n
Aristotle, 7
Arrow, K. J., 170, 200n
Atkinson, A. B., 89, 116n
Austin, 168

Bakunin, M., 150, 159n
Banfield, E. C., 121–3, 156n, 166–7, 200n
Banham, R., 155, 159n, 169, 200n
Barker, P., 155, 159n, 169, 200n
Barlow, J. E., 29, 45n
Baumol, W. J., 219–20, 228n
Beggs, T., 68
Bell, D., 1, 172, 200n
Bendix, R., 205, 228n
Bernstein, B., 113, 117n
Beveridge, Lord, 92, 94
Binstock, R. H., 161, 199n
Blanc, L., 8
Blau, P. M., 201n, 205, 228n
Bodin, J., 48
Booth, C., 23, 44n, 72, 92
Bottomore, T. B., 51–2
Braybrooke, D., 168–9, 200n
Brooks, M. P., 185, 201n
Bruner, 168
Buchanon, C., 135, 158n
Bulpitt, J. G., 127–30, 157n
Burgess, E. W., 23–5, 28, 44n, 68
Burke, E., 7
Burns, W., 4, 16n, 131, 194, 202n

Cadbury, G., 73
Carr-Saunders, A. M., 119, 156
Catherine II, 191
Chadwick, E., 70
Chadwick, G. F., 33–4, 45n, 46n
Chamberlain, N., 78–9
Chapman, S. D., 115–16, 118n
Clegg, 116n
Chetwynd, A., 182, 201n
Clapham, R. C., 182, 201n
Clark, J. J., 16n, 91–2
Coates, K., 96, 117n
Cobbett, W., 67
Cockburn, C., 16n, 181, 184, 201n
Collison, P., 25, 44n
Comte, A., 8, 9, 55
Cooley, 28
Coser, L., 55–8, 111, 117n
Cullingworth, J. B., 105, 117n

Dahl, R. A., 161, 199n
Dahrendorf, R., 55–60
Darwin, C., 8
Davidoff, P., 192, 202n
Davis, 100
Davies, J. G., 120, 126, 131, 139–40, 151, 152, 156n
Dennis, N., 32, 45n, 126, 133, 135, 148–9, 150, 157n, 159n
Dewy, 161
Donnison, D. V., 114, 118n, 173–6, 200n, 228n
Dudley, 28
Duncan, O. D., 205, 228n
Durkheim, E., 9, 16n, 17, 38–41, 94–5, 117n
Dyckman, J. W., 161–2, 165, 170, 199n

Eddison, T., 5, 16n
Emmet, D., 199n
Engels, F., 51, 100, 116, 117n
Euler, 191

Farr, W., 68
Ferguson, A., 8, 49
Feuerbach, 160
Firey, W., 26, 44n
Florence, P. S., 91, 116n
Foley, D. L., 126, 133, 146, 157n, 181, 183, 201n
Freud, S., 39
Friedmann, J., 120, 156n, 160–1, 180, 193, 199n
Friend, J. K., 5, 16n, 195, 202n

Galbraith, K., 94
Gallie, W. B., 173–6, 200n
Geddes, P., 22–3
George, L., 78
Gerth, H. H., 116n
Glass, D. V., 113, 118n, 200, 228n
Glass, R., 32, 120, 147–8, 156n, 158n, 160, 199n
Godwin, G., 100, 117n
Goldthorpe, J. H., 114, 117n, 171, 200n, 205, 228n
Goodman, R., 133, 152, 157n
Goodnow, 168
Gouldner, A., 189–90, 202n
Greenwood, 79
Gumplowitz, G., 49
Guttsman, W. L., 91, 117n

Hall, J., 113
Hall, P., 4, 125–6, 133–5, 140–1, 148, 149, 155, 157n, 159n, 169, 194–5, 200n, 202n
Harrington, M., 97, 117n, 137–8, 158n
Harris, D. C., 25, 44n
Harvey, D., 135–6, 142–5, 153, 158n
Hegel, F., 7, 8, 49, 160
Henderson, D., 117n
Herbert, G., 20–1, 27, 44n, 45
Hill, O., 68
Hobbes, T., 39, 48
Horton, J., 172, 200n
Hume, D., 49
Hutchinson, E., 31, 45n
Home, A. D., 113
Howard, E., 22, 74–5
Hoyt, H., 25, 44n, 68
Hyams, H., 100

Jackson, B., 113, 117n
Janowitz, M., 190, 202n
Jessop, W. N., 5, 16n, 195, 202n
Johnson, T. J., 123–5, 156n, 172, 200n
Johnston, R. J., 25, 44n
Jones, E., 25, 44n

Kantorowich, R. H., 3, 16n, 181, 183, 184, 193, 201n
Keeble, L. B., 3, 16n, 183, 193, 201n
Kitchen, T., 3, 16n, 201n
Kitson-Clark, G., 65
Klein, J., 30, 45n
Korn, A., 228n
Kuper, L., 32, 45n

Laski, H. J., 65
Lavers, 93
Lee, J. M., 127–30, 157n
Levy, J., 91, 100
Lewis, R., 119, 156n
Lindblom, C. E., 161, 168–9, 199n, 200n
Ling, A., 181, 201n
Lipset, S. M., 205, 228n
Litwak, E., 190, 202n
Lockwood, D., 112, 117n
Luce, R. D., 170–1, 200n
Lukes, S., 39–41, 46n

McLeish, J., 18, 44n
McLoughlin, J. B., 6, 16n, 33–4, 45n, 132–3, 157n, 184, 201n
McMillan, Harold, 172
Malinowski, B., 17, 44n
Malthus, T., 49
Mann, P. H., 25, 44n
Mannheim, K., 54, 121, 164–5, 200n
March, J. G., 188, 200n, 202
Marcuse, H., 179, 201n
Marris, P., 223–4, 229n
Marriott, O., 148, 159n
Marquand, D., 116n
Marsh, D. C., 204–5, 228n
Marx, K., 8, 9, 39–41, 49–54, 86, 94, 98, 160, 171, 178–9
Maude, A., 119, 156n
Mead, M., 146, 158n
Meade, J. E., 89, 208, 116n, 228n
Merton, R. K., 151, 159n, 188
Meyerson, M., 121–3, 156n, 166–7, 200n
Michels, R., 51–2

Mill, J. S., 7
Mills, C. W., 51–3, 96, 116n, 117n
Mitchell, R. B., 34, 46n
Mogey, J., 44n
Moore, 110
Morgenstern, 165, 167, 169
Morris, R., 38, 161, 199n
Morrison, A., 151
Mosca, G., 51–52
Myrdal, G., 54

Neumann, 165, 167, 169
Nevitt, A., 105
Nietzche, 7
Nightingale, R. T., 65
Norris, J., 31, 45n

Orlans, H., 17, 31, 33, 43n
Owen, R., 7, 67

Pahl, R., 86, 116n, 134, 139, 141, 145, 147, 157n
Pareto, V., 51–2, 141–2, 209
Park, R., 28
Parsons, T., 17, 18, 42, 44n, 58, 110, 119–20, 156n
Perry, J., 3, 16n, 28, 201n
Pinker, R., 201n
Plato, 7, 121, 163
Plummer, D., 102
Price, C., 155, 159n, 169, 200n
Proudhon, 7

Quinn, S. A., 24, 44n

Radcliffe-Brown, A. R., 17, 43n
Raiffa, H., 170–1, 200n
Ramsdale, G. I., 29, 45n
Ratzenhofer, G., 49
Rawls, J., 177–9, 201n
Rein, M., 223–4, 229n
Rex, J., 30–1, 45n, 54, 56–63
Robins, 206
Robson, B. T., 25, 27, 44n
Rodwin, L., 125, 140, 157n
Rosenberg, B., 111, 117n
Rowntree, S., 73, 92–3, 95–6
Rueschmeyer, D., 152, 159
Runciman, W. G., 95, 177–9, 201n

Salt, T., 67
Saint-Simon, 7, 8
Sames, 100
Samuely, F. J., 228n
Schoeffler, S., 164, 200n
Schopenhauer, 7
Schubert, G., 123–5, 156n
Schuster, G., 4, 16n, 132–3, 157n, 194
Scott, R. W., 201n
Selznick, 188–9
Shaftsbury, 67
Silburn, R., 96, 117n
Silkin, L., 4, 16n, 194, 202n
Simmel, G., 38, 46n, 55–6
Simmie, J. M., 26, 45n, 117n, 137, 158n
Simon, H. A., 161, 167–71, 188, 199n, 200n, 202n
Skeffington, A., 128, 136, 138, 157n
Smelser, N., 19
Smith, A., 49
Smith, D., 131
Smithberg, D. N., 199n
Sorel, G., 51–2
Spencer, H., 7, 9, 17, 49, 55, 66
Stegman, A., 185, 201n
Stewart, J. D., 5, 16n
Stinchcomb, A., 190, 202n
Summer, W. G., 49

Thomas, R., 145, 158n
Thompson, V., 199n
Thornley, J., 6, 16n, 157n
Titmuss, R. M., 97, 117n
Townsend, P., 93–6, 117n, 172–3
Tracy, Destutt de, 160

Ullman, E. L., 25, 44n

Veblen, T., 151, 159n
Vetch, Capt. J., 23, 44n, 68
Victoria, Queen, 42, 65

Weber, M. M., 9–10, 16n, 38, 54, 87, 161, 186–8, 190, 201n, 208, 209–10, 228n
Wedderburn, 174, 200n
Westergaard, J. H., 25, 44n
Wheatley, 79
Williams, R. M., 52–3
Wilson, P. A., 119, 156n
Wirth, L., 38–9, 46n
Witaker, B., 138, 158n
Wood, 28
Woods, 28

Young, M., 151, 159n